SCOTLAND

SINCE 1688

Struggle for a Nation

SCOTLAND

SINCE 1688

Struggle for a Nation

EDWARD J COWAN
& RICHARD FINLAY
with WILLIAM PAUL

CIMA BOOKS

London

First published in Great Britain in 2000 by Cima Books
32 Great Sutton Street
London EC1V 0NB

10 9 8 7 6 5 4 3 2 1

A CIP catalogue record for this book is available from the British Library

ISBN 1 903116 15 5

Designed by Roger Daniels

Printed and bound in Portugal by Printer Portuguesa

Contents

The Legacy of Scottish History

IT might be expected that when James VI of Scotland succeeded Elizabeth as James I of England, in 1603, the occasion would be one of Scottish rejoicing, celebration and triumphalism, but such was not the case. On the contrary, a majority of Scots appear to have been profoundly worried by the implications of the personal union; they feared the fulfilment of Henry VII of England's satellitic metaphor that the greater must inevitably attract the lesser. There was little comfort for the concerned in King James' assumption that 'to England must the greater gain come' for Scotland subject to English laws must become 'but as Cumberland and Northumberland and those other remote and northane shires'. He was echoed by Sir Thomas Craig, a brilliant lawyer, devoted monarchist and convinced apologist for union who wrote, 'voluntarily and in the friendliest spirit we yield to our neighbours in this union, terms such as they could not have obtained save as the result of the bloodiest war and most conclusive victory'.

In the event, the king's plans for the integration of the two kingdoms were defeated by the hostile opposition of his English and Scottish subjects alike, who well understood, as the would-be absolutist monarch did not, that laws, customs, concepts and cultures could not be assimilated at the stroke of a pen. The mutual suspicion, distrust and enmity which had accumulated over several centuries were not to be forgotten overnight. James undoubtedly saw himself as the reborn Arthur of the prophecies of Merlin, since he had proved to be the first monarch to rule over Scotland, England, Ireland and Wales but the Scots both feared and resented the status of London as a second Camelot. The union robbed Scotland of her court as a centre of culture and patronage, the major focus for both identity and national aspiration. Trade would also be adversely affected - 'Towards London the wealth of Scotland will flow'. There were important religious differences also, for Henry VIII had imposed Reformation in order to escape a marriage that had become an unproductive inconvenience

while in Scotland the movement had been 'popular and parliamentary', brought about in opposition to the monarchy, as represented by the young Mary Queen of Scots. Contemporary anxieties were to be fully vindicated in the massive upheavals and profound developments of the seventeenth century.

The first millennium of Scottish history had witnessed the incursions of the Romans who came and saw but decided against outright conquest, though the Emperor Hadrian strung a great rampart or wall across the north of England, a monument to himself, the legacy of which was to separate the peoples on either side of it. In a crucible-like context, the various ethnicities of the early Middle Ages were to battle for supremacy. The Britons of the south of Scotland, Welsh-speaking and partially Romanised, were to be hard-pressed by the Angles who abandoned their sea-girt settlements of the Netherlands, Germany and Scandinavia, as the water levels rose, to penetrate the rich river valleys of the eastern Borders. To the north a Pictish warrior aristocracy held sway all the way to Shetland, a people whose Celtic language is now lost but which receives some compensation in the baffling eloquence of their rich stone-carving tradition. In the west were the Scots, rulers of a maritime kingdom extending through the Hebrides to Ireland whose inhabitants shared their language, Gaelic. At the end of the eighth century a new infusion appeared with the Vikings sweeping down from Norway to seize Shetland and Orkney and much other plunder besides, gradually planting themselves on the northern and western seaboards and occupying the Western Isles. The savagery of their attacks led to the amalgamation of the kingdoms of the Picts and the Scots and the beginnings of the Scottish nation which, fairly rapidly and aggressively, conquered the Britons and the Angles as well, enforcing a frontier marked by the River Tweed and the Cheviot Hills in the east but extending deep into Cumbria in the west.

By AD 1000 a process of assimilation was under way and, patchy, non-linear and at times regressive though it was, it resulted in the emergence of a recognisable kingdom. The tribal or 'clannit' nature of Scottish society was to survive for very much longer in the traditional cultures of both the Highlands and Islands and the Borders.

A series of strong and talented twelfth and thirteenth century kings welcomed and exploited Norman and English innovations in government, institutions and administration while continuing to refine and encourage a sense of Scottish identity but there was no Norman Conquest of Scotland. As in England, some of the wilder elements were despatched to dissipate their energies on the advancing frontiers of the kingdom while officials such sheriffs were manipulated to enhance the power and influence of central authority. David I's upbringing at the Anglo-Norman court did not prevent him invading England with an army which significantly drew manpower from the whole country including Argyll, the Isles, Galloway and Moray in which areas his hold was at best tenuous. By the mid-thirteenth century the English border was much as it is now, though the Scots had acquired the Hebrides and were pushing aggressively towards the Northern Isles which remained under Scandinavian sovereignty for a further two hundred years.

At the same time, those kings exploited a partnership with the Church as a force for stability and control. Christianity had been established in pockets since the fifth century; shadowy traditions about such saints as Ninian and Mungo testify to its existence. Possibly the greatest, and certainly the most venerated contributor, St Columba, arrived from Ireland to establish a monastery at Iona which became 'the luminary of all the Celtic regions' and which sent missions to the Picts and the Northumbrians and, eventually, to Europe. The Celtic Church, as it is controversially known, survived the worst of the Viking attacks to be gradually absorbed into the *Ecclesia Scotticana* in the twelfth century when the organisation of the country into dioceses and parishes had a sound administrative motive as well as a spiritual dimension. Likewise, the fashion for establishing the great abbeys of the Border country was not entirely altruistic for they also served an economic function particularly in regard to the wool trade as well as providing accommodation for itinerant monarchs and their courts. Scotland shared in a period of thirteenth century prosperity which is reflected in the castles and churches established at that time, while burghs developed as centres of trade and administration. Hindsight, however, was to suggest that something of a golden age turned to ashes when, in 1286, Alexander III was accidentally killed so promoting one of the defining episodes of the Scottish experience, the Wars of Independence.

In the confusion following Alexander's death, Edward I seized the opportunity to expand the English empire to the Pentland Firth. At first, he attempted to control Scotland by means of a puppet king, John Balliol, but when the latter rejected Edward's outrageous demands, he had him deposed and in 1296 sent in an army of occupation. Scottish resistance was led by William Wallace, younger son of a knight though later to be characterised in legend and tradition as a 'man from nowhere', who intervened to combat English tyranny when the Scottish nobility, paralysed by reverence for Edward and fearful of losing their estates in England, failed to act. In partnership with Sir Andrew Murray, Wallace won an outstanding victory at Stirling Bridge (1297) but the following year was defeated by Edward at Falkirk.

Wallace always claimed that he was fighting to secure the restoration of John Balliol as rightful king of the Scots. He sought the support of the king of France and of the pope before he was finally betrayed and handed over to the English for a brutal death at Smithfield. Unusually for a national hero, almost everything that is known of Wallace derives from hostile English chroniclers who were intent upon demonising the man, stressing his unnaturalness and base origins. In reality, he was feared by his own nobility and the English alike because his supposed lowly background threatened the entire hierarchical structure upon which medieval society was built; his very existence jeopardised the survival of the Great Chain of Being. His example was never forgotten and was often cited in later centuries as that of the common man who would come to the fore in his country's hour of need and whose interests future kings would ignore at their peril.

Following his death, the cause was taken up by Robert Bruce whose grandfather had advanced a claim to succeed Alexander III. His story is equally inspirational for he not only challenged the mighty Plantagenet; when he killed a rival, John Comyn, in the church of the Grey Friars at Dumfries, he initiated a civil war and earned a sentence of excommunication for defiling the sanctuary. After his inauguration as king at Scone, matters went from bad to worse as he suffered successive defeats at English hands. Forced to flee to an unknown destination, he reconsidered his strategy though his alleged arachnidan inspiration is unrecorded until Walter Scott invented his encounter with the spider five hundred years later. Bruce's subsequent military success derived from his avoidance of conventional warfare and his adoption of guerilla tactics. For some seven years, following Edward's death, he enjoyed an almost unbroken run of triumphs until his hot-headed brother forced him into the battle of Bannockburn in 1314, a hard-fought encounter which resulted in unequivocal victory though it barely marked the half-way stage in the wars.

Bruce was also a master of propaganda, utilising the talents and expertise of a brilliant band of canon lawyers. In document after document, he depicted the Scots as innocent folk who lived in peace until the advent of the tyrannous English, culminating in the momentous Declaration of Arbroath (1320), a letter addressed to the pope in the name of the nobles, barons, freeholders and 'the community of the realm of Scotland', asking John XXII to intervene with the English to persuade them to recognise the legality of Bruce's kingship. The signatories claimed that they were so committed to Scottish independence that if Robert ever showed the slightest signs of submitting himself or his kingdom to the king of England or the English

(an inconceivable eventuality from all that is known of Bruce) they would remove him and set up another better able to govern in his place. They then continued with the memorable flourish:

'For as long as a hundred of us remain alive, we will never on any conditions be subjected to the lordship of the English. We fight not for glory nor riches nor honours, but for freedom alone, which no good man gives up but with his life.'

In this remarkable missive, we have the first articulation in European history of the contractual theory of monarchy, of the idea that the kingship is elective and that the monarch is bound by the laws as is the subject, basic notions of constitutionalism that are now taken for granted. The eulogy on freedom expresses a universal truth wherever decency, justice and human dignity are revered. Such ideas, particularly combined with the legend of Wallace, would produce a powerful mythos which was central to the Scottish experience and which made a crucial contribution to the distinctiveness of Scottish history. It is something of an anticlimax to note that Bruce did eventually make his peace with the English (1328), but that the wars were to continue long after his death.

Ideas, however, are dangerous things. Robert II and Robert III were both set aside as kings because of personal incapacity. Some would argue (not perhaps with total conviction) that both James I and James III were tyrants who were violently removed by their subjects, but there is no doubt that the most significant aspect of the much-romanticised reign of Mary Queen of Scots was that she was deposed by the Scots, another exercise in political pragmatism which anticipated the theories of contemporary political philosophers.

Such notions were not entirely absent in the lead-up to the Scottish Reformation. Scotland was almost the last country in Europe to experience reform of religion. After James IV's disastrous defeat at the battle of Flodden (1513), an encounter occasioned by the French alliance, a body of opinion gradually emerged which advocated closer alliance with England, a view notably advanced by John Mair in his *History*. Such an accommodation would save money, lives and the futile squandering of precious resources. James V, however, was survived by his French wife, Mary of Guise, and the French favoured the religious status quo. Scotland's first Protestant martyr (the first of the few as it turned out) was executed in 1528. The unfortunate victim, Patrick Hamilton, had been smitten by the teachings of Martin Luther. The cause was continued by such men as George

9

Wishart and, after his demise, by his adherent, John Knox. The latter's preferred approach to reformation was to have it imposed, Henrician style, from above, an unlikely development since the Catholic regent, Mary of Guise, administered the kingdom on behalf of her infant daughter, Mary Queen of Scots, who was in France for safekeeping.

Knox then appealed to the Scottish nobility who, in time-honoured fashion, showed themselves to be a spineless lot, at least in the early stages. The reformer, who had imbued some of the more radical ideas of John Calvin at Geneva,

then besought the support of 'the commonalty of Scotland', pointing out that all were created equal in the sight of the Lord and urging them to bring about perfect reformation. Aided by inflammatory sermons which stimulated the faithful into acts of iconoclasm in which a substantial chunk of the artistic and intellectual heritage of medieval Scotland was destroyed, Protestantism was imposed from below in a bout of danger-laden enthusiasm and revolutionary fervour. Admittedly, the cause was aided by a number of extraneous factors. Some of the nobility, notably the powerful

Edinburgh Castle has played a central role in Scottish history since at least the 6th century. The birthplace of James VI, it figured prominently in the Jacobite campaigns. It housed French prisoners during the Napoleonic Wars and it still functions as a military barracks. This view, Edinburgh Castle and the Nor' Loch, *was painted by Alexander Nasmyth in 1824.*

relief, church finance, universities, a school in every parish and the outlawing of bishops who were to be replaced by superintendents. By the late 1570s, Andrew Melville, a more radical Calvinist than Knox, was preaching the doctrine of the 'Two Kingdoms' and stressing the concept of parity, the advocacy of the notion that there was no hierarchical difference between *presbyter* 'priest' and *episcopus* 'bishop'. Predictably, monarchists feared that if such ideas were pursued in the Kirk it would only be a matter of time before they were also applied to the state. Melville also defined and refined the system of church courts such as kirk session, presbytery and synod, and rigorously administered a programme of 'discipline' which touched upon the most intimate aspects of the lives of the women and men of Scotland upon whose shoulders the hoodie-crow spectre of Calvin would perch for centuries.

James VI never knew his parents but he was taught, by George Buchanan, that his father, Darnley, had been murdered by his mother, Mary. His horrendous childhood experiences must have made him often doubt, at the very least, his security, at worst the very legitimacy of his position as king, all compounded by the tenets of Presbyterianism which were dinned into his being. The safety of his person in doubt in a faction-ridden kingdom, it is small wonder that as some little defence he attempted to shelter himself in theories of divine right kingship revived from an earlier era. The king, however, was far too intelligent to believe implicitly in absolutism though it must have been with considerable relief that he set out for England, a kingdom which had fostered the cult of 'Gloriana' and which understood the divinity which doth hedge a king.

There is little doubt that he worked hard at anglicising, not to mention 'civilising' Scotland, from the safe haven of Westminster. He it was who smashed the Border reivers, who tamed the rebel earls in Orkney and Shetland, and who created mayhem in Gaelic Scotland, where he advocated the plantation of Lowland settlers, the deculturisation of the Gael and the genocide of such clans as the MacGregors and the MacDonalds, disastrous policies, the hideous enormity of which can scarcely be exaggerated. From such actions he did not retreat though he is credited with knowing when to pull back in the implementation of his attempts to bring the Scottish Church into line with that of England. If such was the case, and the matter is arguable, his son Charles displayed no such sensitivity. He took his despotic powers for granted and thus ensured that the true legacy of the personal union of 1603, the concern about, and the dissatisfaction with, the absentee monarch, was the Covenanting Revolution of 1638.

Campbells, saw the light and labelled themselves the 'Lords of the Congregation'. Mary of Guise was deposed. Elizabeth of England lent troops to defeat the French forces still in Scotland. History is never simple. A combination of circumstances, and more could be mentioned, conspired in the Reformation Parliament of 1560 which established Protestantism as the religion of the realm.

The *First Book of Discipline* formulated an ambitious programme of reform which embraced such subjects as the abolition of saints' days, the abolition of lay patronage, poor

The Death of Caledonia
and the
Birth of North Britain

1688-1850

SCOTLAND'S parliament is back in business after almost three centuries. If the intervening years have been a roller-coaster ride through an enthralling historical panorama taking in the heights of human ambition and achievement and the depths of human perfidy and depravity, it is perhaps time now to pause and take stock of the journey that has been travelled.

On the cusp of the uncertainties of the 21st century, it is instructive to look back 300 years and try to imagine what Scots then were thinking as they fretted nervously over the future that awaited them. A long period of constitutional chaos followed the Union of the Crowns in 1603 when James VI, King of Scotland, became James I, King of England, and the nation was engulfed in civil war. Religious tensions, issues about the role of the monarchy and relations with England posed major problems through the 17th century. The Revolution Settlement of 1689-90 which banished James VII and replaced him on the throne with his daughter Queen Mary and her husband, the unswervingly Protestant William of Orange, established Presbyterianism as the national religion of Scotland but did not resolve matters. The Scottish parliament had taken on new powers which seemed to threaten the security of England and

questioned the future of the shared monarchy of the two nations. Evidence of the new powers of the parliament were to be found in the decision to establish a trading colony at Darien on the isthmus of Panama. Hopes were high that the scheme would lead to national salvation, and when it collapsed it destroyed morale and self confidence. The failure of the Darien expedition to carve out a line of economic development, that was not dependent on England, added to the growing tensions between the two nations. By 1704 there was a major crisis in Anglo-Scottish relations. The Treaty of Union was conceived as an endeavour to ease these tensions and both countries had their different agendas and interest. Far from setting out the template for the future British state, it was a mish-mash of a compromise which had to cater for a whole range of different interests. The overriding objective was to secure peace between the two nations and secure the Protestant succession to the crown. Long before anyone thought about giving ordinary people the vote, Scotland's ruling elite imposed its will on an unwilling country where it provoked riots in the streets.

Once in place, the Union did not deliver its promised benefits overnight. Indeed, it made little difference to most Scots. A good comparison would be to consider the signing of the Maastricht Treaty. Technically, we are all European citizens now and historians in the future may talk about Maastricht as the day the European Union was created. The reality is that most of us have noticed no change.

In the early 18th century, a fully fledged, functioning and independent Scotland was a threat few English politicians were prepared to contemplate, especially when they were at war with France. The Union was a security imperative, won through unequal negotiation and then confirmed by the destruction of the Jacobites at Culloden.

By 1750, with Jacobitism a lost cause, Scotland's leaders were determined to bury the past, quite literally, and concentrate on being 'North Britain', even if there was no complementary move on the part of the English to become 'South Britain'. The Scottish Enlightenment followed, cementing the Union.

There have been few periods in the history of Scotland which witnessed such a radical transformation in society as the 1770s to the 1850s. Scotland moved from being a predominantly rural country based on subsistence agriculture, where each farmer grew just enough food for his own family with maybe a little left over to sell at market, and became one which was overwhelmingly urban and industrial where people sold their labour.

It was an age of revolutions in every aspect of everyday living as the new forces of commercialism spread inexorably through the whole of Scottish society. Manufacturing and commerce altered the traditional economic base, allowing Scotland to leapfrog its way from a position as one of the poorest and most backward countries in Europe to a leading role at the cutting edge of contemporary technology.

The economic revolution entailed a social revolution. The middle classes expanded as the wealth they accumulated from commerce and industry increased. With money went status and their political expectations grew accordingly and inspired a more questioning attitude to the long-established hegemony of the old aristocracy. People were no longer content to believe that entry to the ruling class was dictated by an accident of birth. American and French revolutions awoke ideals of participation in government for the majority rather than a self-perpetuating minority.

The middle class as taxpayers and wealth-creators thought it only natural that they should be given their due when it came to the government of their nation.

Yet, for all the sweeping changes in the social and economic structure and the onset of new ideas about democracy and responsibility, the aristocracy did not face a serious challenge to their authority. For while the land-owning elite of Scotland may have been politically conservative, they were not as reticent when it came to matters of making money. The Scottish aristocracy were not slow in exploiting the opportunities offered to them by the growth in commerce and business. Estates were improved, royalties extracted for mineral rights, investments in industry were made, property bought and sold. With economic muscle, the Scottish aristocracy were able to ensure that the tentacles of patronage continued to hold society tightly in their grip.

Patronage meant that lawyers, intellectuals and clergymen 'the cream of the middle-class aspirants' owed their living to the beneficence of the aristocracy, so it was hardly likely that they would question the status quo and risk their own advancement. It was only in the Church that a middle-class assault on the citadels of patronage paid off.

The Industrial Revolution which changed Scottish society out of all recognition, far from being a technological revolution, was heavily dependent on the labour of women and children. While many Scots rejoiced in Enlightenment notions of virtue and liberty, Scottish society was not very liberal or very virtuous. Politicians were generally corrupt and trapped by a cynical network of patronage that could not, however, defy for ever the advance of the democratic movement.

Change was a slow burn. In much of Scotland, life went on as before. The Enlightenment may have ushered in a new way of thinking about the world, but many Scots manifested anxieties about their identities. While Scotland did change dramatically at this time, not all Scots abandoned their old ways.

JAMES VI & I

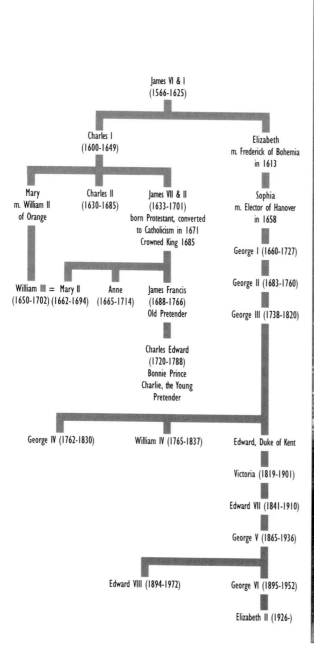

James VI & I
(1566-1625)

Charles I
(1600-1649)

Elizabeth
m. Frederick of Bohemia
in 1613

Mary
m. William II
of Orange

Charles II
(1630-1685)

James VII & II
(1633-1701)
born Protestant, converted
to Catholicism in 1671
Crowned King 1685

Sophia
m. Elector of Hanover
in 1658

George I (1660-1727)

George II (1683-1760)

William III = Mary II
(1650-1702) (1662-1694)

Anne
(1665-1714)

James Francis
(1688-1766)
Old Pretender

George III (1738-1820)

Charles Edward
(1720-1788)
Bonnie Prince
Charlie, the Young
Pretender

George IV (1762-1830)

William IV (1765-1837)

Edward, Duke of Kent

Victoria (1819-1901)

Edward VII (1841-1910)

George V (1865-1936)

Edward VIII (1894-1972)

George VI (1895-1952)

Elizabeth II (1926-)

CHAPTER 1

The Age of Union
1688-1707

THREE hundred years ago Scotland was in crisis. The final decade of the 17th century was to be the culmination of an unhappy century blighted by war, political uncertainty and famine. With the Union of the Crowns in 1603, James VI of Scotland inherited the crown of England and became James I. He removed himself to London, returning only once in 1617 but otherwise confining himself to his southern kingdom.

James might have been King of Scotland but he and his Queen, Anne, became strangers to its people and they were unable to bring about the promised 'perfect union' with England. The two countries remained constitutionally and legally separate, and mutually antagonistic. The English were suspicious that rapacious Scots would help themselves to the richer nation's wealth, while the Scots feared absorption into a larger and more powerful neighbour. King-sharing from such a distant London base meant there was a vacuum at the head of the Scottish state with no one to symbolise nationhood and no royal court to display the trappings of power.

The last British king to be born in Scotland was James' son, Charles I. He entered the world in 1600 in the ancient Scots capital of Dunfermline but left for England at the age of three. A sickly child who succeeded to the throne in 1625 only because of the death of his teenage brother, he proved himself a hapless monarch without his father's political acumen. His idea was to bind his two kingdoms together by combining the Scottish and English churches. In the north, this was regarded as unjustified Anglicisation and it was greatly resented in a country where the King's long absence had allowed national identity to focus increasingly on the Kirk with its distinctive brand of Presbyterianism.

Charles' dictatorial style further alienated the Scots. In 1637, he used the royal prerogative – bypassing the Scottish parliament and the General Assembly of the Church of Scotland – to try to impose an English Book of Common Prayer, clearly at odds with Calvinist doctrine. Although withdrawn, the botched attempt led directly to the signing of the National Covenant by a wide sector of Scottish society and the outbreak of civil war across Britain, the War of the Three Kingdoms: namely Scotland, England and Ireland. The Army of the Covenant then did not endear itself to the English by invading the north of their country.

The English parliament under the influence of the republican-minded Oliver Cromwell, the Protector, denounced Charles I as a tyrant and had him executed. The Scots, placing their faith in a covenanted King rather than republicanism, crowned his son Charles II at Scone in 1651. They then promptly invaded England in a bid to impose Presbyterianism on the rest of Britain only to be defeated at the Battle

15

of Worcester by Cromwell and his new model army which was then able to move north unchallenged to occupy Scotland. It stayed for the period of the Interregnum (1651-1660), doing little to improve neighbourly relations.

After Cromwell's death, the monarchy was restored in England and with it Charles II to the joint throne. Many Scots allowed themselves to believe that things would improve. After all, Charles had signed the Solemn League and Covenant endorsing Presbyterianism at his Scone coronation, albeit at gunpoint. But this was just wishful thinking because Charles, like all monarchs, had no time for Presbyterianism. He regarded it as dangerously radical because it did not operate on any hierarchical structure and the Scottish aristocracy were similarly hostile, despite paying lip service and being immune by virtue of their status to ritual humiliations like the stool of repentance in church as had to be endured by commoners. Presbyterianism was deemed to give too much

power to the people. Therefore, Presbyterianism and good order, it was thought in the fearful higher echelons of Scottish society, could not properly go together.

When Presbyterianism failed to be legally established as the national religion, Covenanting took to the open air, kept alive by large crowds of sympathisers who gathered to hear itinerant preachers in outdoor venues, which were known as conventicles. These gatherings were illegal and the crowds were often armed and ready to take on government troops seeking to break them up. The continuing persecution of Covenanters only served to reinforce their resolution and increase their radicalism.

In 1679 the Duke of York, the heir to the throne and a high profile Catholic, arrived in Edinburgh to oversee military operations against the Covenanters. This resulted in what has passed into folklore as 'the killing time' with no mercy shown to the Covenanters by the authorities.

A King, a Commoner, and a Queen: Scots-born Charles I (left) was denounced as a tyrant by Oliver Cromwell (above), then Charles II was restored to the throne to be succeeded eventually by Queen Anne (right), final facilitator of the Union

———— ◈ ————

In 1685 the Duke succeeded to the throne, as James VII and II, after the death of his brother, provoking the Presbyterian Earl of Argyll to stage an uprising. It was suppressed but James then took the opportunity to make a significant concession; all religions would now be tolerated in his kingdoms. If this was intended to appease increasingly hardened Covenanters, it did not. Instead, it had exactly the opposite effect as it was interpreted as James preparing the ground for the imminent introduction of Catholicism. The parliaments of Scotland and

union that was to be achieved in 1707. There is little credibility in claims that it was brought about by far-seeing statesmen and some say it was all a bit of a messy compromise as the Scots traded political independence for the economic benefits of access to English and colonial markets against a very confusing background of shifting political intrigue.

Whatever the reasons, the Anglo-Scottish relationship had reached crisis point as the 18th century dawned. The Scots were unhappy with their constitutional arrangements. Scottish trade with Europe had withered away as a result of English wars. The Darien Scheme was conceived as an attempt to gain economic independence and reduce reliance on English markets through establishing Scotland's own overseas colony. England had strategic interests in preventing it from taking root and, when it finally collapsed, a consensus was born among the governing elite of Scotland that something had to change.

The death of Queen Anne's last surviving child, the Duke of Gloucester, in 1700 – she gave birth to 17 – turned up the constitutional heat. Anne was James VII's daughter (Mary, wife of King William was another) so although the Stewart monarchy had been deposed, had Anne's boy child survived, the line would have been passed down the immediate family. It was the fact that the next monarch would have to be found in another line of the family which concentrated minds on the matter. In such trying circumstances, the Protestant succession was far from certain and anarchy would break out if Scotland and England backed different candidates for the throne. Therefore, to ensure the peace, Scotland and England would have to speak with a single voice. The Scottish parliament was to be sacrificed for the greater good.

England rebelled at the prospect, and James' daughter Mary, along with her Protestant husband William of Orange, were invited to take the throne. In Scotland James was said to have been deposed. England put it more diplomatically; it was reported that he had abdicated.

In 1690, the Scottish parliament armed itself with a new range of constitutional powers and Presbyterianism was finally proclaimed as the national religion of Scotland. Other religions, Catholicism and Episcopalianism, were not outlawed but their followers were discriminated against by having no legally enforceable rights in land or property ownership.

The scene was now set for a new episode to open in the far from friendly relationship between Scotland and England. Historians have been, and remain divided on the compelling causes of the eventual parliamentary

Massacre of Glencoe

THE origins of the massacre can be traced back to a decision taken by Dalrymple of Stair, the Lord Advocate, in 1691, in order to demonstrate the power of the state and to suppress the Jacobite activities in the Highlands. It would also demonstrate the Lord Advocate's loyalty to King William.

The Jacobites took their name from the Latin form of James, the king whom William had supplanted, so if a disobedient Jacobite clan was singled out for punishment it would keep the others in check.

Glencoe was renowned for lawlessness due to its geographical isolation which made it impossible to effectively police. As was often the case in matters of 17th-century law and order, terror and reprisals served as an effective deterrent. By deliberately obtaining orders signed by King William himself to 'extirpate Highland rebels', Dalrymple had secured carte blanche for his Highland policy. All that was needed was the scapegoat.

The MacIains of Glencoe (a sept of MacDonald Clanranald), were the unlucky victims. The clan had been notorious for cattle thieving and the fact that they were either Episcopalian or Catholic made them likely Jacobite supporters. Dalrymple believed that the punishment of a 'popish clan' would be popular with the people.

Government policy had stipulated that all clan chiefs had to give an undertaking of loyalty to the new regime by January 1, 1692. The elderly chief of the clan, Alastair MacIain, set off in atrocious weather with every intention of meeting the deadline. Unfortunately, he mistakenly journeyed to Fort William where the commander refused to accept his oath. The old man set off in a blizzard, south, was arrested and detained, found no sheriff when he eventually arrived in Inverary and eventually took the oath five days late. The government now had its target.

Early in the morning of February 13, 1692, a detachment of soldiers under the command of Captain Robert Campbell of Glenlyon butchered 38 members of the clan and torched the settlement. It was far from a textbook massacre. Glencoe was hedged in on both sides by mountains and escape should have been impossible, especially in winter. The original plan was for a dawn raid with troops advancing along both sides of the glen, preventing escape and wiping out the MacIains. About 850 armed men would take on the 100 men of the clan and 500 women and children.

The operation, however, was botched and the attempt to seal the passes failed. The original plans required precision and took no account of the problems of marching over difficult terrain in inhospitable weather. The element of surprise was lost and most of the intended victims escaped, although many of them perished in the snows as they fled. The survivors, including two sons of the chief, were able to tell the outside world what had happened and the result was that, far from setting an example, the news of the massacre horrified most people. The stories of rape and murder were seized on by Jacobite propagandists and half-hearted disclaimers by the government failed to allay disquiet. Indeed, the unseemly efforts of the politicians to dissociate themselves from government Highland policy and an attempted cover up made them appear more guilty. In 1695, the Scottish parliament condemned the atrocity as an act of murder. Dalrymple, was forced out of office, although he remained unrepentant. Glenlyon, who took to drink in the taverns of Edinburgh, carried his written orders to convince everyone he was not to blame. The fact that Glenlyon was one of the Campbells, traditional rivals and enemies of Clan Donald, hardened attitudes against the new regime, although actually most of his soldiers were not Campbells at all. Ultimately, the massacre only served to stiffen Jacobite resolve in the Highlands.

Glencoe was a botched military operation ordered by a government which then condemned it as murder, although more perished in the snow than died by the sword

The Darien Adventure

JOHN CAMPBELL
2nd Duke of Argyll
1678-1743

JOHN succeeded to his father's dukedom in 1703 and was known among his clansmen by his Gaelic nickname of 'Red John of the Battles'. In 1705, Queen Anne appointed him Scottish High Commissioner and set him the task of preparing the way for the Union between Scotland and England. Argyll was a soldier and planned his campaign for Union with military precision and great ruthlessness. He had little time for politics or politicians and used court patronage to ensure and buy compliance from members of the Scottish parliament. His own support for Union was bought by the award of an English peerage as the Baron of Chatham and Earl of Greenwich.

WILLIAM PATERSON, an avaricious financier from Dumfriesshire, predicted that the colony at Darien on the inhospitable isthmus of Panama would prove the 'door of the seas and the key of the universe' by providing a link between the Atlantic and the Pacific. Instead, for many it proved the gateway to disease, despair and death. The unfolding tragedy involved a cast of characters to make any playwright drool – adventurers, charlatans, buccaneers, Spanish grandees, cunning native chiefs, expectant investors, sea captains, soldiers, loyal wives and dutiful children.

Andrew Fletcher of Saltoun captured the mood of the country when he distinguished the whole ambitious scheme as 'a greater venture at sea than at any time since we have been a nation'. To contemporaries, Darien was a symbol of commercial and national aspiration set against a devastating scenario at home of famine and homelessness; a venture embroiled in an international crisis which absorbed half the world – the fate of the Spanish Empire. To posterity, it was to become a metaphor for Scottish hubris, mismanagement and failure.

The Company of Scotland Trading to Africa and the Indies was founded by an Act of the Scottish parliament in June 1695. Initial hopes that investment capital could be raised in London were dashed when the East India Company put pressure on King William to oppose it, as it also blocked later schemes to find alternatives in Amsterdam and Hamburg. The issue then became a matter of national pride, as the Scots were left to raise a target of £400,000 on their own.

Paterson promised 'riches and a golden age' to all who joined in the project. It was anticipated that Scottish settlers already in the Caribbean would flock to the new colony.

Fearful of offending Spain, King William pulled the plug on local assistance for the adventurers, an action

Leith 1800: in July 1698, five ships set out from the harbour.
William Paterson, who founded the Bank of England before promoting the
Darien scheme as Scotland's economic salvation, was on board

which further fuelled Scottish resentment. Pamphleteers, quoting William Wallace and the Declaration of Arbroath, protested that Scots were treated worse than foreigners.

There were two expeditions to Darien; the first fleet of five ships carrying some 1,200 sailed from Leith in July 1698. The commanders' instructions specified that 'by consent of the natives' they were to plant a colony in an uninhabited place in America not possessed by any other European power. As the travellers approached their destination they noted islands reminiscent of the Bass Rock and Inchkeith in the Firth of Forth, while another at night-time appeared 'just as the Castle of Edinburgh does to any going up from Leith'.

The expedition arrived at Golden Island on 3 November to be greeted by native Indians who mistook them for English. On being told that the Scots wished to settle among them and be their friends, the natives reassured them that their arrival had been predicted two years earlier and the omens were excellent for a successful venture.

What was rapidly to become apparent was that the naively patronising colonists were to be manipulated by the Indians who had already experienced 200 years of European contact. Within a day, the natives were flying Scottish flags on their canoes to further flatter the visitors, as they might today for some passing cruise ship.

The Indian agenda involved recruiting Scottish support against Spain while the Scots offered trade at a preferential rate – though the substantial quantities of clothing and footwear in their cargo seemed redundant when the chiefs appeared in the latest fashions of Spain and France. Savage nakedness, as presumed from Scotland, was disappointingly uncommon.

On St Andrew's Day, the Council of the Colony of New Caledonia entered into a Treaty of Friendship, Union and Perpetual Confederation with Chief Andreas. It was anticipated that the liberation of the natives 'from the hideous conditions under the Spanish' would follow, the Scots refusing to acknowledge the papal edict which had originally conferred the vast Atlantic territories on Spain.

The colonists established Fort St Andrew, defended by the sea and a canal, above their anchorage in Caledonia Bay, known today as Puerto Escoces. Nearby was projected the community of New Edinburgh.

The main enemy proved to be lack of supply and the unfamiliar fevers of an alien environment. The Scots dropped like flies, but the final blow came with the appreciation of the true depths of English hostility to Scottish success – 'It is in the interest of England to take all fair ways to defeat the settlement of Darien.' Failing to receive aid or supply, hundreds died as the colonists retreated to what they

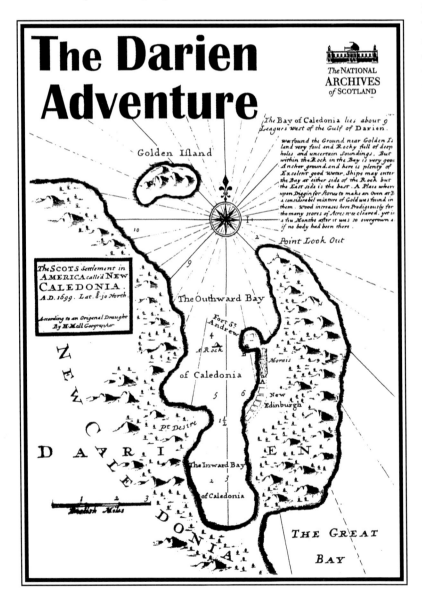

imagined were the more hospitable climes of the Caribbean and New York.

Meanwhile, a second expedition numbering 1,300 people was preparing to leave the Clyde in September 1699. A kind of Darienomania seized Scotland as poems and songs were composed and volunteers rushed to embark. Such euphoria, unsurprisingly, was not receptive to reports that Darien had been abandoned.

Yet so it proved, save for a couple of sloops commanded by Thomas Drummond, a veteran of the previous sortie. Once again, strife seized the community before Robert Campbell of Fonab arrived to take charge. It was he who, with the help of the Indians, defeated a Spanish force at Toubacanti, Scotland's one victory in Latin America and arguably the most creditable episode of the entire dismal venture. Spanish ships blockaded the colony and large numbers of the would-be settlers died. On 31 March, 1700, the Scots surrendered on honourable terms.

When the parliament met two months later, King William's perfidy was manifest. Pamphleteers fulminated about the injuries sustained by 'this gallant and ancient nation', her

WILLIAM PATERSON

1658-1719

PATERSON was born on a farm in Dumfriesshire. He became a trader in the West Indies, and founded the Bank of England in London before returning home to Scotland, where he persuaded his fellow countrymen that the establishment of a colony at Darien would be the making of the nation.

He sailed with the first expedition as a private individual and returned an all but broken man in December 1699. He then directed

his energies into suing for the Treaty of Union, which had become the most obvious way out of the economic hole dug by the failure of the Darien scheme.

After 1707, he was elected as the first MP for the Dumfries burghs. There, he used his financial talents to tackle the problem of reducing the National Debt.

A few years before his death, he was awarded £18,000 as indemnity for his Darien losses.

sovereignty and freedom violated, laws trampled upon and trade interrupted. When news of the Toubacanti triumph reached Edinburgh on 20 June, the city was convulsed by anti-government riots. Worse was to come as news of the Darien surrender filtered through; many who had escaped the Panamanian graveyard were now prisoners of

the Spanish. Investors demanded compensation as the Scots apportioned blame to everyone save themselves.

The company survived until the Union. Famously, one ship did return from the African trade, to yield a substantial profit. Yet so deep-rooted was the Darien rage, that Captain Green of the *Worcester* and two of his crew were executed in 1705 on a trumped-up charge of having seized a company ship in Madagascar.

The Darien experience undoubtedly stoked the fires of Scottish chauvinism, helping to ensure that the Union negotiations were tough and aggressive. The insane folly of challenging the might of Spain was quietly forgotten, as was the ignorance and ineptitude which characterised the entire venture, consuming, as it did, as much as one quarter of Scotland's wealth. But the craze for trade and the greed which motivated the investors also dictated their willingness to be bought out with the Union. The most significant legacy of Darien was thus, for good or ill, the United Kingdom of Great Britain.

Dead end at Darien: in Puerto Escoces, Caledonia Bay, where heroic aspiration was to be revealed as insane folly

The Matter of Union

SCOTLAND in 1707 had a population of around 1.1 million, and the capital city, Edinburgh, around 30,000. Politicians at the time feared that Scotland faced a bleak economic future because of the failure of Darien. The 1690s, commonly known as the 'Lean Years', had been a period of severe harvest failure and famine. At least 25% of the national wealth had been lost in the attempt to create a Scottish trading colony in the Darien adventure, deliberately scuppered by King William (King Billy) in order to protect the economic interests of England and its colonial trade.

Scotland's economic and trading interests had traditionally been strong with Europe, but by the early 18th century Scottish exports, principally cattle and linen, went mainly to England. Scotland also faced political problems, the most important of which was her future with England. Since 1603, Scotland and England had shared the same monarch but were independent kingdoms. The current monarch was Queen Anne but she had no surviving heirs and the main concern in London was to ensure a Protestant succession in both England and Scotland. England was also involved in the War of the Spanish Succession fought against the aggressive foreign policy of France. English politicians wanted to ensure a quick resolution to the political problem of Scotland where the Edinburgh parliament was becoming more politically and constitutionally nationalist. Edinburgh sought control over its own foreign policy and the right to decide on its own successor to the Scottish throne. It also resented interference in Scottish affairs by English politicians and the 'Court interest', whose job it was to manage Scottish affairs on behalf of the monarch in London. This rise in 'constitutional nationalism' met with a swift response from the English parliament which exploited Scotland's weak economic position and threatened to treat the Scots as 'aliens', excluding them from English markets.

By 1705 the only acceptable political outcome for Westminster politicians was an incorporating union between England and Scotland. Political treachery by the Duke of Hamilton, one of the leaders of the opposition in Scotland, ensured that the Scottish MPs who negotiated the Treaty of

---

Queen Anne and her courtiers discuss the Treaty of Union prior to 1707. Once it was signed, the Earl of Seafield lamented: 'There's an end to an old song'

In black and white: 25 Articles of Union that created Great Britain

Union with their English counterparts were chosen by Queen Anne and all bar one of the Scottish negotiators was in favour of an incorporating union. This did not represent the majority of Scottish political opinion. Most politicians wanted some kind of closer links with England but federalism was the preferred option. This would have kept the Scottish parliament and placed restrictions on a future Scottish monarch. However, a federal union was unacceptable in London and the treaty was drawn up in the summer of 1706 before being presented to the Scottish parliament for final ratification in January 1707.

Scotland's parliament was a single chamber institution of 147 men which comprised three 'Estates'; the nobility, shire representatives, and burgh representatives. Ordinary people had no say in elections in the modern sense, and the parliament's membership was based on representation of the elite classes. It was these elites, rather than the people of Scotland, who voted for the Treaty of Union.

There were anti-union riots in Glasgow, Edinburgh and Dumfries in the winter of 1706 as the Treaty of Union passed through the parliamentary system. Glasgow Town Council imposed a curfew and 200 dragoons were sent to the city to help maintain public order. Rioting in Edinburgh was particularly intense. One of the MPs for the burgh of Edinburgh, former provost Sir Patrick Johnston, was attacked by the mob. Several of the leading MPs who were in favour of the Union were jostled and manhandled as they approached the parliament in their carriages. Anti-Union petitions were delivered by burghs, presbyteries and individual church parishes, all designed to stop the Union the parliament was about to endorse.

The Church of Scotland was at first one of the most vociferous opponents

ANDREW FLETCHER OF SALTOUN

1653–1716

IRONICALLY for one known as 'the Patriot', Fletcher spent most of his life furth of Scotland. As an MP he bitterly opposed Stewart absolutism. Forced into exile, he supported Monmouth's rebellion of 1685 and in his absence he was attainted a traitor, returning home with William of Orange in 1688. He wrote several discourses and speeches, later published as *The*

Political Works. A proponent of the dismantling of the Scottish feudal system, he harboured certain republican sympathies though his debt to the tradition of Scottish political philosophy has been overlooked. He is best known for his opposition to the Union in 1707 but as a radical loner he represented no real party or interest and held no sway over the final decision.

of the Union, but when it became clear that the Presbyterian religion would be safeguarded the hostility of the Church faded away.

The government of the day was also frightened by the prospect of an armed uprising. Lanarkshire was perceived to be one of the hotbeds of potential plans to raise an army to march on Edinburgh. Shotts, Stonehouse and Lesmahagow were identified as the more fertile recruiting grounds. Troops in the north of England and on continental Europe were put on standby. England was confident it could suppress any uprising but left nothing to chance. In Scotland, the MPs knew that they were making a major decision on the country's future. Some genuinely believed their best prospects lay in union with England. Others, however, had other reasons.

Robert Burns would later argue that Scottish MPs were 'bought and sold for English gold' and that the Union was passed by bribery and corruption. A sum of £20,000 sterling (£240,000 Scots) was sent to Scotland at the time, ostensibly for back payments of parliamentary salaries, but it also seems

to have been used to secure key votes to enable the Treaty to be passed. David Boyle, first Earl of Glasgow, was entrusted with the task of secretly distributing this money amongst the MPs. A key political group within the parliament was the Squadrone Volante – the Flying Squad – which controlled 25 crucial votes, enough to tip the balance in a London parliament where political groupings were notoriously hard to deliver as a single block. The Squadrone Volante comprised MPs such as the Marquesses of Montrose and Tweeddale and the Earls of Roxburgh, Marchmont and Leven, who were basically a bunch of chancers motivated entirely by self interest. They all received money from Boyle, although it was not until 1711 that these corrupt payments were actually exposed via a Westminster commission of inquiry.

The outcome of these secret deals was that the Treaty of Union was passed in opposition to the will of the people. Scotland gained free trade with England, access to English colonies and came to play a leading role in the British Empire. It lost its independence and its parliament.

CHAPTER 2

The Jacobite Threat

1707-46

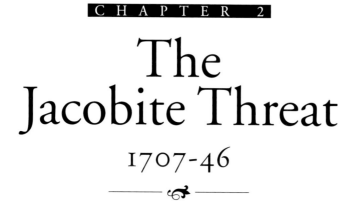

LITTLE changed in Scotland during the first years of the Union. The country was governed essentially by the same people as before and everyday life was not drastically altered for most. In many ways, the Union was invisible, delivering none of the much-vaunted trade benefits. It had been brought about by a constitutional crisis in Anglo-Scots relations yet it did not solve the core of these problems. Five years after the treaty was signed and sealed, the Scots nobility transferred to the House of Lords in London voted, unsuccessfully, for its repeal.

Jacobites – supporters of the deposed Stewart dynasty – bided their time, as did most people, waiting to see how the political dice would fall. The politics of the time was motivated as much by self interest as by ideology and although the Hanoverian succession was guaranteed on paper, few were sure that it was a *fait accompli*. After all, Queen Anne was a Stewart and until a Hanoverian sat on the throne, the political situation in Scotland and England would remain unstable.

The critical moment came in 1714 when Queen Anne died and 'German Geordie', George I, arrived to claim the throne. A key player in Scottish politics at this time was the Earl of Mar, John Erskine, known as 'Bobbing John' on account of his indecisiveness in politics and his tendency to try to

be everyone's friend. Mar had been one of the signatories to the Union and believed that he would be rewarded for his sterling services in ensuring the Hanoverian succession. When no material rewards were forthcoming, 'Bobbing John' switched sides in the hope of bettering himself by restoring the Stewarts. From his base at Braemar, Mar led the Jacobite rebellion of 1715.

The Highlands were the staging posts for Jacobite insurrections for a number of reasons: the area was very hard to police and operations could be initiated with little government harassment; Highland society retained a quasi-military structure and troops could be put into the field quickly; a number of large clans had lost territory to the powerful House of Argyll, which effectively acted as a police force for the government in the western Highlands. The clans believed a return of the Stewarts to the throne would restore their lost lands and privileges.

There were others who were attracted to the Jacobite cause. The Episcopalians of the north-east had seen their religion degraded from one which was officially sanctioned by the state to one persecuted by it. Although the Stewarts were Catholic,

A mounted Bonnie Prince Charlie leading the charge during the '45

Episcopalians believed they would get a better deal as loyal subjects of James VIII, the Old Pretender, than the current Presbyterian-backed Hanoverian regime. Some even believed in the justice of the Stewart cause, arguing that to depose a true monarch was unlawful in the eyes of God. Others, such as Mar, were more pragmatic and assessed the odds to see which of the sides would offer the best opportunities for self-advancement.

The wily Roderick Chisholm of Chisholm, remained neutral, while two of his sons fought for the Hanoverians and the other for the Jacobites in the '45 Rising. It was the perfect insurance policy.

In that spirit, with rebellion in the air, the Duke of Hamilton diplomatically retired to his estates with a 'toothache' and waited to see how the events would turn out.

The Union was particularly unpopular north of the Tay and Mar made easy progress, occupying Perth and Inverness before making ready for an assault on the lowlands. On 20 September, 1715, James VIII was proclaimed king at Aberdeen while he waited in France. But Mar's indecisive trait, while an asset for a politician, was a major liability for a soldier. It was a mistake to hedge his bets and divide his forces, pushing east against Edinburgh and west against the Argyll stronghold of Inverary. Both assaults were repulsed. Worse was to follow.

On 13 November, 1715, at Sheriffmuir, north of Stirling, Mar's army of 10,000 men faced the 4,000 assembled by the Duke of Argyll. Despite the numerical advantage, the battle was indecisive. The Jacobites were forced to retreat and lost the initiative. The arrival of 6,000 Dutch troops and the surrender of the Jacobite army in the south tipped the balance in favour of the Hanoverians. The Old Pretender stepped ashore at Peterhead three days

Too late the hero: the Old Pretender landed in 1715 when the Jacobite rebellion was already collapsing. His son, the Young Pretender, tried again later

☙

before Christmas in 1715. He set up court in Scone but the rebellion was collapsing around him and on 4 February, 1716, he sailed from Montrose back to exile in France.

The Duke of Argyll tried to impress on the government just how lucky they had been. Intelligence reports backed up his case and a third of Justices of the Peace north of the Tay were reckoned to have supported the rebellion. Jacobite estates were confiscated and run by trustees, Clans were made to disarm, garrisons were stationed to ensure the peace of the Highlands and roads were built to facilitate easy troop movement to quell another rebellion. Hanoverian resolve, however, was not as steadfast as the Jacobites' and after the rebellion of 1715 the safeguards were gradually dismantled. Troops were withdrawn, many Jacobites were pardoned after an oath of good conduct, and the only clans to disarm were those loyal to the government.

International politics had their bearing on the fortunes of the Jacobites.

France was keen to use the Stewart cause to promote internal instability within the territory of its greatest threat. Charles Edward Stewart believed that the French ought to give wholehearted support to his cause in the name of the divine right of kings. The French, however, were keen to use Jacobitism for their own purposes. It was French inaction which prompted Prince Charles to initiate the uprising of 1745 in the hope that a successful insurrection would spur the French on to an invasion of the south of England. With a handful of supporters he raised his father's standard at Glenfinnan on 19 August, 1745.

From the outset, the adventure seemed doomed. Charles did not have official French support, although that did not stop him from claiming to his followers that he had. Without such claims, few would have supported him. Furthermore, far from a wild rush to support the rightful king, recruitment was slow and uneven. Yet the Jacobites had a number of advantages. The military garrisons left in the Highlands had been depleted and were staffed mostly by raw recruits. The Jacobites had the element of surprise. And far from enabling the government to respond to any rebellion, the roads constructed by General Wade in the aftermath of the '15 enabled the Jacobites to move quickly and effectively. Garrisons and forts were cut off, and to everyone's amazement, the Jacobites were allowed to occupy the eastern Lowlands, almost without a shot being fired. Raw recruits were no match for the hardened Highland shock troops who formed the backbone of Charles' advance guard. At Prestonpans, the Jacobites defeated an evenly matched army and then prepared for the invasion of England.

Jacobite military success was based on the Highland charge. Highlanders would approach the enemy lines and hover just out of range of the muskets. Warfare at this time demanded a great deal of nerve and discipline. Muskets were hopelessly inaccurate and took time to load. The Highlanders would try to unnerve the enemy by jeering,

Lord George Murray: the prince wouldn't listen to his military commander

———— ❧ ————

taunting and making false charges which were designed to break the Hanoverians' firing discipline. If soldiers fired too early, it was a wasted shot, during which time the line was vulnerable to a charge as muskets had to be reloaded. Having psyched out

the enemy, the Highlanders would advance, fire their muskets into the enemy lines, discard them, and charge with broadswords, reaching the Hanoverians before the soldiers had the chance to get off a second volley. It took nerves of steel to face a full-blooded Highland onslaught and this nerve was lacking in the government forces at the outset of the campaign. Fleeing soldiers left gaps in the line and left their comrades vulnerable, and were themselves liable to be hacked down by their pursuers.

Charles was lucky in the fact that he had a gifted military commander, Lord George Murray. Having secured most of Scotland, Charles did not consolidate his position, nor did he break the Union and recall the Scottish parliament as he had promised. Instead he advanced on northern England in the hope that Jacobite strongholds would emerge to support him. Unfortunately, Charles fancied himself as a strategist and did not listen to his advisers. An occupation of the north of England would have stopped coal supplies to London, created panic in the south and would have meant that the lines of communication were not overstretched. Charles, however, wanted to press south. Furthermore, he made great play of the French invasion of the south and the supplies which would be coming over the channel. The truth was that the French were caught hopelessly unaware. Indeed, the main reason why the Jacobites encountered little resistance from the south was that the bulk of the government's forces were being held in reserve for the expected French invasion. Also, the government was remarkably slow in taking the threat from the north seriously. By the time the Jacobites had reached Derby it was clear to all that there was no French invasion force and only inadequate supplies. Dangerously overextended and with troops going

THE DUKE OF CUMBERLAND

1721-65

WILLIAM AUGUSTUS was the third son of King George II. He was a professional soldier who gained his military experience serving in the campaigns in the Low Countries during the War of Austrian Succession. He was a ruthless and stern disciplinarian. His 'pacification' of the Highlands following his victory at Culloden earned him the nickname in the north of

'Butcher Cumberland'. The common flower popularly known as Sweet William became Stinking Billy to his detractors. Although reprisals were part and parcel of warfare in early 18th-century Europe, the ferocity with which they were carried out on Cumberland's orders has led one modern historian, Allan Macinnes, to describe his policy as a form of ethnic cleansing.

home, Murray took the decision that the best option was a strategic retreat back to Scotland.

Having given the game away that there would be no French invasion and having failed to muster English Jacobite support, Murray made the best of a bad job. The retreat to Scotland was conducted efficiently and the Jacobites were able to snatch victories at Penrith, south of Carlisle, and at Falkirk on 17 January, 1746. The prospect of a Jacobite invasion of the south of England had forced on the Hanoverian regime the seriousness of their situation and had led to the recall of the Duke of Cumberland and battle hardened veterans from the war in Flanders. At the same time, the Duke of Argyll was raising the muster among his supporters in Scotland. The Jacobite army was pursued into its Highland hinterland and Charles, full of romantic bravado, issued a do or die call at the Battle of Culloden on 16 April 1746.

Tactically, the choice of Culloden was a disastrous one. The Jacobites faced a well-trained, highly disciplined army of 9,000 men, almost twice their number. Hanoverian artillery was superior and the famous Highland charge had to be made uphill over marshy terrain. The result was a total rout and, amid the carnage on the moor, Charles turned and fled, leaving his followers to fend for themselves as he went off to practise a legendary bout of Highland transvestitism before escaping to France.

The story does not end there. The Jacobite rebellion of 1745 arguably had the least chance of success but it had almost brought the Hanoverian regime to its knees. The leniency which was shown after the '15 would not be

Morier used defeated Scottish prisoners as models in his painting, An Incident in the Rebellion of 1745

CHARLES EDWARD
The Young Pretender
1719-1788

Popularly known as Bonnie Prince Charlie, he was the son of James Edward Stewart (the Old Pretender). Charles had little real contact with Scotland and grew up in the exiled Jacobite courts in France and Italy. After leaving his defeated forces at Culloden, he made his legendary escape dressed as a woman, helped by Flora Macdonald. After 1754, drinking excessively, he went into physical and mental decline. Finally in 1760 his Scottish Mistress Clementina Walkinshaw, who suffered much physical abuse at his hands over the years, left him. His subsequent marriage to a minor German princess, Louisa of Stolberg-Gedernin, collapsed by 1780 due to his violent alcoholism. With the death of his brother Henry in 1807, the Jacobite line ended, although this has not deterred some colourful claimants coming forward. Neither he nor his life were as romantic as subsequently painted.

repeated. After all, Edinburgh had fallen and England had been invaded. The most powerful nation in the world had seen its capital city, albeit for a very short time, threatened by 'barbarians from the north'. Not only had the rebellion caused panic and fear, the fact that the Jacobite army had got as far south as it did was a source of humiliation. The Hanoverians were not to know that Prince Charles was broken and had given up his campaign and was destined to die a dissolute alcoholic. It was resolved that there must be no repeat of the rebellion.

Even before Culloden, government propaganda was busy blackening the name of Highland society. The Highlanders were portrayed as bandits, thieves and 'a savage limb of the antichrist in Rome'. Black propaganda was issued by the government to account for the reasons why the Highlanders formed the backbone of the Jacobite army. It was claimed that the uneducated Highlanders were superstitious and easily controlled by their priests and chiefs. They were denounced as lazy and lacking self-discipline and the opportunity for plunder was more enticing than the rewards of industry. In short, Scotland had territory beyond the pale of civilisation. There were three phases of the military repression which followed Culloden. The first, lasting through the summer until the departure of Cumberland, involved the 'hot pursuit' of Jacobites and those believed to have been sympathetic to the cause. Rebels were sought out and given no quarter as they were subjected to arbitrary justice. Second, known Jacobite districts were treated to longer and more sustained repression. Coastal villages were bombarded from the sea. Third, cattle and crops were wilfully destroyed to impoverish the people. This economic warfare meant deprivation continued in the Highlands well beyond 1747.

Throughout these three phases, soldiers roamed in search of Jacobites. Women who helped starving or wounded prisoners were likely to be strip-searched and raped. Houses were searched and if arms were found, the occupier was put to death. Many Highlanders, Jacobites or not, fled the advancing troops, fearing draconian justice. Their abandoned houses were torched or, if left intact, were used for the 'quartering' of troops encouraged to live off the local inhabitants, like locusts, as a salutary lesson of the fate of all rebels.

Not all soldiers behaved in such a barbaric way. Many Highlanders who fought on the government side were more liberal in their interpretation of orders to root out rebels. Knowing them to be more sympathetic, Jacobites were more likely to give themselves up to fellow Gaels rather than lowlanders or English. Despite the purge in the Highlands, Jacobite sympathisers were still able to use the Highland terrain to smuggle supplies into Inverness and Fort William. Banditry and attacks on troops, classic guerilla warfare, still continued during this period, showing that state repression had not cowed everyone and the Highlands remained a dangerous place to be, and not only for the remnants of the Jacobite army.

Once the soldiers retired to barracks, evangelical clergymen invaded the Highlands. The military campaign may have been over, but the ideological war was just beginning. For many Hanoverians, the reasons for the rebellion were to be found within the nature of Highland society itself. Gaelic culture faced a cultural and legal onslaught. The 'barbarisms' of the Highlands were to be replaced by civilised values. Presbyterianism and the English language would convert the Highlander from his old ways and 'improve' the area so that decent

no truck with a movement which found the substance of its support among the Episcopalians and, at that time, Scotland's tiny Catholic population. Nor was it a Highland/Lowland war. The most powerful Hanoverian in Scotland was the Duke of Argyll, whose clansmen fought at Culloden alongside the professional government forces and gloried in the final defeat and humiliation of Bonnie Prince Charlie, the man who presumed to be their natural leader.

It was in the 19th century, when the real threat had faded into the past, that history was turned around. The Jacobites and Prince Charles were rediscovered and recast as the dashing romantic figures of popular imagination that are very far removed from the reality of being on the losing side in a savage struggle for power.

The moor at Culloden, near Inverness where the Jacobite cause was lost

people might be able to live in it. The systematic destruction of the traditions and culture of Highland society became a political priority.

There are a number of common misconceptions about the Jacobite rebellions which persist despite the evidence. The war between the Jacobites and the Hanoverians has sometimes been presented as a war between Scotland and England. It was not; rather it was a bloody civil war waged to decide who held ultimate political power within the British state. Prince Charles' claim was to both Scottish and English thrones, joined a century and a half before. Glasgow and the western lowlands remained implacably hostile to the Jacobite cause. Presbyterianism, which was the most popular religion in Scotland at that time, would hold

FLORA MACDONALD

1722-90

'A NAME that will be mentioned in history. and if courage and fidelity be virtues, mentioned with honour'. So famously said Dr Johnson when he met Flora in 1773. Best known as the 'lass' who brought Charles Edward Stewart, disguised as Betty Burke, 'over the sea to Skye' from Benbecula as he sought to avoid his pursuers after the defeat at Culloden. The episode was later immortalised by Samuel Johnson and Boswell. Flora, born in South Uist, was actually a lady of some status raised in the Clanranald household. In 1750, she married Allan Macdonald of Kingsburgh, Skye, and a quarter of a century later, emigrated to North Carolina where, as British loyalists, they became involved in the American War of Independence. She sailed back over the sea to Skye in 1779 and was buried there when she died in 1790.

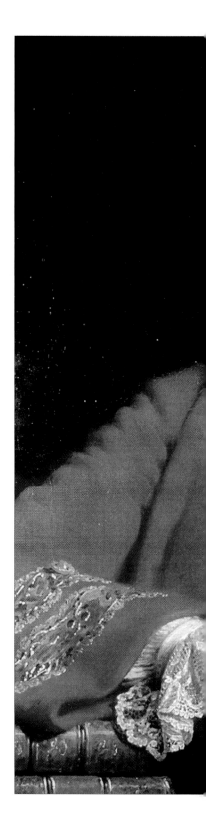

CHAPTER 3

The Age of Enlightenment

1750-1800

❧

'Is it not strange that at a time when we have lost our princes, our parliaments, our independent government, even the presence of our chief nobility, are unhappy in our accent and pronunciation, speak a very corrupt dialect of the tongue of which we make use of; is it not strange, I say, that, in these circumstances, we should really be the people most distinguished for literature in Europe?'

With these words the philosopher David Hume summed up the attitude of many of his contemporaries. Scotland, which for long had been regarded as a small, peripheral and poor nation, suddenly in the mid-18th century witnessed a great outpouring of intellectual endeavour. As one English observer noted: 'Here I stand at what is called the Cross of Edinburgh, and can, in a few minutes, take fifty men of genius and learning by the hand.' As Voltaire, the great French philosopher, said: 'It is to Edinburgh that we must look for our intellectual tastes.'

Just why Scotland should have produced such a prolific outpouring of genius at this time has puzzled many, but it is worth pointing out that Scotland was not the intellectual desert that many believed before this time. Before the Union when England had only two universities, so did Aberdeen, Marischal and King's College.

Scotland also had Edinburgh, Glasgow and St Andrews. Newtonian physics was taught in Scotland before England and in 1690 the Society for the Improvers was founded. Scotland had long established intellectual links with Europe. The place was not the un-educated backwater many made out.

The cultural background was very important in creating the fertile ground where intellectualism could take root. Scotland was undergoing a social and economic revolution at the time of the Enlightenment and this is reflected in many of the important subject areas which attracted Scots at this time. Adam Smith, the author of *The Wealth of Nations*, was a professor at the University of Glasgow, a city which was experiencing the development of the transatlantic economy. Smith could see the ships carrying goods from the window of his office.

Similarly, developments in medicine and science were given a considerable impetus by the development of industry and growing cities. It is noteworthy that the University of St Andrews trailed the other centres of learning in Scotland and was the only university town which did not experience major economic growth.

There was also an increase in toleration which was reflected in the more moderate style of the Church of

DAVID HUME

1711-76

DAVID HUME was the greatest of Scotland's philosophers.

He was a freethinker and atheist, and as such was denied a chair at a university. He had studied at Edinburgh but never graduated, working for a period as a counting house clerk in Bristol before living in France while writing his first and most important work, *A Treatise on Human Nature*.

This work was not received well to begin with but his later *Essays Moral and Political* were an instant success. Hume was a leading empiricist, a dominant and lasting influence, arguing that proof was needed to establish a truth, and he did much to promote the growth of rationalism.

Prone to bouts of depression, Hume lived in Edinburgh and on the family estate at Ninewells in Berwickshire, but he spent much of his time in Paris and London and was obsessed with the idea of eradicating Scotticisms from his speech and writing.

In spite of the importance of his philosophical works, Hume was also a historian. His *History of England* was a bestseller and remained in wide circulation until the late 19th century.

Portrait of David Hume by Allan Ramsay, dated 1776

Scotland. The fire and brimstone favoured by the 17th-century leaders of the Covenanting movement gave way to a more gentile and liberal approach. The introduction of patronage in 1712, whereby the landowner was given the right to appoint a minister to a church on his land, ensured that the aristocracy favoured ministers who were conservative in political outlook and reflected the same social and cultural characteristics as themselves.

The Scottish gentry wanted intelligent conversation and good manners from their clergy rather than hell-and-damnation preaching. But the introduction of patronage was not popular throughout the 18th century; many ordinary Scots preferred the 'wild enthusiasm' of the Covenanting tradition. This led to numerous disputes in which incumbent appointees were harassed and assaulted by the parish, and to the creation of some breakaway churches.

'A Nation Betrayed...'

THE 18th century was the golden age of Scottish intellectual life. From chemistry to economics, from philosophy to geology, Scottish scientists, thinkers and men of letters featured at the international forefront of their disciplines. Scotland's universities, St Andrews excepted, overflowed with talented academic leaders. But the achievement of the Enlightenment was not confined to the ivory towers of Edinburgh, Glasgow and Aberdeen. The ranks of the Kirk included a number of ministers famous for intellectual achievements far removed from theology, notably William Robertson, one of the greatest historians of the age. Similarly, the triumphs of Scotland's judicial bench, whose brightest stars were Lord Kames and Lord Monboddo, ranged far beyond the narrow confines of the law. Even the rural Ayrshire of Robert Burns was caught up in a vigorous debate between the enlightened and the orthodox over the merits of Calvinist theology.

The Scottish Enlightenment was no mere accident. Nor was it a by-product of the Union of 1707. Rather, the Scottish Enlightenment had deep roots in the culture of late 17th-century Scotland, and it flourished not as an exotic outgrowth of the universities, but as part of the fabric of educated Scotland. Many of the topics which featured in the works of the intellectuals were rehearsed in discussion clubs and debating societies where lawyers, clergymen and gentlemen mingled as the intellectual peers of the professors.

The core of the European Enlightenment was, of course, the France of Montesquieu, Voltaire and Rousseau, but Scotland has a good claim to be recognised as the most significant provincial outpost of the new learning. At any rate, the successes of the Scottish academy put England into the shade. The dons of Oxford were, according to one disenchanted student, sunk in port and prejudice. Although the experimental method

ADAM SMITH

1723-90

A PIVOTAL figure in the Scottish Enlightenment, Smith had survived a childhood scare when he was thought to have been kidnapped by gypsies in his home town of Kirkcaldy. Inspired by seeing the growth of maritime trade in the Fife port, he conceived the first principles of what we now call economic theory before going on to study at Glasgow and Oxford universities.

His single-volume masterpiece, *Inquiry into the Nature and Causes of the Wealth of Nations* (1776), laid the foundations for the

development of economics as a social science. He was the first man to identify the principle of the invisible hand of market forces as the key factor in the development of trade. His economic doctrine did not support unrestricted *laissez-faire* but was informed by his early work on morality and ethics.

Smith was professor of logic at Glasgow University, and later became professor of moral philosophy. He died in Edinburgh in 1790 at the age of 67 and was buried in Canongate churchyard.

associated with the English scientist Isaac Newton had provided an inspiration to intellectuals throughout the rest of Europe, including Scotland, 18th-century England produced no philosopher to rival David Hume, no economist of the stature of Adam Smith, no geologist as systematically brilliant as James Hutton. Not that Scotland was renowned only for isolated men of genius who established themselves at the head of particular disciplines. Some fields of enquiry were virtually founded in 18th-century Scotland. Taken together, Adam Ferguson, Lord Kames and John Millar acted as midwives to the new subjects of sociology and anthropology.

Behind the patriotic boasting, however, there lurks a more sinister story: the tale of how Scots were won over to the idea of Britain. In the 18th century, Scots grew to cherish their political connection to England, in large part because the thinkers of the Enlightenment persuaded the educated elite that little of value had been lost with the Union of 1707. In particular, they claimed the old Scottish parliament, far from being a symbol of nationhood, had been an albatross around the neck of an oppressed people.

The Enlightenment represented, above all, freedom from prejudice. Most often this took the form either of radical assaults on the substance of the Christian faith (which won Hume notoriety) or of attempts to reconcile the faith with the insights of science and philosophy. Of course, the Scottish Enlightenment was not a unified movement which followed a single party line. Disagreement, politely expressed of course, was integral to 18th century Scotland's culture of intellectual conversation. The Common Sense philosophy of Thomas Reid and his disciples evolved in response to the dangerously sceptical and anti-Christian philosophy of Hume.

Sometimes, and this was clearly the case in 18th-century Scotland, the Enlightenment led to attacks on another sort of prejudice, the traditional myths which sustained a nation's identity. Despite divisions over other matters, there does appear to have been a broad consensus within the Scottish Enlightenment about the condition of Scotland and the benefits of Union. History, according to the 18th-century

James Hutton 1726-1797

sages, was a story of the progress of mankind from primitive rudeness to modern commercial refinement. In this long trek, they perceived, England had clearly stolen some ground on Scotland. But admission to the Union, all agreed, had allowed Scotland to catch up with her more advanced neighbour. Scotland's first major intellectual journal, the short-lived *Edinburgh Review* of 1755-6, pinpointed Scotland's position: 'If countries have their ages with respect to improvement, North Britain may be considered as in a state of early youth, guided and supported by the more mature strength of her kindred country.'

The ancient nation of Scotland had been relabelled the modern province of 'North Britain' but a uniform

Britishness failed to materialise because of English cultural intransigence and a refusal to see England as 'South Britain'. The English radical, John Wilkes, denounced the Scots as a threat to liberty and his magazine *The North Briton* was openly racist. In 1763, the Prime Minister, Lord Bute, was forced to resign because of the rampant Scotophobia of the London mob, prompting Hume to comment: 'Some hate me because I am not a Whig, some because I am not a Christian, and all hate me because I am a Scotsman.'

Nonetheless, the *Edinburgh Review* was positive. Scotland had been stuck in a rut but, it argued, the Union of 1707 had invigorated Scottish life. Many commentators went further, arguing that the loss of independence was a necessary stage in the making of modern Scotland. The old parliament had been dominated by the aristocracy. The commoners now enjoyed greater protection for their liberties within the House of Commons than they ever had in the parliament of Scotland.

The leaders of the Enlightenment positively welcomed the Anglicisation of Scotland. Elocution lessons were mandatory for Scots fearful of making their debut on the metropolitan stage as incomprehensible provincial embarrassments. Writers such as Hume and the Aberdonian philosopher, James Beattie, compiled lists of Scottish words and phrases to avoid, because they would grate on an English ear.

However, although the Scottish Enlightenment betrayed older ideas of Scottish nationhood and identity, its leaders did not think of themselves as unpatriotic. Rather, they considered themselves to be cosmopolitan realists who were doing their best to bring Scotland's culture and economy up to the highest standards. The loss of Scotland's historic identity and political autonomy seemed a small price to pay for such wealth and civilisation.

35

BOSWELL: PROTEAN SCOT

JAMES BOSWELL is now hailed as the greatest biographer in the English language for his *Life of Samuel Johnson* (1791). Raised a Calvinist, he later wrote that 'the first great idea I ever formed' was the notion of eternal punishment in Hell; his imagination 'was continually in a state of terror', as throughout his life it would remain during bouts of alcoholic excess and venereal disease. Intent upon avoiding the legal profession, he went off to London in 1762 in search of an officer's commission. Instead he discovered 'all the sweets of being', aristocrats, politicians, actresses, men of letters, prostitutes, and the irresistable companions of taverns and coffee houses, all of whom were to be immortalised in his *London Journal*. In 1763, he first met Samuel Johnson; when Boswell confessed 'I come from Scotland but I cannot help it', he elicited the rejoinder, 'That, Sir, I find, is what a very many of your countrymen cannot help'.

Boswell embarked upon his own Grand Tour, securing interviews with Rousseau and Voltaire. Both recognised his failings and his desire to gain acceptance, but both also appreciated his perceptiveness and willingly responded to his questioning. He also visited Pasquale Paoli who led an independent Corsica. There, he assumed the local costume and briefly lived the legend of

'Corsican Boswell'. His *Account of Corsica* (1768) detailed his friendship with Paoli, and earned him critical acclaim. In 1773 Boswell accompanied Johnson on a tour of the Hebrides. Both men wrote accounts of their experiences in which both affectionately pointed out the eccentricities of the other as they sought to document Gaelic-speaking Scotland, which they perceived to be on the verge of extinction. The historical importance of their observations has been exaggerated, but the astounding complementarity of both journalists is unrivalled in the world of letters.

Boswell returned to a legal career in Edinburgh alleviated by trips to London. Friends and associates noted increasing dissipation. Disastrous debts were temporarily relieved when his father died in 1782, but thereafter he moved to London to concentrate on his *Life of Johnson* while misguidedly attempting to make a living at the English Bar. Three years before his death he wrote, 'I feel no pleasure in existence except the mere gratification of the senses.' It was his ability to describe such gratification which modern audiences find attractive, his genius for capturing the essence of experience, for documenting the richness and excitement of people and places, and his relentless honesty in discerning his personal flaws and weaknesses in the greatness of others.

Ladies of Pleasure A-plenty

THE past, for some reason, is often seen as a place of great innocence and purity. In the world of Jane Austen, everything seemed so much more refined. Take the following few sentences. 'The guests at tea were largely oblivious to the young couple's intercourse in the corner. Indeed, few paid attention to their quiet love making.' While this will no doubt raise a snigger among modern readers, it meant no more than Mr Darcy poured our young heroine a nice cup of tea.

After all, the 18th century was the period of the Scottish Enlightenment where virtue and sensibility were the order of the day. And, by 1850, we were well into the reign of Queen Victoria who would not be amused at any smuttiness or crudity. The reality, however, was quite different.

In the 18th century, *An Impartial List of Ladies of Pleasure* was privately printed in Edinburgh to be circulated among well-to-do young dandies. It offered advice and descriptions concerning Edinburgh's brothels. All the major Scottish towns had their brothels and, as one might expect, these were tailored for the different social classes, although practically all the girls were drawn from the lower orders. In 1763, one commentator claimed that there were only five or six brothels in Edinburgh, but within 20 years 'every quarter of the city and suburb was infested with whores'.

In 1797, Edinburgh opened its first Magdalene hospital which was designed to 'cure' women of both venereal disease and prostitution. It was held as conventional wisdom that women were totally responsible for both problems.

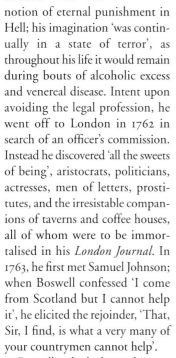

The Magdalene hospital was a ghastly place where women were forced to live in a state of virtual imprisonment and were made to pray and wash clothes, to signify a cleansing of the soul. After many years, when deemed cured, they would be sent back into society.

It was the middle class ,with their new notions of respectability, who railed against the evils of prostitution. With evangelical fervour they sought to denounce the work of the devil and the prostitute was singled out for special opprobrium as the very antithesis of what a woman should be. The nobility, on the other hand, were much slower in coming to shame. The prostitutes who flocked to Musselburgh races were welcomed by the 'young blades of the turf' and as one noted authority on the subject, Dr William Tait, noted: 'As an encouragement to brothel keepers, some noblemen of the highest rank and title prefer taking up their quarters in a house of ill fame rather than in a respectable hotel, and unblushingly visit

By 1800, it was claimed that 'every quarter of the city and suburb was infested with whores'

all the "lions" in company with the keeper and one or more of her ladies. It was reported that a minister in the west of Scotland let his manse to a certain nobleman for the purpose of lodging his concubines.'

Men of the cloth were not immune to temptation. In 1814, a magistrate wrote: 'I have the police court at present and I will be needed very much to keep the whores and ministers in order during the sitting of the Assemblies.'

As the cities and the economy expanded in the early 19th century so too did the number of prostitutes. It was estimated in 1842 that in Edinburgh there were about 800 full-time prostitutes, 200 of whom lived privately with the rest housed in 200 brothels. In addition to these numbers, it was also estimated that there were 1,200 'sly' prostitutes who operated from 'houses of assignation' where a room could be let with no questions asked. In Glasgow, in the same year, it was estimated that there were between 450 and 1,500

WHAT'S ON WHERE, 1775
The 18th-century equivalent of a city's *What's On* listings could be found in *Ranger's Impartial List of the Ladies of Pleasure in Edinburgh*

Betty Clark, at Miss Walker's
This lady is about 21, of the middle size, red hair, and very good teeth. She is far from disagreeable, if it were not for her sulky temper, which sometimes cools the keenest desire even in the height of their mutual embraces. Notwithstanding, when she meets with a lover, she gives him the utmost satisfaction, as she understands the power of friction admirably well.

Jenny Stewart, to be found at Mrs Young's
This lady is rather short, brown hair, good teeth, about 19, and very good natured. Among the worshippers of Venus, there is not, perhaps, a more faithful votary than this. She is entire mistress of her trade, and her whole person is pleasing.

Molly Jones, within the Cowgate Port
This lady is about 20, rather short, good complexion, brown hair, and very good natured. She is very well calculated for her business and knows how to behave in a proper manner to her lovers, and gives general satisfaction in the Critical Minute.

Miss Fraser, at Miss Nairn's
This is as pretty a little filly as ever man clapped leg over. She is not above 16 and has not been above six weeks in the service. Her youth and beauty procures her a great many admirers and she is of so good a disposition that she does her best to oblige them all. She has rather short brown hair, good teeth and a very fine skin.

brothels and 4,000 part-time and full-time prostitutes.

As ever, it was the women who bore the blame for this state of affairs. Men were warned against the temptations of the flesh. Yet middle-class respectability meant that men had to wait until late in life for marriage. To afford the required house and the servants meant a long period of abstinence and saving. Temptation proved too great for many forced to postpone marriage until their forties. Prostitutes were almost always economic marginals, forced on to the streets by necessity. Many were abused serving girls, seduced by the master or sons of the house then thrown out. Examination of records for venereal disease reveals the vast majority of sufferers were in their teens. Also, child prostitution existed. Of those admitted to hospital, 4% were under the age of 15 and some children had venereal disease at the age of nine or 10.

A Different Story from the Dark Side

THE 18TH CENTURY was an age of reason, progress and intellectual enlightenment, a true 'Golden Age' in Scotland's cultural history, or so the story goes.

Somewhere around 1700, as if by magic, the Scottish people were allegedly dragged out of a medieval darkness of superstition and guided towards the light of rationality and improvement. Any survivors left still clinging to credulous beliefs such as witchcraft, ghosts, fairies or second sight were marginalised, either intellectually as ignorant fools or geographically as living remote from the centres of advanced and civilised thinking. There is, however, as with most stories, another side to this

well-told tale, a side which has, until recently, been largely ignored by scholarship. Belief in the supernatural did not suddenly vanish in a flash of spectral speed as has been supposed but clung on tenaciously, not only throughout the 18th century but arguably into the 19th and 20th centuries as well. Enlightenment, rationalism and scepticism did undeniably have an impact upon belief in the supernatural. However, at a popular level it is difficult to distinguish to what extent such developments had an influence upon the integrity and survival of such beliefs. Furthermore, these conceptions were by no means restricted to the 'unlettered peasant'. A number of learned men and women

The Legend *by George Paul Chalmers: an old woman admits a few of the next generation to the secrets of the spirit world*

expressed if not a sincere conviction in the existence of ghosts, apparitions, witchcraft, and the like at least retained an open mind about them.

Towards the end of the 17th century and the beginning of the 18th, the educated classes debated the reality of supernatural phenomena. This surge of interest in traditional folk beliefs was so great that these beliefs were being used as propaganda in the polemics of the day. Through the writings of such individuals on both sides of the debate it is not only possible to understand something of learned opinions on the topic, but also to garner some insight into general folk attitudes.

Defence of supernatural belief is found in, among others, the work of George Sinclair, *Satan's Invisible World Discovered* (1685), Robert Kirk, *The Secret-Commonwealth* (1691), John Bell of Gladsmuir, *The Tryal of Witchcraft* (1705), John Frazer, *Deuteroscopia* (1707), and Theophilus Insulanus, *A Treatise on the Second Sight* (1763). These men were less willing to banish to the past and the 'vulgar' what had come to be regarded as 'superstition', and indeed wrote vehemently against such notions. They were engaged in a fight against 'sadduceeism' or unbelief, attempting to conquer the rise of atheism and materialism by upholding and defending witchcraft, ghosts, and the entire world of spirits. For these men, incredulity of the supernatural world meant disbelief in God. They sought to authenticate and offer proof of the existence of supernatural phenomena and thus combat the tide of scepticism. Case histories of alleged metaphysical experiences were compiled and offered as empirical evidence. George Sinclair, professor of natural philosophy at Glasgow, argued that devils, spirits, witches, and apparitions were realities and used 'authentic records' and the 'attestations of witnesses of undoubted veracity' as confirmation.

Bell McGhie (1760–1836), the last witch in Ayrshire

———— ❧ ————

Robert Kirk, an episcopalian minister successively in the parishes of Balquhidder and Aberfoyle, similarly defended the veracity of fairies and second sight. Belief in the existence of fairies was, in Kirk's opinion, not inconsistent with Christian belief. In fact he set out to collect and record 'evidence' of this belief, using first-hand eye-witness accounts and Biblical references, in part to uphold and strengthen belief in the existence of angels, the Devil, and the Holy Spirit and 'to suppress the impudent and growing atheism' of his age.

His main objective was not solely to record for posterity the beliefs of his parishioners, but rather to present a well-reasoned argument that unified spirituality, supported religious tolerance and would further the strength of the church.

These treatises are of interest for the way in which supernatural phenomena were defended as essential to Christian orthodoxy, but also as reservoirs of folk belief. Kirk's *Secret Common-Wealth* is not the only account of fairy belief in this period but it is the most fulsome. From him we learn that the fairies of Scottish folk tradition were far removed from the Victorian legacy of mischievous, frolicking nymphs of tiny physique and butterfly wings. Rather, the fairies had

JOANNA BAILLIE

1762–1851

THE poet and playwright was born at Bothwell, the daughter of a minister, and lived in Lanarkshire until moving to Hampstead in 1792. The intellectual environment of the household prepared her for her writing career. Her first play, *De Montfort*, was performed in London, but *The Family Legend* was produced with the support of Walter Scott in Edinburgh in 1810. She wrote a number of verse dramas and a Gothic horror story, *Witchcraft*, set in Scotland with a cast of intriguing female characters.

Baillie sought to explore the predicament of women, viewed from her rather confined world. It has been suggested that she was attempting to find a female voice in the male-dominated world of Romanticism, her inspiration derived from her Scottish upbringing and background.

once been regarded as potentially dangerous, capable of causing bodily harm to humans and animals, damaging property or stealing babies and replacing them with one of their own unwanted 'changelings'. Nor were the fairies considered to be small, but were generally described as being of human size and appearance. They were thought to live inside certain hills, removed from the community but never really far away. It was Kirk's contention that the fairies were a distinct order of created beings, living unseen by most mortal eyes only because they lived in another sphere. This division was, for him, no different than the separation between humans and the undersea world. The fairies lived in another state and in the course of time he envisaged an open correspondence between humans and these 'nimble and agile clans', once they were

uncovered like any other of the world's many mysteries.

Fairies were considered to live on the boundaries of village life while the witch resided within the community. Not so much a supernatural creature, the witch was a human, usually though not always female, believed to be invested with supernatural powers.

About 2,000 alleged witches were executed during the Scottish witch-hunts. The last full scale 'witch-craze' to affect Scotland took place in 1662. The Witchcraft Act was repealed in 1736, making it no longer possible formally to try and convict someone of this crime. The need to persecute witches was noticeably in decline after the 1660s, but the belief in witchcraft was not so quickly scotched. Extreme cases of random witch-panics, which resulted in executions, erupted, for example, in Paisley (1697), Pittenweem

(1705), and Dornoch (1727). Accusations of witchcraft continued well into the 18th century, with some particularly late instances in Kenmore (1757) and Kirkcudbright (1805).

As it is difficult to know the level of supernatural belief of those living at the close of the 20th century – people still report seeing ghosts, fairies, UFOs and continue to have psychic experiences or read horoscopes – it is even more challenging to grasp the beliefs held by 18th-century people. Attitudes then, as now, can be inconsistent and contradictory. What is reasonably certain is that the synonymity between the past as an age of irrationality and darkness and the present as an age of reason and light is a prejudice that can no longer be sustained. According to present-day popular culture 'the truth is out there' and it seems we still want to believe.

The Fairy Rade: Carrying Off a Changeling, Midsummer Eve *by Sir Joseph Noel Paton, dated 1867*

A Nation Under the Influence

DRINK was very much a way of life for the average Scot at this time. In this very harsh environment it was a source of solace, a drug to lubricate good feeling and hospitality at every opportunity.

In the 1830s, the average Scot aged over 15 drank just under a pint of whisky per week. There were no legal restrictions on who could buy drink and in some places alcoholism was a recognised problem in women and young children. Both Edinburgh and Glasgow had a pub for every 130 people and, if the places which could sell drink over the counter are added, it is clear that Scotland was a fairly drunken society. Also, until the mid-19th century, illicit whisky was another source of drink, much of it manufactured in the Highlands, so the official figures are very much an underestimate of the true extent of consumption.

When a child was born, the custom was for one bottle of whisky for a girl and two for a boy. On entering the workplace, one entered a culture of drink. Starting a new job, finishing one, completing an apprenticeship, the birth of a workmate's child, marriage, death, and getting paid were all great drinking occasions. Contemporary accounts from the streets show them to be littered with drunks. Before 1853, when the Forbes Mackenzie Act obliged premises to close at 11pm and forbad them to open on the Sabbath, the wynds of the inner cities were awash with alcohol in all its forms.

It was in response to public displays of drunkenness which haunted every Scottish village, town and city, that employers and clergymen united in their campaign against the demon drink. Although the middle class did their heavy drinking behind closed doors, gratuitous and public displays

In the 1830s, there was the equivalent of a pub for every 130 people in Edinburgh, Glasgow and many other Scottish towns and cities

of inebriation offended their sensibilities. Also, employers were keen to enforce greater discipline in the workplace. Monday morning was for many an unofficial holiday and work came to a halt for all kinds of celebrations. Performance and output suffered as a consequence. Emboldened by drink, workers talked back to their bosses. Temperance would have the effect of making the workers more efficient, productive and better disciplined.

The Church also denounced the 'demon drink'. Alcohol led to corruption and vice. One social commentator calculated how much money was spent on drink in a close

in Blackfriars, Glasgow, against what the inhabitants earned. He found a shortfall of £2,000. How was this money raised, he asked his middle-class readership. Crime, gambling and prostitution was the answer.

The 1853 crackdown on drinking in the cities meant that the only places which could legally sell alcohol on a Sunday were day-trip boats going 'doon the watter'. The prospect of being able to get booze was an integral part of the appeal and success of these boats. As a result, the words 'steaming' and 'steamboats' have entered the Scottish vocabulary as metaphors for being drunk.

CHAPTER 4

The Age of Transformation

1780-1850

SCOTLAND was among the poorest European nations at the beginning of the 18th century. Its agriculture was primitive, manufacturing non-existent and the only exports amounted to timber, linen, some cattle and a few animal skins. Yet, within a century, Scotland would be well on the way to having one of the most modern economies in the world.

One of the main reasons for popular hostility to the Union in 1707 was a fear that the Scottish economy would be swallowed up by the more modern and competitive English economy, swamped by cheaper and superior goods. These fears over the economic impact were balanced by assurances that there would no longer be blockades on trade in cattle and linen as had happened periodically in the past.

Any wild expectations that Scotland would straight away share in the greater wealth of England were sadly disappointed. The Scottish economy remained on the same trajectory for the first half century after Union as it had before. The reason for this was that the English had no real economic interest in Scotland; the country was too poor and it did not have a big enough market to produce tempting profits. In practice, this failure to initiate trade allowed poverty to act as a protective barrier and allowed the Scottish economy to develop in a complementary way to England's because there was no direct competition between the two nations.

The first sector of the Scottish economy to find the opportunity to expand was overseas trade with the Americas in tobacco. One distinct advantage of the Union was that it permitted the Scots open trade with the English empire. The Scots were trading there illegally before 1707. and, in an increasingly protectionist world where markets were being closed, this gave the Scots legal entry into a valuable market just at a time when the whole focus of the world economy was moving away from the Mediterranean towards the Atlantic. Scotland was well placed, and not only in a geographical sense, to take full advantage.

Once they started, imports of tobacco into Glasgow rose significantly year by year until they accounted for half of all the country's trade. The Scots were ruthlessly efficient at undercutting rival traders from Bristol and Liverpool, who in any case were attracted by the more lucrative slave trade. Tobacco encouraged the development of banking and a commercial infrastructure. The tobacco

Smoke marks the spot where Scotland's heavy industries began to be forged at Carron Ironworks in Falkirk

A prosperous tobacco baron enjoys the material benefits of a highly lucrative transatlantic trade

—❧—

Pride in the job: a tobacco worker's apron

merchants with their new found wealth and a desire to flaunt it in the building, impressive offices and mansions contributed greatly to the development of Glasgow.

Commerce and industry were dependent on the development of banking. Scottish banks were among the first to issue paper notes which helped to improve credit facilities. The banks' willingness to lend was important for industrial expansion. (In the 1760s, there were some spectacular crashes as banks lent beyond their capacity.) In 1742, the British Linen Bank was formed to provide the

necessary financial facilities to help the expansion of trade in linen, and transform it from a rural cottage enterprise into a modern commercial industry.

The domestic linen industry expanded rapidly as a result of guaranteed access to transatlantic markets. Output increased from 2.2 million yards in 1728 to 12.1 million yards in 1776. As many as 100,000 people were employed in mills across the country at the industry's peak. The industrialisation of Scotland was gathering pace.

In turn, linen provided the basis for the expansion of the cotton industry. The first cotton mill was established at

Pencuik in 1778 and within a generation the industry would emerge as the leader of Scotland's industrial revolution. Workers from the linen industry could adapt to cotton, which was more flexible and easier to weave than linen. New technology made possible massive leaps in productivity. Cotton was cheap to import, and made cheaper by the invention of the Cotton Gin which mechanically harvested the plantations in America. Water, and later steam, power meant that the industry could tap into Scotland's abundant sources of river and coal energy. Until the invention of the steam power loom in the early 19th century, most mills were situated next to rivers. Scotland's extensive number of rivers also acted as a convenient means of transport in the days before railways. The fact that Scotland was part of the first industrial nation meant that Scottish merchants were free to ply their trade throughout the world. A simple record of statistics demonstrates the power of 'King Cotton' in this period. The imports of raw cotton rose from 0.43 million pounds in the years 1781-86 to 7.19 million pounds in the period between 1799-1804. The number of cotton mills grew from 18 in 1787 to 192 by 1839. By 1872 it was estimated that the industry employed over 150,000 people.

CHARLES TENNANT
1768-1838

A MANUFACTURING chemist and one of the key pioneers in the Scottish industrial revolution, he first started bleaching at Darnley near Paisley and was ready to cash in on the expansion of the cotton industry when he found himself an ideal position to take advantage of a market that began to take off.

In 1798 he took out a patent for liquid bleach and then a solid bleach powder which was not only cheaper to make but easier to use, transport, and store. In 1800, he set up a chemical works at St Rollox, Glasgow. It proved to be a vital centre for chemical manufacture which underpinned the industry's expansion in the 19th century, although the resultant air pollution did not enhance the local environment. It quickly became one of the most polluted sites in Glasgow and the whole of Scotland.

Engines of Change
Start to Roll

NEITHER in Europe nor the rest of the world was the march of industry so rapid or far-reaching in its effects as it was in Scotland. A relatively powerless nation and backward rural society in the later 1600s, by 1851 Scotland had become an integral part of the Great British Workshop of the World. Industrialisation was accompanied by a massive shift in the population towards the central belt of Scotland and a rate of urban growth which was faster than anywhere else in western Europe.

Whatever its potential as an independent nation – and historians disagree about this – Scotland was suffering exceptional economic hardship on the eve of the Union of 1707. With a minuscule navy, the Scots had found economic survival increasingly difficult in an age of muscular mercantilism where the expansion of trade and therefore the attainment of wealth depended on military and naval might. Other than in and around Glasgow where the tobacco trade flourished, partly through tax evasion, conditions worsened over the next 30 years. Under-employment spread and for most, living standards barely rose above subsistence level.

In order to counter major public disorder and dispel government fears that Jacobite threats to the new Hanoverian regime would lead to rebellion, the British state was forced to intervene directly in the Scottish economy by encouraging manufacturers and creating employment through the use of quasi-state agencies such as the Board of Trustees for Fisheries and Manufactures (1727). The Scottish landed and urban elites were determined to turn Scotland into an opulent and virtuous society. Thus the Enlightenment was particularly pragmatic in character and encouraged –

JOSEPH BLACK
1728-99

BORN in France, the son of a Scots wine merchant, he was the first scientist to realise that air is made up of a variety of different gases. In 1786 he was appointed professor of anatomy and chemistry at Glasgow University, but also found time to practise as a physician. Additionally, he was a successful consultant to the industries of bleaching, dyeing, iron-making, fertiliser manufacture, and water supply. Black evolved the theory of 'latent heat' that confirmed his scientific reputation and later accepted the chair of medicine and chemistry at Edinburgh University. His fame as a teacher spread far and wide in both Europe and America, and many foreign students travelled to Scotland especially to be able to participate in his chemistry classes.

ultimately through the writings of
Adam Smith – the division of labour.
This was applied in agriculture as well
as manufacturing. It was part of what
was an extraordinary process of
national social engineering. Employers acted collectively to discourage
collective action by workers. Custom-
ary practices such as drinking during
work time, or talking to friends, were
eliminated as walls, gatemen, overseers
and clocks revolutionised the
experience of work.

Scotland was still vulnerable to
foreign competition in the early 1770s.
With the opening of the first cotton
mills in 1778 at Penicuik and Rothesay,
however, a new and radical phase in
Scottish history was opened, boosted
later by the blow to overseas rivals
which was dealt by the wars with
revolutionary France. Cotton became
synonymous with Glasgow and Paisley.
No longer lagging, Scotland's share of
British output of coal, iron, ships,
linen, woollens and other products rose
steeply. Scots began to innovate and
invent on an unprecedented scale, their
confidence soaring as market opportunities opened. James Watt is the best
known but there were many others.

The tentacles of economic and
social change entered virtually every
corner of the nation. Highlanders and
islanders, cleared from their townships
to make way for sheep (for wool and
mutton) were relocated in coastal
small-holdings to subsist by part-time
kelping (for the soap and glass industries) or fishing (for consumption in
the manufacturing towns). Numerous
'planned villages' were established, at
Tobermory, Ullapool and at Helms-
dale, the last-named an element in the
notorious Sutherland clearances.

But while industrialisation became
increasingly concentrated in regional
centres like Glasgow and Clydeside,
Dundee, the Monklands and the Borders, from around 1820 the bottom

began to fall out of the markets for
kelp, black cattle and even illicit
whisky distilling. This left a deliberately enlarged population in the western and north highlands and islands
increasingly poor and dependent upon
the potato for its sustenance. Blight
caused it to fail in 1846. Although the
availability of work in the lowlands, on
railway construction for instance, eased
the blow, the consequence was massive

*Machinery adds to the muscle of jute
mill workers at the Mid-Wynd works
in Dundee, 1850*

⊷

emigration, while, ironically, more
Highland estates were purchased for
shooting, fishing and contemplation
of the (man-made) wilderness.

The causes of the Industrial
Revolution in Scotland are the subject

THE daughter of a naval lieutenant she was brought up in Burntisland but was exposed to a minimal education. She was virtually an autodidact in her chosen field of mathematics, discovering almost by chance a passion for algebra and geometry of such intensity that her parents feared for her sanity. Warmly encouraged by her second husband she was introduced to the scholarly communities of London and France. The author of several influential books and papers on scientific subjects, notably astronomy and light, she was honoured by the Royal Society who commissioned a bust of her. In later life she wrote her *Recollections*, an illuminating but non-censorious account of the prejudice which she encountered and a celebration of the 19th-century scientific community.

of debate. It has been argued that it was part of a process of 'complementary development', that is, within the Union, Scotland and England each played to their separate economic strengths. This, however, overlooks the lasting rivalries there were between certain business interests in the two countries. Others argue that roots of the phenomenon lay in the 17th century, that it represents a monument to Scottish ingenuity, in business, banking and technology, and owes much to favourable features of Scottish rural society. Unlike Ireland, where land was continually sub-divided, in rural Scotland, enclosure and the creation of larger farms broke the links between agriculture and industry, creating a mobile army of workers for the manufacturing sector.

Denied a choice, people did move, but not at first, or willingly, into the mills and factories. Ironically, labour bottlenecks in Scottish industries such as cotton-spinning were broken not only by the forced labour of paupers but also with the aid of immigrants from rural Ireland.

Scottish responses to the risks and opportunities of the Union of 1707 were clearly important. Scottish banking helped but there seems little doubt that Scotland's place within the British fiscal-military state was fundamental. This gave the Scots legal access to markets and outlets for enterprise in America, the West Indies and India. Vital too were the aid and concessions obtained from Westminster for key industries. Thus were created the conditions so that by 1780 Scotland was poised for industrialisation.

English skills and technologies – but also those from Ireland, France and Holland – were adopted in virtually every manufacture. The great ironworks at Carron imitated the leading English works at Coalbrookdale, and were built by labour imported from the south. Mechanisation in cotton and linen, the industrial pathfinders in and around Glasgow and Dundee respectively, depended on English inventions, the best known being those of Richard Arkwright (the water frame) and Samuel Crompton (the spinning mule).

Scotland's favourable natural resources – water, coal and iron ore – were crucial too, even before the age of heavy industry commenced in the 1830s. Ample supplies of clean running water were essential to power mills and for textile bleaching, printing and dyeing. Without coal for domestic heat and fuel, the great urban expansion upon which so much else depended could not have happened.

Two crucial breakthroughs were David Mushet's appreciation of the

JAMES WATT
1736-1819

WATT was the father of the steam engine which was a major technological breakthrough that contributed to the Industrial Revolution. It was at Glasgow University, where he was employed as a mathematical instrument maker, that he first became interested in steam power. In 1765 he constructed an engine with a separate chamber for condensation and patented his invention in 1769. The steam engine was the vital catalyst that drove the industrial revolution because it provided the mechanical muscle that was needed to transform the coal and textile industries and increase their capacity by huge amounts.

By 1800, it is estimated that there were more than 1,000 steam engines in place and working for a wide variety of industries across Britain.

Watt's discovery and the impact of steam power was very probably the 18th century equivalent of the worldwide web.

James Watt and the Steam Engine
by James Eckford Lauder

innate value of Scottish blackband ironstone and James Neilson's introduction of the hot blast furnace in 1828. The latter conserved energy by using hot air for the bellows and thus made much higher temperatures possible. By 1845, a quarter of British pig iron was produced in Scotland rising to a peak of 1,206,000 some 25 years later. The production of steel followed shortly thereafter.

Industrialisation in its early stages was a brutal process. A higher proportion of women and children – the 'shock troops' of Scotland's reluctant industrial army – was employed in manufacturing (and in agriculture) than in England. Of necessity, in order to compete with English and other rivals, employers had to cut labour costs to the bone. Labour relations in key industries such as coal and cotton

were bitter with angry confrontations between masters and workers carrying on through the period 1800-1840. Helped by Highland migration to the central Lowlands, Irish immigration and a rise in the indigenous population, the workforce expanded and capitalist manufacturers and farmers gained the upper hand.

Protests against the ill-effects of the transformation were widespread and,

in overcrowded towns such as Glasgow and Greenock, often involved violent rioting and looting. Poetry and song provided other outlets for dissident voices. But there were countervailing forces too: burgh police, church missions, temperance reformers, growing prosperity amongst skilled workers. While in 1819 and 1820, the west of Scotland seemed to some in authority to have been on the brink of

revolution, by the 1840s a strong strand of respectability and restraint had emerged amongst sections of the working class. By no means were disorder and strikes things of the past. But a new society was in the making and, despite the squalor and disease, the pains of adjustment and the recognition within it of great inequalities, it was accepted in its essentials by the majority.

A Better Deal for the Workers

NEW LANARK was founded in 1786 by David Dale, a cotton master and self-made businessman. Dale was an enlightened employer who believed that effective regulation of the workforce made very sound business sense. The location of New Lanark on the upper reaches of the River Clyde was such that it was difficult to find an abundant supply of local labour for the mills. Housing for the workers, therefore, was one way of attracting people. Another was the use of pauper children.

By 1797, Dale had built barracks which housed more than 500 orphans. The children rose at six in the morning for a 13-hour shift with an hour and a half permitted for breaks. Once they had finished work, they were taught at the school for two hours.

Dale was held up as a model employer by the rest of society. Visitors were impressed by the clean orphans who were well fed and educated. As one contemporary wrote of the factory: 'What a number of people are here made happy and comfortable who

would, many of them, have been cut off by disease or, wallowing in dirt, been ruined by indolence.'

The management of New Lanark passed to Dale's son-in-law, Robert Owen, a Welshman, in 1800. Owen, like his father-in-law, was a self-made man and the manager of a cotton mill in Manchester. Once in control, he abolished the use of pauper children. He wanted to create an idealised community among the 2,000 people he inherited as the workforce at New Lanark. Unlike Dale, Owen was not religious and his ideas were driven by a form of pragmatic humanitarianism. Although Dale was considered a benevolent employer, Owen thought the condition of the workers 'wretched' when he took charge. Housing for families consisted of one room, sanitation was pitiful, food was dreadful, drunkenness was endemic and, critically, productivity was poor because of absenteeism and slack working habits. Owen, flying in the face of conventional wisdom, argued that human character was influenced by

social environment and therefore improvements in productivity and efficiency could be achieved by providing the workers with better conditions. With only limited resources, he began to build new houses which were more spacious and hygienic and added an extra storey to the existing properties so that families would now have a minimum of two rooms. Owen needed to attract families to the community to replace the pauper children. The surroundings were tidied up. A central company was established which would sell essentials to the workers and thus cut out the profiteering middlemen.

Owen was not driven solely by altruistic concerns. He intended his paternalistic system of management to bring economic dividends and there were strict sanctions for any worker who stepped out of line. A police house was establlished in the village to regulate the behaviour of the inhabitants. Fines were imposed on workers for drunkenness and for the 'irregular intercourse of the sexes'. Fines and one sixtieth of workers' wages were used to pay for education, medical care and sickness benefits. The creation of this unique social infrastructure, he confidently predicted, would make for a happy workforce that would bear economic fruit in improved profitability.

The details of Owen's management techniques, as described in his *A New View of Society* (1813–14) were designed to ensure that working efficiency was maximised. All workers had precise records kept of their progress and supervision was constant to make sure there was no slacking. He

Model mills:
New Lanark where the workers were treated better in the pursuit of profit

introduced what was called 'the silent monitor', a colour-coded block of wood that was the earliest manifestation of what would today be called 'name and shame'. Each worker was assigned a block and its colour represented that worker's previous performance. As a result of this quality management, Owen was vindicated by increased profits.

Education was an important part of Owen's philosophy. The extra profits he made built The Institute for the Formation of Character which contained the school for the factory children, the world's first day nurseries, and community rooms. Owen, again well ahead of his times, argued that education was a civilising force which would improve society as a whole. Children were to receive teaching which would turn them into good citizens and 'rational beings'. Geography, history and maths as well as basic reading and writing were taught.

In 1825, unhappy that his ideas had not been more widely taken up, he left the industrial operation at New Lanark in the care of his partners, and set sail for America. Here he attempted, unsuccessfully, to realise his utopian visions in the New Harmony Community, Indiana. Other communities were established at Orbiston, Lanarkshire, in Devon and in Ireland, the 'Social Father' Owen himself, enjoying the support of the Owenites for the rest of his life, despite the disapointing failure of most of his schemes. In 1829, after business disagreements with his partners, he sold his shares in New Lanark and returned to his native Wales where he continued

Robert Owen: a pioneer who proved his ideas at New Lanark but couldn't make them work elsewhere

to experiment with various socialist schemes such as trade unions and co-operatives. He then became closely involved with the Chartist movement, but for the last twenty years of his long life – he died in 1858 – he pursued various millennial projects, attractive in themselves but somewhat lacking in practicality. Having proved his theories of social engineering and set the tone for the Victorian paternalism that was to follow, Owen was content to see out the remainder of his life contemplating the abstract as opposed to the physical. New Lanark has now been restored as a fitting monument to Owen's humanitarian and inspirational vision.

Character forming: dancing classes at New Lanark to test the theory that all work and no play wasn't good for business

CHAPTER 5

Demise of the Old Order

1780-1850

THE aristocratic grip on power aroused powerful middle-class jealousies. After all, the middle class were paying taxes, acting as responsible citizens and contributing to the growing power and prosperity of the British nation. To them it seemed only fair that they should have the vote.

When news of the French Revolution reached Scotland in 1789, hopes were high that a similar form of democracy would reach Scotland. The French regime was regarded as one of the most absolutist in Europe and if it could topple, it seemed to many it would only be a matter of time before the British regime followed. Robert Burns welcomed the prospect of imminent change in the wake of the French Revolution with his poem *The Tree of Liberty* 'with its branches spreading wide, man'. Effigies of Henry Dundas were burned on the streets. In 1792 the Scottish Convention of the Friends of the People was formed to press the case for an extension of the franchise to 'responsible' citizens. The air was full of optimism and the middle class was convinced that its time had arrived.

This optimism proved ill founded. When news of the post-revolutionary 'Great Terror' reached Scotland, it filled middle-class hearts with fear. The French Revolution, a source of such hope and optimism, appeared to have gone badly wrong and the forces unleashed by agitators for reform on the Continent seemed to be completely beyond their control.

The news that not only arrogant aristocrats but respectable middle-class citizens were being led to the guillotine by fanatics who had come to power riding the tide of a popular democratic frenzy was too much for the Scots middle class to stomach. Yes, they would like the vote, but not if it meant risking social breakdown, the loss of their property, and their necks. Gradually, the middle class retreated from the reform movement, only to be replaced by radicals who were making more and more outlandish, as it seemed then, demands.

By the Convention of 1793, radicals had begun to seek universal suffrage, an idea unthinkable to the middle class, who threw in their lot with the ruling regime. Radicalism suffered an even greater setback the same year when Britain went to war with France. There was a patriotic backlash and radicalism was denounced as the ideology of the enemy.

Burns had thought twice about his initial support for the revolution and turned against the French:

Does haughty Gaul invasion threat
Then let the louns beware, Sir

For never but by British hands
Maun British wrangs be righted!

But men like Thomas Muir openly welcomed a French invasion and the war was used as a pretext by the state to clamp down on reform activity.

Spies and agent provocateurs were used to weed out radicals. Despised as sympathisers of the enemy, hunted down by the state and lacking popular support, the radical movement dwindled.

One effect of the rapprochement between the middle class and the aristocracy was that the state consolidated its power. Trade unions or, as they were called at the time, combinations, were permitted under Scots law in the 18th century. Workers could combine to present a grievance to the sheriff's court against an employer who was thought to be treating the workforce unfairly. The class-dominated Scottish legal system had little love for upstart artisan employers.

Also, the means of enforcing the will of the state at that time were very limited. There was no modern police force and the only effective way to enforce law and order was to call out the troops. That could take days, by which time the damage was done. As a result, courts were inclined to try to keep the peace and it was no skin off their noses if the middle class had to pay for this. Consequently, the legal system was not shy of improving wages and conditions for the working class, much to the chagrin of the middle class.

By the time of the Napoleonic Wars, combinations were being denounced as fronts for revolutionary activity and were made illegal, helping to keep the middle class on side.

Following the end of the war in 1815, there was a widespread depression in

HENRY DUNDAS
1st Viscount Melville and Baron Dunira
1742-1811

Henry Dundas *by David Martin, 1770*

WILY DUNDAS or 'King Harry the Ninth', as he was known, dominated Scottish politics at home and at Westminster for the last two decades of the 18th century. Through patronage and judicious sharing out of 'jobs for the boys' he built up a loyal following among Scottish MPs whom he could rely on to do his bidding and vote for whatever issue he decided was worthy of his support. He used his position of privilege within the government to procure the elevation of Scots in the East India Company and ultimately helped to create the phenomenon of the nabob, someone who returned home from India having made his fortune and who was forever in the debt of Dundas for being given the opportunity. Dundas was a close friend of Pitt the Younger, the Prime Minister, and the pair of them would regularly attend debates in the House of Commons blind drunk. His passion for claret was also responsible for the induction of some rather wild Scottish patriotism, within a British context, especially his now famous assertion that 'any ten Scots could beat any ten English'.

The Disruption of 1843: hundreds of ministers walked out of the General Assembly and gave up their livelihoods in a split over who should appoint a minister – the landowner or congregation?

trade with high unemployment and falling wages. With factory owners free to draw on plentiful supplies of cheap labour and keen to enforce workplace discipline, workers could find no legitimate way of expressing their grievances as the law still made combinations unlawful. For many, the source of the depression was 'old corruption' in the government and the only way that they could win back their traditional rights was to change the law. To change the law you needed political power – workers needed the vote. The connection between economic grievance and political rights was made.

The period witnessed a rise in class tensions as strikes among cotton spinners, miners, iron workers and masons broke out only to be met with harsh repressive action. Employers were free to use the agencies of the state to enforce discipline and troops were often called out. A general strike in Glasgow in 1812 attracted 40,000 supporters and was put down by dragoons. Soon the government was receiving reports of secret drilling and several caches of arms were found. To make matters worse, posters and bills appeared calling for an armed insurrection against the state.

The extent of revolutionary sympathy in Scotland is unknown. The secret nature of revolutionary societies, such as the United Scotsmen, and the fact that government intelligence was prone to exaggeration, make it difficult to assess the numbers involved. Yet, it is clear that Scottish society in the second decade of the 19th century was volatile.

In 1820, a band led by Hardie, Baird and Wilson attempted a march on Carron Iron Works with the intention of inciting an uprising that would spark a revolt across Britain. They were intercepted by a detachment of cavalry at Bonnymuir outside Falkirk and executed. Soon after, the economy picked up, and so removed many of the economic grievances which had driven the radical movement. The *ancien régime* survived to fight another day.

As the wind of economic and social change swept through Scotland in the early 19th century, it was to carry the Scottish middle class to new heights of prosperity.

Scotland started out in the grip of the *ancien régime*, and unlike in England, where one in eight adult males had the vote, only one in 125 adult Scottish males had the franchise. The power of the Scottish aristocracy was such that it would countenance no reform and the rulers of Scotland were unflinching in their support of the status quo. A form of liberal Toryism developed in England, but there was no similar movement in Scotland where the middle class would have no truck with reform if it threatened stability and property.

Yet despite the turmoil of the French Revolution and agitation in the period following the end of the Napoleonic wars, many people still felt that they were denied their proper place within society. The passing of the Great

Reform Act in 1832 was a result of a crisis over Catholic emancipation and it gave the middle orders the vote almost by accident, but it was a bitter disappointment to the working class who regarded it as a devastating betrayal. Framed by two Whig lawyers, Henry Cockburn and Francis Jeffrey, the Scottish Bill increased the Scottish electorate by 1400% to match the situation in England. According to Cockburn it gave Scotland a constitution for the first time. One immediate consequence of this change was that the Scottish Tory Party, which had fought tooth and nail against reform, was almost wiped out by the enlarged Scottish electorate.

In the following year, 1833, the aspiring middle class flexed their muscles in the General Assembly of the Church of Scotland by passing the Veto Act. This was in response to criticism against patronage which allowed landowners the right to appoint ministers to churches on their land. Patronage, it was claimed, went against the Presbyterian tradition and it was argued that it was the right of

the Presbytery to select ministers. Patronage was viewed as yet another example of the aristocracy's abuse of privilege. Given that the Church was a very important social institution, many ordinary people resented the fact that their churches could be dominated by ministers more in sympathy with the aristocratic view of the world. The majority preferred their ministers to be evangelical, enthusiastic and committed, rather than other-worldly and intellectual. This was especially the case as godlessness was reckoned to be a major problem in the sprawling cities, which were expanding as a result of the Industrial Revolution.

The growing influence of the middle class in Scotland can be seen in the fact that by 1833 there was a majority in the General Assembly against patronage, not including the one third of Presbyterian adherents outside the established church who had left because of the issue. These seceder or voluntary churches were again dominated by the middle class.

The fact that a majority of the Church believed that patronage was an

ecclesiastical issue and of no interest or consequence to the state did not prevent the House of Lords ruling that patrons or landowners did have the right to appoint ministers. In effect, they overturned the church's Veto Act. Despite the best endeavours of the leader of the Evangelicals, Thomas Chalmers, the government refused to intervene, largely it must be said because few English politicians could grasp the intricacies of Scottish ecclesiastical affairs. Indeed, the perception of Chalmers at Westminster was that he was a fanatic.

Unable to convince the politicians of the Church's case, in 1843, at what became known as the Disruption, he led a breakaway Church from the General Assembly. Almost half the congregation and a third of the ministers walked away from their comfortable livings and out into the street with him to form the Free Church of Scotland.

The Disruption was essentially a debate about the place of the Church in a modern industrial society, and as such is one of the most significant metaphors of 19th-century Scotland.

It was during this time that the middle class began to reinvent Scotland in their own image around the values of laissez-faire. Thrift, hard work, self-reliance and independence were recast as Scottish values. It was at this time that the cult of William Wallace began to grow. The middle class saw in Wallace characteristics which, they fondly imagined, mirrored their own. Wallace had stood up and led Scotland on the basis that he was the best man for the job, not, like the aristocracy, because of birth. William Wallace believed in liberty and freedom, and so did the middle class (in the *laissez-faire* sense). The Wallace story demonstrated the perfidy of the aristocracy and he was recast as Scotland's first 'lad o'pairts', the archetypal self-made Scot.

THOMAS CHALMERS

1780–1847

THOMAS CHALMERS started his clerical career as a moderate, but he rapidly became an evangelical. He moved to Glasgow in 1815 where, at St John's parish in the Trongate, he tried to adapt the Scottish parochial system to a new urban environment. Chalmers was an earnest proponent of self-help who encouraged the working class to be self reliant and stand on their own two feet. An unswerving critic of patronage, he found himself as leader of the evangelical wing of the Church of Scotland. His attempt to persuade the British government to overturn a House of Lords ruling on the use of patronage eventually came to nothing and, in 1843, he led his supporters out of the General Assembly in the Disruption which saw the foundation of the Free Church.

Power, Politics, Perfidy

I~N~ spite of the claims of the intellectuals that Scottish society was governed by ideas of virtue and enlightenment, the nation's politicians could best be described as a motley crew of self-seeking chancers.

Though the Union of 1707 had abolished the Scottish parliament, the political system which elected MPs remained the same, the only difference being that the number of MPs was cut from 159 to 45. The electorate was less than 4,000 and the rules governing who got the vote were archaic and corrupt. Constituencies were divided into burghs and counties, the former representing urban areas and the latter rural. Elections were held every seven years and some constituencies were bundled together to elect a Westminster MP while others took turns. In the burghs, having the vote could be determined – among many things – by medieval charters and, in the counties, land was the principle qualification. Given the small number of voters, elections were subject to bribery and fixing in advance.

Most of the time, the majority of seats were not contested. When they were, it was a riotous occasion and could last up to three days. Drink was supplied to the voters, who had to make their declarations of support public. Not surprisingly, there were many allegations of corruption and intimidation.

Based on taxable wealth, as a proportion of the UK, Scotland's representation at Westminster was smaller than that of Cornwall. Scotland was also entitled to send 16 aristocrats to the House of Lords. Politics in the 18th century was fluid; ideology and party discipline in the modern sense did not exist and prime ministers, who were appointed by Royal prerogative, had

String-puller supreme: Archibald Campell was adroit at manipulating politicians. His successor Henry Dundas was even better at it

———— ❧ ————

to gather together a coalition of MPs to pass legislation. Self-interest, personal prejudice and naked ambition were important facets of the political system and had to be accommodated to make the system work.

It was within this system that Scottish politicians had to operate, and a number of features exacerbated a tendency towards corruption in Scotland. Firstly, the Scots MPs were recruited largely from the second and third sons of the aristocracy or minor gentry. MPs were not paid and tended not to have private means and were vulnerable to financial pressures. This could be exploited by 'Scotch managers' who would withhold pensions and favours to ensure that they were compliant creatures in the Commons.

The precarious financial position of most Scottish MPs meant that they could easily be controlled. The 18th century House of Commons was subject to shifting allegiances and it was the ability of the 'Scotch managers' to deliver a solid phalanx of Scottish MPs which made them so valuable to governments struggling to control more than 500 English MPs in a system totally unlike modern party politics.

The wheels of the Scottish political system were lubricated by the oil of patronage. Access to pensions, jobs, and contracts were essential weapons in a Scotch manager's armoury.

The system of political management through patronage was first demonstrated to good effect by Archibald Campbell, Earl of Islay and 3rd Duke of Argyll. Having taken over the mantle from his brother John in 1743, Archibald built up an elaborate system of political control which was administered by Andrew Fletcher, the future Lord Milton. Critical to the success of a manager was the ability to be seen to have access to the levers of power. Patronage had to be dispensed wisely, as there was not enough to go round. It had to be given without alienating potential supporters. Archibald Campbell was not only able to use patronage to keep his MPs in line, but he could also use patronage in the constituencies to bribe voters. Government posts, such as that of customs officer, might be offered to the son of an important elector. University professorships, clergy appointments and teaching posts could also be held out as incentives.

One effect of the dominance of patronage in –Scottish society was that the leading figures of the Scottish Enlightenment all owed their positions to the ruling elite and used their intellectual powers to promote the existence of the status quo.

When Archibald Campbell died in 1761, having created a system in which over half the Scottish MPs were regularly in his pocket, the mantle of Scotch manager fell to the Earl of Bute, who became Prime Minister briefly in 1761 but who had to resign two years later. The vacuum was eventually filled by Henry Dundas. Appointed as Lord Advocate in 1775, he quickly learned the rules of patronage and by 1780 controlled 12 Scottish MPs. Keen to enhance his influence with the government, Dundas extended his tentacles. Pragmatic and hard-headed, he supported Pitt the Younger, and by 1784 controlled 22 MPs. As Lord Advocate and Secretary of the Navy, he used his position to enhance his powers of patronage and in the general election he was able to deliver 34 of the 45 Scottish MPs.

His dominance of Scotland made him an indispensable ally of Pitt the Younger and he was appointed Home Secretary in 1791, which greatly increased his power of patronage. Dundas made use of his position to open up opportunities for Scots in the East India Company, making India, in the words of Sir Walter Scott, 'the Corn Chest of Scotland'.

In 1794 Dundas was made Secretary for War and in 1804 First Lord of the Admiralty, responsible for much of the war effort against Napoleonic France. Access to such power, however, proved to be his downfall. Dundas was impeached in 1806 for improper use of Navy funds for private speculation. Though acquitted by one vote, the damage to his reputation had been done. The death of his ally Pitt in the same year ended his career anyway.

The old political system trundled on until the passing of the Great Reform Act in 1832 but Scottish politics never again experienced the same degree of mis-management, patronage and corruption.

THOMAS MUIR OF HUNTERSHILL
1765-1799

BORN in Glasgow, Muir was a radical and idealistic lawyer who helped found the Scottish cell of The Society of the Friends of the People in 1792. He was dedicated to political reform and the cause of the United Irishmen, commitments which led to his arrest. His intervention for the life of Louis XVI smacks of egomania. In Paris, he met not only the revolutionary leaders but also Thomas Paine, author of *The Rights of Man*. He returned to Scotland via Ireland to stand trial. Accused of sedition he promised that 'the echoes of this trial would rumble down the centuries'.

Sentenced to 14 years' transportation in New South Wales he escaped on an American ship to enjoy further escapades in Latin America and Spain before he died in Paris from wounds received fighting the British.

CHAPTER 6

People and Identity

1780-1850

❧

IN 1700, nine out of 10 Scots lived in the countryside. It was a far cry from a rural idyll. Most existed as subsistence farmers, that is growing just enough food to feed themselves and pay the rent. Farming was primitive and organised around 'ferm touns'. The land was divided into two kinds of areas: the outfield, which was poor quality land used for grazing, and the infield, which was divided up into cultivated strips.

It was during the period from 1760 onwards that fairly dramatic changes began to alter the nature of life in rural Scotland. Imbued with Enlightenment values, and driven by the need for more income, Scottish landowners began to dramatically change the system of agriculture. Strips of land and subsistence farming were abolished and replaced by single tenant farmers who operated enclosed fields which increased production of crops significantly. Chunks of the population became landless rural labourers employed in the reorganisation of estates. Market principles became the guiding force in the life of rural Scotland.

Displaced people from the countryside could work as rural labourers, or if that option was not available, they could move to the expanding urban areas. At the start of the century, Scottish society was one of the least urbanised in Europe, yet by the end of

the century it was one of the fastest urbanising societies in the world. By 1850, almost a third of the population had moved to live in an urban environment.

The speed of change was utterly traumatic. There were few mechanisms in place to deal with such a rapid expansion and the social problems which attended the development of the cities became legendary.

Scottish housing was almost certainly among the worst in western Europe. The reasons for this state of affairs can be traced to certain features of the Scottish legal system. First, Scottish building regulations were very stringent. After a great fire in Edinburgh in the late 17th century, it was made law that Scottish buildings had to be constructed of thick stone and made to withstand the potential of fire. This made building relatively expensive. The second factor associated with housing was feuing. An arcane feature of Scots law meant that feus were purchased for building property, often speculatively. A fixed down payment was made and an annual fee was then charged. This could not be

❧

Glasgow's Jamaica Bridge forms the main north-south axis over the River Clyde for the rapidly exanding city in the 19th century

renegotiated and was paid in perpetuity so it would decrease in value as a result of inflation.

Consequently, when land was earmarked for building purposes, the seller would try to extract as large a down payment and set as high a feu as possible. Builders therefore had to borrow large sums of money to pay for land they needed to stay in the business of building houses. And once the property was built there were no clauses stipulating that it had to be kept in good repair, unlike in England.

Builders had every incentive to maximise the earning potential from their investment and they did so by packing houses as close together as possible to exploit the land to the full. Many tenements in Glasgow had rooms which saw no sunlight. Also, it was easier to get more money by dividing tenements into as many residences as possible so that separate feus could be charged. Most were one or two rooms. It has to be remembered that Scotland was a low wage economy where the majority of workers were in unskilled and casual labour. High rents were something that few could afford so large families were crammed into cramped spaces they had little option but to call home.

The speed of Scottish urbanisation can be illustrated by a few telling statistics. Of the 13 largest towns in early 19th-century Scotland, five at least trebled their population between 1750 and 1821. Glasgow grew from 31,700 to 147,000 and, by 1841, it was reckoned that half the population of the city had not been born there. The speed of such growth brought many social problems. Inadequate sanitation was the major problem. Contaminated water supplies, the piling of waste in the streets and open sewers, together with the fact that people were huddled together in close and cramped housing, took their toll. Although the larger towns were mainly free from epidemic fevers in the period 1790 to 1815, thereafter diseases such as typhus

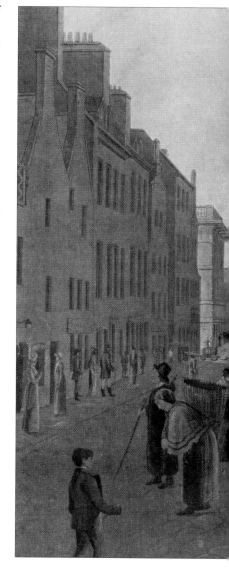

Aberdonians gather at the Castlegate in a city built from the granite quarried at Rublislaw

---

The pillars of the Royal Scottish Academy building begin to rise at the foot of the Mound in Edinburgh

appeared repeatedly in 1817-20, 1826-7 and 1836-7. A major cholera outbreak in 1831-32 claimed 10,000 lives.

The reasons for the persistence of major heath problems in the towns and cities were varied. There was little response to the outbreak of cholera in 1831 because many believed it was a visitation from God and that it would be wrong to interfere with Divine will. Another problem was that official scientific wisdom believed that the disease was carried through the air in a cloud, rather than through contact.

Local authorities were not armed with sufficient powers and much legislation which could have improved conditions was dependent on a parliament which took little interest in local affairs. Furthermore, from the mid-18th century the middle class began to evacuate the city centres in search of more congenial pastures. The creation of Edinburgh's New Town and the emergence of suburbs in Glasgow's west end meant that the middle class removed themselves physically from the major problems. As ratepayers, they were not

keen on funding improvements which would not affect them directly but would benefit others.

This state of affairs was reinforced by the development of an ideology which stressed the responsibility of individuals to look after themselves. Many commentators associated the symptoms of poverty, drinking, gambling, crime and prostitution with the causes of poverty. Conventional wisdom held that charity and handouts would do nothing to solve the problems. The only solution to the condition of the working class was to initiative a change within themselves. Self-help, moral improvement, abstinence, hard work and thrift were the recommended solutions. Until people realised that they were responsible for their own plight, it was argued, nothing could be achieved. It was a moral vindication of the policy of inaction that allowed the majority to continue living in intolerable conditions. Thomas Chalmers, the leading Scottish clergyman, once had a beggar visit his house asking for a penny. Chalmers was determined that it was best for the man that he stood on his own two feet. At the moment, however, he relented. His act of charity haunted him for many weeks, believing that he had kept the man in beggarly ways.

Life in the lower classes was nasty, brutish and short. In 1800, you had a one in six chance of reaching your first birthday. You would get married in your mid-twenties and die in your late thirties. If you were a woman, you would have a one in five chance that you would never marry. If you did, you would have four to five children, although it was foolish to expect all of them to reach adulthood. If you lived in a town or city, you would probably live in one or two rooms. You would start work before your teens and might even be employed from the age of five or six. Your average working day would last 14 hours. Once you reached 15, you would be consuming just under a pint of whisky per week. Your diet would consist of more than two-thirds bread and oatmeal, less than a fifth of meat, with cheese, butter and eggs a luxury. You would also face periodic unemployment and suffer a high risk of industrial injury which would leave you dependent on your children, who would already have troubles enough of their own.

Crime and Punishment

SCOTLAND in the 18th century was a lawless country. Riots were a regular feature of society. They could break out over the price of food, or the introduction of new taxes, or when popular celebrations got out of hand. The normal means for dealing with disturbances was to call out the militia, who could easily take several days to arrive, by which time the damage had been done.

Until the middle of the century, the Scottish legal system was a hotchpotch of different courts and, because of the lack of any effective police force, it fell to the judiciary to make strenuous efforts to try to ensure social stability.

In the Highlands, because of the problems of geography and terrain, it was impossible to enforce the rule of law. Cattle thieving was part and parcel of everyday life.

In the countryside, landowners normally had a free hand to dispense justice for all crimes committed on their land as they saw fit. The exceptions were treason, murder, rape and arson which had to be tried in Edinburgh, In the towns and cities, misdemeanours were punished by fines or alternatively a spell in the notoriously unhygenic tollbooths where the jailers were paid from the collection of fines and had every incentive to make

a prisoner's life miserable to encourage payment. Caning was used on petty criminals and serial fornicators were put in the stocks.

The Church also played its part in trying to regulate the good conduct of its parishioners. It had the power to fine for various misdemeanours such as fornication (one notable victim of this public shaming was Robert Burns) swearing and general bad conduct. In parishes, minister and elders would try to get unmarried mothers to disclose the name of the father. It was permissible to squeeze the nipples of young women suspected of being pregnant to see if they were producing milk.

Witch burning had largely stopped by the late 18th century but it was outlasted by forehead branding with a hot iron, a punishment normally meted out to beggars who, if they were able-bodied and not mentally disabled, were deemed to have no excuse. Public execution by hanging was a day out for the family with the criminal paraded in an open cart to the gallows. Many would try to say a few last words before the drop but drummers were always on standby to drown out the speech if it was considered provocative or obscene.

Treason was punishable by beheading before the body was quartered. At the execution of Baird, Hardie and Wilson for their part in the 1820 insurrection, this task was performed by medical students.

❧

1788: Scottish society turns out to witness the hanging of Deacon Brodie, a respectable Edinburgh citizen by day, cat burglar by night – hanged on the gallows he himself presented to the city

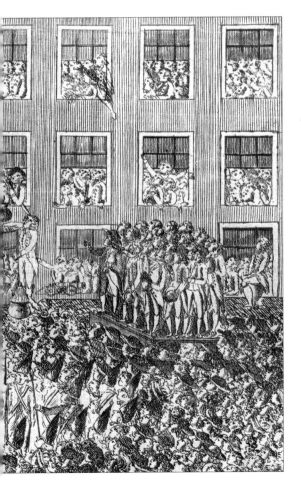

LORD BRAXFIELD
1722-99

Robert MacQueen was born near Lanark and became a highly respected advocate specialising in the obscure and esoteric area of feudal land law, until he was appointed to the High Court and quickly established a notorious reputation as a hanging judge.

It fell to him as Lord Justice Clerk to pronounce the death sentence on Deacon Brodie, another colourful character of the time. Presiding over one of the notorious treason trials, Lord Braxfield famously responded to a defence plea in mitigation that Jesus Christ had also been a reformer with the stinging reply: 'Muckle he made o' that. He was hangit.'

The author Robert Louis Stevenson was later to use Braxfield as the model for his hard-hearted, hard-drinking judge in his unfinished novel, *Weir of Hermiston*.

A Call to Arms

SCOTLAND has a long history as a military nation. The fact that the nation was only briefly conquered twice, by the English, contributed to the fond belief that the nation had preserved its liberty by feats of arms against overwhelming odds.

The truth is that Scottish soldiering had as much to do with poverty at home as innate military prowess. A military wage sent home from abroad for an impoverished household was a desirable goal and what one man achieved as an original soldier of fortune, his neighbour often copied. In the 17th century, it is reckoned that as many as one in eight adult males in Scotland may have been employed abroad as a mercenary. Scots were employed as soldiers in the Swedish army of Gustavus Adolphus, used as bodyguards by the French and Prussians, and saw service with the Russian army of Peter the Great. When the civil war broke out in England and Scotland was called on to defend itself, returning mercenaries turned the country into an armed camp overnight.

In the aftermath of the Jacobite Rebellion, the Scots had a range of opportunities to prove their martial prowess in the Seven Years War (1756-63) and the American Revolution (1776-83). During these campaigns the Scots, and in particular the Highland regiments in their highly distinctive

kilted uniforms, had distinguished themselves, although plans to create a Scottish militia in the mid-18th century were spurned by the government. Memories of the similarly clad Jacobite army were too recent to allow Scots to practise their military skills too close to home.

It was the Napoleonic wars, however, that firmly established the popular images associated with the enduring Scottish military tradition. During the latter part of the 18th century, the poems of Ossian, the ancient Celtic bard 'discovered' by James Macpherson, became very popular. They gave an idealised vision of the 'noble savage'. These attributes were believed to have survived in Highland society, which was beyond the reach of Mammon and corruption. Highlanders were believed to be loyal warriors whose keen sense of kinship made them ideal soldiers.

This was pure romanticism. The Highlands were an ideal recruiting ground for the British army, not because the people there were inclined to fight and die for king and country, but because the area was over-populated and landowners were able to use the threat of eviction to force tenants to join up.

Religion was also important. Evangelicalism had gripped the Highlands and insinuated itself into the ranks of the soldiers. When Highland regiments disembarked at Portsmouth in the early 19th century, the locals were amazed when they headed, not for the gin shops, brothels and pubs like so many of their fellow soldiers before them, but for the Bible classes and churches.

The publication of Sir Walter Scott's novel *Waverley* confirmed the growing notion that the Highlanders were fearless warriors whose loyalty had been so cruelly misplaced in the service of the Jacobites. But, with the Jacobite threat well and truly buried, this loyalty was now transferred to the service of the British state. Even the Prime Minister, William Pitt, was moved to pay tribute to the qualities of the Highland soldier.

At the battle of Alexandria, in 1801, it was the 42nd Highland regiment which was given the credit for turning the battle and capturing the French standard. William Cobbett, the English radical, subsequently proved that it was the Queen's German Regiment which deserved the glory but if the facts do not fit the story it is often overlooked.

At the climactic Battle of Waterloo in 1815, however, the evidence is that the facts did fit the story. The London *Times* reported how the Scots Greys charged to the cry 'Scotland Forever' and tore into the ranks of the French with infantrymen from the Scottish regiments hanging on their stirrups to give them greater momentum, the better to cut a swathe through the enemy. On the day, the Scots spilled more than enough blood to confirm their reputation and be feted as the heroes of the field and heroes of the British nation.

The Scots Greys at Waterloo

What is Scottish Culture?

IT IS A curious fact that, in the century and a half after Scotland had lost its native parliament, the country enjoyed an unprecedented period of international fame. During the late 18th and early 19th centuries especially, Scottish history and literature was broadcast across Europe and America so that Scotland became a land of ancient and modern romance in the mind of the western world.

The nation's contradictions in identity – land of the Scots, the British, Covenanters, Jacobites, lowlanders, Gaels, Enlightenment rationalists and folk-songsters – which have since so perplexed those in search of the essential Scotland, made in the eyes of contemporary observers for the warp and woof of a colourfully venerable culture.

The Scottish Enlightenment presented to the world the spectacle of the philosophical, practical and cultured Scot. This was a period where not only Edinburgh could be described in Tobias Smollett's phrase as 'a hotbed of genius' but other metropolitan centres could as well, notably Aberdeen and Glasgow, as they also brimmed with Enlightenment activists producing works of belles-lettres, moral philosophy, history, and the natural and social sciences.

In terms of the creative imagination, the Enlightenment represents a much more ambiguous period of inspiration. A range of often strange and spectacular literary experiments resulted from the sponsorship of the dominant Scottish mindset.

The most famous and enduring of these was the poetry of Ossian, which Napoleon Bonaparte notoriously came to admire at the height of his military exploits. Between 1759 and 1762, James Macpherson (1736-96) published poetry which he claimed to be translations of 'Erse' verse of the 3rd and 4th centuries celebrating the virtuous martial exploits of the ancient Celts.

These poems, hugely lauded at the outset by Hume, became one of several significant points of Anglo-Scottish cultural tension during the 18th century. Berated by Samuel Johnson as a barefaced forger, the truth is that Macpherson did indeed utilise some original materials culled from the Gaidhealtachd but stitched these together and amplified them with a great deal of creative ingenuity.

The taste for Ossian in Scotland shows how vibrant the compass of the Scottish Enlightenment could be. If the Scottish literati were fired by the desire to demonstrate to its post-1707 partner, England, and the world at large how civilised Scotland was, the enthusiasm for the primitivism of the Ossianic epics showed Scotland shaking off its stereotypical image as a place of dour Calvinistic retentiveness. Scotland's immersion of itself in this highly emotional secular expression represents one of the harbingers of the great age of Romantic art which was to sweep Europe later in the century.

One of the great European novels of the 18th century is *The Expedition of Humphrey Clinker* (1771) by Tobias Smollett (1721-71). It draws on the Enlightenment interest in psychology and anthropology and explores, via the perspectives of a series of travelling letter-writers, the cultural geography of Britain. In one of the book's many comic moments a character is in trepidation as she is about to cross the Border into Scotland. She has heard that the Scots have only sheep heads to eat, and it takes some time to dawn on her that where there are sheep heads there must also be the bodies of sheep.

The novel is about stereotypical misunderstandings and it argues that if new-fangled Britain is to work, its widely-differing inhabitants must

SIR HENRY RAEBURN

1756-1823

ARGUABLY Scotland's greatest portrait painter, Raeburn was born at Stockbridge, Edinburgh. Apprenticed to a goldsmith, he began his career as a miniaturist. Having spent some time in Rome he returned to Edinburgh where he spent most of his career. He was influenced by Sir Joshua Reynolds and members of the Scottish School. According to Duncan MacMillan, Velasquez and Rembrandt also impacted upon his art. Raeburn captured on canvas a number of the luminaries of late-Enlightenment and Georgian Scotland such as David Hume, James Boswell, Henry Dundas and Walter Scott, as well as kenspeckle figures such as Neil Gow and Macdonnel of Glengarry. At his death, he was planning a portrait of a kilted George IV which might have proved one of the defining moments of Scottish Romanticism.

SIR WALTER SCOTT

1771-1832

SCOTT was addicted to writing. The son of middle-class Edinburgh parents, his first major publication was a collection of ballads, *Minstrelsy of the Scottish Border* (1802-3), which inspired his own narrative poems such as 'Lay of the Last Minstrel' (1805). He was a strange mixture of ambitious businessman and hopeless romantic who wrote to rescue himself from bankruptcy. His first novel, *Waverley*, was anonymously and successfully launched in 1814. Arguably his greatest novels deal in Scottish themes – *The Antiquary*, *Old Mortality*, *Rob Roy* and *The Heart of Midlothian*. In his fiction, Scott brought ordinary people back into the historical process, but as a historian, he seemed embarrassed by his country's past,

Sir Walter Scott *by Sir Henry Raeburn, 1822*

particularly as represented by the Highlands. Nowadays, Scott is more criticised than read, but although he had problems confronting the reality of his times, he cannot be held responsible for the cultural travesties which are claimed by some as his legacy.

work to know one another. Chillingly, Smollett observes the pre-Clearance Highlands and observes the populousness of the place; he also has one character remark on the fighting abilities of the clansmen which might be best put to use in British regiments (something, of course, that was to happen increasingly from the later 18th century, so establishing the 'fighting Jock' myth). If Smollett shows his British mentality, his Scottish nationalist side is also seen in this novel as he voices the complaint that in some economic aspects (especially with regard to European trade) Scotland has lost out by the Union with England.

In the 18th century, the most potent form of what we would today call cultural nationalism was to be found in the work of poets writing in Scots. Such writers are often regarded as standing in stark opposition to the cultural energies of the Enlightenment, as might be witnessed by Hume's cheeky remark about the 'corrupt' tongue of Scotland (though it is possible that, in this instance, Hume had his tongue in his cheek). Such writers were often inspired by a mixture of political and sentimental Jacobitism since the Tory nostalgia for the Stewarts brought with it assumptions, which countered a sometimes puritanical Presbyterianism in Scotland, and an alien Hanoverian-led Britishness which could be presented as having little appreciation of the ancient cultural autonomy of Scotland.

Ideas of this kind are to be found very explicitly in the work of the man who was to become Scotland's national poet, Robert Burns (1759-96). However, Burns was to live through the American and French revolutions, world-shaking events which called into question many of the old and assured assumptions about what it was to be a coherent nation. Much of his poetic formation can also be put down to the traditional Presbyterian respect for education and interests in philosophy and psychology derived from the Scottish Enlightenment. Commentators sometimes point to these multifarious influences on Burns and diagnose him as suffering from a typical Scottish "crisis of identity", but one might instead argue a richness of vision on the part of Burns which enabled him to entangle so many aspects and themes in his poems and songs.

Burns, along with Walter Scott (1771-1832), was hugely responsible for collecting, editing and broadcasting to the world the ancient history and folk-culture of Scotland. Scott also utilised many of these materials as he invented the modern historical novel with its keynote charting of the collision of large-scale social and cultural traumas with the carefully particularised psychologies of fictional protagonists (and so again Scottish literature's debt to the Enlightenment is apparent).

He is endlessly fascinated by periods of tension in history and especially by such periods in Scotland. Scott has been accused of unleashing 'tartanry' on the world, but his fictional attempts to explore what beats beneath the tartan (and indeed what lies behind, for instance, the mentality of medieval Scotland or the Reformation) should not be forgotten. Like Burns, he is very much the modern writer as a man of many big historical questions and few simplistic answers.

The claim is sometimes made that with the death of Scott, the increasing emigration of intellectual and literary talent such as Thomas Carlyle (1795-1881), and the emergence of the Victorian British superstate, the last vestiges of Scotland's cultural autonomy entirely receded by 1850. Positive and negative aspects of the Scottish identity, forged from around 1750 continued to resonate, however, and have done so to the present day.

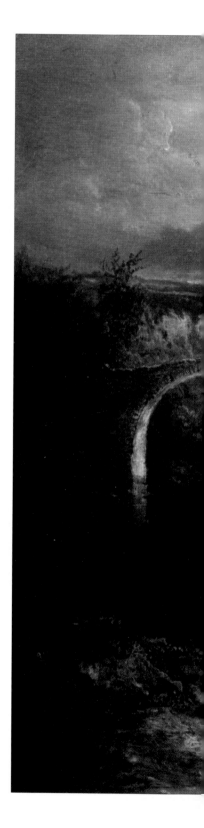

ROBERT BURNS
1759-96

Scotland's national bard gained fame through the publication of one book, *Poems Chiefly in the Scottish Dialect* (1786), the astonishing 'Kilmarnock Edition'. He continued to write poetry, most notably the brilliant narrative 'Tam o Shanter'.

A bit of a lad even by contemporary standards, he fathered 15 children in all, six of them 'out of wedlock' but he never denied responsibility for any of them. He also wrote some of Scotland's and the world's greatest love poems including 'My Love is Like a Red Red Rose'.

In the guise of 'Heaven-taught ploughman' he celebrated basic human decency and the brotherhood of man, while traducing all types of hypocrisy. His satirical pieces still have bite. A native of Ayrshire, he died in Dumfries, having spent the latter part of his short life collecting traditional Scottish songs and music. He had no idea he was to become a world-spanning cult in the form of the Burns Supper which poetic purists abhor and ordinary Burns lovers swear by.

Robert Burns by Alexander Naysmith, 1828

A People on the Move: Empire, Industry and Dispossession

1850-1914

THIS period of Scottish history is marked by a number of contrasts. It was an era of great industrial achievement. Scotland was undoubtedly an international economic powerhouse whose industries were at the forefront of modern technology. Scotland justified its title as the 'workshop of empire' and inspired the stereotypical ideas about Scots being hard-headed businessmen, entrepreneurs, doctors, engineers and scientists. Scots preened them-

selves on these notions. There was a darker side to the story too. Economic success did not come without costs. Scotland had some of the worst slums in western Europe and poverty and chronic ill health were endemic. The magnificent opulence of Glasgow's city chambers was a fitting testament to its position as 'second city of the empire', yet in the Saltmarket, just several hundred yards from the marble pillars and hallways, people lived in dire poverty that crushed the spirit. Innovation and enterprise were important, but Scottish industrial prowess was built on the back of cheap labour.

The Scottish economy of the 19th century was founded on specialisation. As other modern industrial nations moved towards mass production, Scotland retained craftsmanship in design and production. Nowhere in the world, it was argued,

could you find better companies and engineers to design and build high quality ships, engines, locomotives and heavy machinery to such exact standards and specifications. Armies of workers gathered on the Clyde to crawl like ants over great ships that grew piece by piece on the city skyline.

Transport was an essential element in the industrial alchemy which created the modern economy. Trains helped to unify Scotland and shift goods cheaply and quickly from one part of the country to another. They also gave quick and easy access to England and record-setting steam locomotive races became a virility test for rival railway companies. Time, to satisfy the timetables, was standardised throughout the United Kingdom.

Glasgow was the Scottish city which best demonstrated the twin features of progress and poverty. If the 18th century belonged to Edinburgh, the balance then shifted to the west and the 19th century surely belonged to Glasgow. The city was particularly adept at responding to the challenges thrown up by urban expansion and its attendant social problems. These problems were not unique to Glasgow. There were clearly identifiable reasons why all of urban Scotland suffered from poor housing, inadequate sanitation and terrible health.

While remembering the winners of Scottish progress, it is important not to forget the losers. The problems of the cities pale into insignificance when compared to the catastrophe of the Highland famine of 1846. After years on the economic margins, the Highland population was left dependent on one crop for its survival, the potato, and the area was only just saved from the worst effects of famine. Just as Scotland was beginning to glorify itself in a Highland tartan guise, the real Highlanders were exposed to horrendous suffering. The alleged inability of Highland society, in sharp contrast to the potential for change eagerly embraced by the central belt and east coast, to adapt to the demands of a modem commercial economy meant that forced emigration was used as the only realistic solution to the problem. 'Progress', as many at the time termed it, meant that all obstacles to the mantra of free trade and economic self-sufficiency were removed.

An empire such as ours requires as its first condition an imperial race 'a race vigorous and industrious and intrepid.' Lord Rosebery's words in 1898 are frequently quoted to demonstrate how the British Empire was the major influence in the politics of the day. What is less well known is that Rosebery was speaking to a Scottish audience and his references were to the Scottish role in Empire.

Far from being a colonised country, Scots regarded themselves as natural empire builders. It was a frequent boast that the Empire dated from the 1707 Union and that without Scottish soldiers, administrators, engineers, emigrants, explorers and businessmen there would be no Empire at all.

The Empire was an important part of Scottish life. It provided endless job opportunities for individuals and the Scottish economy made a great deal of money exporting railway locomotives to India and exploiting overseas tea and rubber plantations. Enterprising businessmen were always alive to lucrative new deals as they emerged in the ever-expanding Empire, though these could often be more imagined than real.

It was hard to escape the Empire in the 19th century. You would read about it in the morning paper. The streets on the way to work were named after imperial heroes and watched over by their statues. Banking involved imperial investments, industry made imperial exports, retail used imperial imports and the public service was imbued with the values and deeds that 'won the Empire'. The family could visit museums and galleries stuffed with imperial relics, or spend the evening going to the music hall to listen to patriotic ditties. At school, geography lessons were a constant reminder of just how much of the atlas was coloured imperial red, while history lessons focused on the heroes who had formed the Empire. The universities offered courses in tropical medicine and Sanskrit languages in preparation for imperial service.

Ideas about the Scottish role in the Empire played an important part in the development of Scottish politics. Even before the Reform Act of 1868 extended the vote to skilled workers, Scottish politicians were demanding increased representation at Westminster to take account of the fact that Scotland was contributing more than its fair share of imperial revenue.

The demand for Scottish home rule in the period before the First World War was bound up with notions of Empire. National efficiency, social reform and improvement of government were mixed in with Scottish nationalism to produce the first serious demands for a parliament in Edinburgh.

With the extension of democracy, politics was increasingly forced to cater to the demands of the working class and to allow women to become involved. Also, by the end of the 19th century, social reform was moving higher up the agenda; not only as a means to contain the advance of socialism, but as a way to maintain the good running of the Empire. The Boer War in South Africa showed that an unhealthy and uneducated population could not be relied upon to defend the precious Empire. As a result, physical education and home economics were introduced into schools to produce better imperial warriors.

Sporting prowess and worthwhile leisure activity were seen as the building blocks of good character. Though many people clung to baser pleasures than those sanctioned by the imperial mind-set, personal enjoyment was saddled to the theme of making model citizens. The first football clubs were formed and displaced quoiting as Scotland's most popular sport.

CHAPTER 7

The Age of Heavy Industry

1850-1914

⤳

B Y the middle of the 19th century, Scotland had begun to seriously question its place in the world. There were fears that the nation was losing its historic identity and that creeping tentacles of centralisation and modernisation were making Scotland and England uniform and indistinguishable from each other. The traditional Scottish institutions which had survived the Union of 1707 – law, education and the Church – were all thought to be in a state of disrepair. More and more the legal system was being changed to bring it into line with England, especially to facilitate greater commercial interaction. In 1826, a Royal Commission on the Scottish universities had claimed that far from being the celebrated seats of learning associated with the European Enlightenment, they were out of date in teaching and research and riven with corruption. Some venerable professors were found to have been using the same lecture notes as their grandfathers. The much vaunted universal education system with a school in every parish, which was supposed to have given the nation the most intelligent population in Europe, had collapsed as people left the countryside for the cities and towns, where no check was kept on whether they were receiving schooling or not. At least half of all school-age children in urban areas missed out on any education.

This state of affairs had one leading commentator, George Lewis, warning in his 1834 book, *Scotland: A Half Educated Nation*, that the nation would be deluged by a wave of crime and immorality as children grew up in ignorance of Christianity and good behaviour. Finally, the Church, in which so many Scots had vested their national and spiritual capital, had split in the Disruption of 1843 over the issue of patronage.

By 1847 there were three Presbyterian churches: the Established Church of Scotland, the Free Church of Scotland and the United Presbyterian Church. All were of equal size and all claimed to be the 'true' national church of Scotland. Poor relief and education suffered as each of the three claimants jostled for status. One legacy of this religious conflict was a furious spate of church building in which even the smallest of villages was blessed with two, sometimes three, competing churches. Presbyterianism, once a source of national unity, was now a source of debilitating division.

⤳

*The Forth Bridge,
still standing after more than a century
of everyday use, is an enduring symbol
of all that was best about the qualities
of Scottish engineering excellence*

The decline of the traditional institutions, which were arguably the most distinctive feature of a separate Scottish civic identity, was coupled with the accelerating and unsettling effects of urbanisation and industrialisation to produce a pessimistic prognosis for the future of Scotland. According to one Free Church fundamentalist, the Rev James Begg: 'Scotland was sinking under an increasing combination of evils'.

In 1858, Alexander Brown, using the pen name Shadow, published a book of documentary-style episodes of inner city life. *Midnight Scenes and Social Photographs*, being sketches of life in the streets, wynds and dens of the city, were not photographs at all but pen portraits of the evils visited on society. Rather than prick the social consciences of the middle class they seemed instead to titillate with vivid accounts of the strange and exotic Godless masses infesting a whole other world. Readers of Shadow were informed of the habits and customs of an underclass who had degenerated into outright barbarism where prostitution, drunkenness, gambling and crime were endemic.

The cholera outbreak in 1832, the growth of political instability and Chartism, the movement to extend the franchise and the famines in Ireland and the Highlands in the mid 1840s were all thought by many churchmen to be a punishment from God as the nation had turned its back on goodness and endorsed sin. Leading men of letters, such as Sir Walter Scott and Henry Cockburn, had believed that industrialisation and modernity would eradicate the nation for good. They informed the opinions of some people who, as a defensive mechanism in response to the perception that Scotland was somehow disappearing, collected old ballads, historical records and artefacts to preserve as much as possible of the ancient nation before it vanished for ever.

Some groups – such as the National Association for the Vindication of Scottish Rights, formed in 1853 and full of 'romantics and radicals' like the Tory Earl of Eglinton and the Liberal Provost of Edinburgh Duncan MacLaren –

SIR WILLIAM ARROL

1839-1913

THE man who built the Forth Bridge was born in Houston, Renfrewshire. He started his first job in a thread mill at the age of 10 after lying about his age. An apprentice blacksmith as a teenager, he studied mechanics and hydraulics in his spare time and had started his own engineering business by the time he was 29. His firm constructed a railway viaduct at Greenock in 1865 and was brought in to build the second Tay Bridge after the 1879 disaster. Work was under way on the ambitious and pioneering design of the Forth Bridge at the same time. The Tay Bridge was completed in 1887, the Forth two years later.

Tower Bridge in London is another that bears the distinctive Arrol stamp. He also managed to be an MP for South Ayrshire from 1892 to 1906.

sought to turn back the clock by appealing to national pride and sentiment. Although nationalism was part of their agenda, the Scottish Rights campaigners did not want to repeal the Union. Rather, they wanted greater sensitivity from the British government in dealing with Scottish affairs. They demanded the restoration of the position of Secretary of State for Scotland (which had been abolished in 1747 following the defeat of the Jacobites), greater say in the government of Scotland, greater Scottish representation at Westminster and an

Romancing the stone: in 1861 a crowd of 50,000 turned out to witness the laying of foundations for the Wallace Monument at Abbey Craig outside Stirling as Scotland sought to reinforce its identity

end to the use of the disparaging 'Scotch' to describe the Scots. It was this group who appealed to national sentiment in their campaign to erect the monument to William Wallace at Abbey Craig in Stirling. The laying of the foundation stone in 1861 attracted an astonishing audience of 50,000, tapping into the 'Braveheart' strain in Scottish psychology a century and a quarter before Mel Gibson exploited it for his Hollywood film. Such stirrings of patriotism, however, were frowned upon down south where the London *Times* acidly commented that 'the more

Scotland strives to be a nation, the more she becomes a province'.

History tends to be viewed as a straight line, with all that happens along the way seen as inevitable. We know now that Scotland in the 19th century would emerge as a great industrial power, proud of its economic achievements and service to the empire. We also know that few would question the wisdom of the Union, or the fact that Scotland was a nation in her own right, albeit in imperial partnership with England. This was not necessarily how some saw it at the

time when there were two schools of thought. There were those who bemoaned the decline, as they saw it, of Scotland under an unprecedented industrial tide and those who believed Scotland was riding this tide of modernity to national greatness.

The National Association could draw out a respectable number of supporters but, ultimately, few endorsed its gloomy view of the nation's progress. The altogether more positive view of the nation's achievements was prevalent. After all, it was pointed out that Scotland had one of the highest per capita incomes of any society in the world. Its economy was second to none and had made magnificent progress in a wide range of industries. Did not visitors come from Europe to marvel at the efficiency of Scottish agriculture? Was Scotland not a leading pioneer in technology and science? Even the sovereign, Queen Victoria, seemed to regard the Scots as her favourite subjects and revelled in the company of strong-willed Highlanders like her ghillie John Brown. And, as critics pointed out, these achievements had been completed in little more than 100 years. For them, the rise of Scotland was spectacular and the gripes of a minority were of little or no consequence.

In any case, just as the traditional institutions were in decline and industry and urbanisation were scarring the landscape, new myths and visions of the nation were emerging to replace the old ones. Queen Victoria's obsession with the Highlands, prompted by the landscape's similarity to that of southern Germany, encouraged the Scots to recast their national identity in a tartan format. The Highlands became a potent symbol of Scottish national identity because many regarded the place as an older and purer part of Scotland, unsullied by urban industry with all the dirt and squalor that surrounded it. Rather than face the urban reality of modern Scotland, the Scottish middle class took refuge in the romanticism of Sir Walter Scott, the poetry of Robert Burns and the 'Kailyard' novels which glorified the virtues of mythical rural Scotland. Scott's heroes are all principled and valiant; Burns' *The Cottars' Saturday Night* gained the author a reputation as a champion of family values, despite his own notoriously amoral personal life; and the Kailyard theme was always the same, that the best human qualities were to be found in small towns and villages well away from the evils of city life. Scottish self-confidence in the 19th century was built on the firm foundations of economic success. Nowhere was this more evident than in Glasgow, the second city of the British Empire, with its resplendent City Chambers and George Square which was deliberately intended to resemble Trafalgar Square in London.

The first phase of industrial development (1790-1870) has been called the 'generalist' phase. The industries in which Scotland excelled – textiles, iron and coal – all had a number of common features. They produced general products which required little or no skill; they were dependent on cheap and abundant labour and the bulk of their market was overseas. Cotton began to lose its pre-eminence in the

'Shadow's documentary account of the state of the masses both shocked and titillated the respectable folk who bought his book in 1858

Steam and sail share the Clyde in 1865: the navigable waters of the Clyde were extended to meet the growing needs of Scottish industry, pushing further inland towrds the centre of Glasgow

early 19th century as a result of foreign competition and over-production at home. Just as it began to experience difficulties, there was the rise of iron. The development of Neilson's Hot Blast in 1828, the use of hot air in the smelting of iron, permitted the exploitation of Scotland's vast reserves of coal and blackband ironstone (a native iron ore).

While the general industries were successful in the short term, their long term survival could not be guaranteed. One of the most important advantages the Scots had at this time was that they were part of the first industrial nation and there was little competition. However, they were to be squeezed out of foreign markets by the rise of both indigenous UK industry and foreign competitors.

From the 1870s onwards, the direction of Scottish economic development began to shift towards a greater degree of specialisation. The hub of the Scottish economy increasingly focused on shipbuilding and heavy engineering producing goods like rail locomotives, boilers, ships' engines and steam hammers. There were a number of reasons for this. First, heavy goods could not be mass produced. Volume

production and standardisation led the way in the 'second industrial revolution'. The industries of Germany and America pioneered the utilisation of cheap mass-produced goods such as guns, bicycles and chemicals in which economies of scale were important. Large ships and specialised heavy engineering goods, however, could not be so easily produced in bulk and

Scotland had the necessary skills to take advantage of this. Design of one-off ships or engineering plants was very much a Scottish speciality. Customers could insist on high quality specifications which gave rise to the prestigious sobriquet 'Clydebuilt' which quickly became a symbol of Scottish excellence, covering innovative examples of engineering prowess such as the impressive Forth Bridge.

In other economies, there was a tendency towards de-skilling as machinery took over, replacing craftsmanship. Given the high degree of specificity of Scottish products, machinery could not replicate the skills that had been forged among the workforce. Also, as the global economy expanded, there was a ready market for ocean-going ships and railway locomotives to transport the goods which were often produced by Scottish heavy engineering plant. Few could beat the Scots when it came to placing orders for specialist capital investment goods.

The strength of the Scottish economy can be illustrated by a few facts. On the eve of the First World War, the

SIR THOMAS LIPTON

1850-1936

Born in a Glasgow tenement of Irish immigrant parents, he was soon put to work as a delivery boy before emigrating to the US at the age of 15. However, a stint on a tobacco plantation and some shop work on the other side of the Atlantic was enough for him to decide that he didn't fancy it and he came home.

He opened his first shop at Stobcross Street, Finnieston in 1871, and was a millionaire before he was 30. He branched out, buying overseas tea and rubber plantations, and followed the Carnegie doctrine of charitable giving, as well as the accumulation of wealth.

A keen yachtsman and friend of royalty, his humble roots and occupation as a grocer nonetheless were a source of sniffiness and objections to his membership of the Royal Yachting Club.

Clyde produced 18% of all the ships launched in the world that year and the Scottish shipbuilding industry was bigger than that of either Germany or the United States. Glasgow was the largest locomotive production centre in the world and Scotland produced about 20% of the steel made in Britain. With only 10% of the population, Scotland accounted for 17.5% of all manufactured goods in the UK.

But while things may have looked rosy on the surface, there were dangers lurking underneath. Scottish economic well-being was entirely dependent on exports and therefore on the health of the global economy. So long as there was the confidence to invest in ships, heavy engineering and locomotives, Scotland would do well. If there was a downturn in the market, Scotland would be the first to feel it. Also, Scottish competitiveness was based on keeping wages as low as possible which had the effect of preventing the development of a healthy home market that could have helped to promote lighter domestic industry. The failure of the Scottish economy to diversify led to greater reliance on the export industry which kept wages low. That further reinforced pressures against a domestic industry. The problem was that Scottish industry was all inter-related. Shipbuilding provided orders for steel and engineering. Steel provided orders for coal and iron. The inherent danger was that this 'food chain' was self-contained and vulnerable if no one wanted ships any more.

In the midst of a vibrant and thriving economy on the eve of the First World War, however, siren voices warning of theoretical dangers were easily drowned out and dismissed. Only in the wake of the post-1918 collapse were the consequences of having a lop-sided economy dependent on too few industries and too few customers there for all to see.

Trains Take the Strain in a Shrinking Country

IN MARCH 1802, the *Charlotte Dundas* set out along the Forth and Clyde Canal. Built by William Symington, it towed two barges and a combined weight of 100 tons. This was the debut of the first reliable steamer, but it washed the clay banks of the canal away and was as swiftly laid up. Within six years, however, a vessel like it built by an American of Scots-Irish descent, Robert Fulton, was in passenger service on the Hudson River, and in 1812, Henry Bell's *Comet* took to the water at Port Glasgow. Scotland had made the big practical leap towards the application of fossil fuel to transport and all the risks and opportunities it brought with it.

The river steamer was the harbinger of the Industrial Revolution. 'The Birmingham Fire Eater has visited the fabulous East', wrote Thomas Carlyle in 1829. 'And the genius of the Cape, were there any Camoens now to sing it, has again been alarmed, and with far stranger thunder than Gamas.' Which was his particular way of saying that steam navigation had arrived.

There were hitches; salt water was lethal to high pressure steam engines. Only when scientists (among them the future Lord Kelvin) had perfected forms of reliable condensers, which enabled boiler water to be purified and reused, could steam compete with sail for trans-ocean cargoes. Until then the Scots perfected wood-and-iron clippers like the Dumbarton-built *Cutty Sark* which rushed tea and wool from China and Australia to Britain. When the breakthrough came with the compound engine, it came from the Clyde. In 1865, the Blue Funnel's *Agamemnon*, owned by Scotts of Greenock, could steam to China and back on one load of coal. It

was a timely innovation, for the huge sail fleet of the US had just been decimated by the Civil War and needed to be replaced.

The Clyde launched 50,000 tons of steamships in 1860, half a million tons in 1900: equal to the entire production of the German Empire. The Clydesiders didn't just build ships, they owned them: the Donaldson line, the Hogarth Line, the Clan Line. Elegant vessels with their raked smokestackers, white ventilators and boats, they would anchor at Tail o' Bank while the folk of the west came down by the south-western train to Princes Pier, or by Caley to Gourock, to embark the paddle steamers that carried them to the liners and a new life overseas. These – the *Athenia*, *Samaria*, *Duchess of Richmond* – represented an unconscious elegance of line and functionality of design. No wonder that the prophets of the modern movement – Le Corbusier, the German Werkbund – built houses and schools that looked like them.

The Scots weren't in the van of railway engineering, as they had earlier been in road and canal building. Trevithick was Cornish, the Stephensons were Geordies, Brunel French, Crampton and Gooch English. Yet the Scots came to dominate the business after the headlong expansion of the 1840s: with the Fairbairn and Drummond brothers, Patrick Stirling and Henry Dubs (originally from Germany) in the ranks of the Glasgow locomotive builders. By 1900 Glasgow was the locomotive capital of Europe, and the diamond-shaped makers' plate of the North British Locomotive Company was to be found on engines throughout the Empire, China, Russia and South America. The only works bigger was Baldwins of Philadelphia, producing engines the Springburn men regarded as trashy and short-lived, but which were constructed to have interchangeable parts and to be easy to maintain. American mass production reached Scotland, true, in the shape of the huge Singer sewing machine works at Clydebank, which had its own terminus and rail network, but the principle was never extended to the actual manufacture of locomotives.

Railways had begun in Scotland as wagonways which transported coal and minerals from Lanarkshire and Fife to the coast. In 1842, a passenger line was running between Edinburgh and Glasgow. Throughout the 1840s, there was railway mania and links were established between all the major towns and cities. Berwick was connected to the network in 1846, Carlisle in 1848. Travelling time from the centre of Scotland to London was cut from 43 hours to 17. By the 1880s, it was reduced to eight hours.

In the 1870s, however, came a period of 'short breath'. The Tay Bridge disaster was technological hubris. The design was flawed, work was skimped. The forces of control began to move in: a railway rates act was put through in 1886 against the protests from railway directors. The companies fought back, using the building of the Forth and second Tay bridges to glamorise trains with the railway races of the 1890s.

The thoroughbred express engines and plush carriages served the well-to-do, but the railways made their money from serving industry. The network itself grew out of agricultural traffic, carrying coal and fertiliser inwards, cattle, sheep and grain out. Its branches snaked to (or often not quite to) the smallest burgh: Moniaive in Dumfriesshire, Greenlaw in the Borders, Oldmeldrum in Aberdeenshire.

The Scots working class did comparatively well out of the railways. In England in the 1850s, only one train a day carried third class passengers; in Scotland nearly all carried them, and respectable artisans got used to making pilgrimages to the country. Paddle steamer excursions were much less approved of – passengers could and did drink, which was not something to be contemplated in non-corridor lavatoryless railway carriages.

After 1918 everything changed again as the steamer companies went into collapse and the internal combustion engine – in cars, lorries and aircraft, none of which were Scots success stories – brought lean times to the railways. By 1990, car engines were to have boosted human mobility by a factor of four compared with 1920, with the results that can now be measured by global warming. Carlyle's words about the railway mania of the 1840s – 'they know not where the end of the death-dance will be' – now have an ominously contemporary ring if applied to the favourite means of transport today.

LNER's Mallard *notched up 126mph to break the world speed record as journey times shrank from days to hours in the glory days of steam*

CHAPTER 8

Origins of Socialism

1850-1914

Almost two million Scots left their homeland between 1850 and 1914. It was not, although many liked to think it, because Scots were an expansive and virile race who had innate qualities which made them wander the globe. In fact, it was because Scotland was not a nice place to live for most of the population.

One consequence of being so dependent on an export-led economy was the holding down of wages to maximise competitiveness. Also, orders for ships and heavy engineering could be intermittent with cyclical downturns in the global economy having immediate and significant repercussions in Scotland, causing short-term unemployment and job insecurity until a new order was placed with a yard. This perpetuated the endemic problems of poverty and ill health among workers.

The statistics of the time illustrate the point. In 1861, 34% of all Scottish homes had only one room, 37% had only two rooms and 1% had no windows. In 1886, one third of Glaswegian families lived in a single room. By the eve of the First World War, half of the Scottish population still lived in one or two-roomed houses. Such cramped conditions spread disease and encouraged many

Contemporary cartoon treatment of the many strands of popular unrest in the late 19th century

JAMES KEIR HARDIE
1856-1915

Born near Holytown, Lanarkshire, into poverty and forced to go down the mines, he became one of the early trade unionists and educated himself to become a journalist. He is widely acknowledged as the founding father of the Labour Party. His belief was that the political interests of the working class could best be represented by themselves, his outlook and philosophy shaped by ethical Christian humanism rather than doctrinal socialism. He contested the Mid Lanark by-election in 1888 as an independent working man's candidate and, although he lost, he helped to form the Scottish Labour Party later the same year. It met with little success and Hardie moved south to start and edit *The Labour Leader* and become an integral part of the setting up of the Independent Labour Party. He won the seat of West Ham in London but lost it because of his opposition to the Boer War and the First World War, clinging resolutely to his pacifist convictions until his death.

working men to escape to the pub to take refuge in alcoholism. Booze, it was said, was the quickest way out of Glasgow.

Estimates show that per capita in the 1860s, Scots earned about 75% of wages in England. The figure increased to about 90% before the First World War, where it remained with minor fluctuations until the pay gap finally closed altogether in the 1980s. In a British context, however, these figures do not do justice to the true extent of the differential between Scotland and England because the prices of staple goods in Scotland remained consistently higher. Bread, for example, cost 10% more.

Not only were Scots paid less than the English, the distribution of income was more uneven north of the Border. Using estimates of Scottish national income in 1867, 70% of Scots were in the lowest economic bracket of unskilled and low-skilled where wages were under £50 a year. The higher skilled workers who earned over £50 comprised less than 10%. 'Lower small' incomes who earned up to £100 made up 11%, while 'middling and upper small' incomes of £100 to £1,000 amounted to 8% of the population.

Finally, at the top of the tree, there were the very wealthy who earned over £1,000 and accounted for a tiny 0.33% of the population. Statistically, this reveals that the society of Victorian Scotland consisted of a large group of unskilled and semiskilled workers who formed the vast bulk of the population. There was a significant number of skilled workers and lower middle class who made up about a fifth of the population, and a small middle class of less than 10%. The bottom 70% of the population earned a third of total income, while the top 8% earned almost 46% of the nation's wealth. Just under 5,000 individuals earned 25% of the total national income. Clearly, Scotland was a society divided by wealth.

Rise of Town and City

Industrial growth brought a population explosion for many of Scotland's towns. Glasgow, for a time in the early decades of the 19th century, grew at rates faster than anywhere in Europe, overtaking Edinburgh between 1811 and 1821 as Scotland's largest city.

Small villages, like Coatbridge, were transformed into blackened, polluted industrial towns in two or three decades experiencing many of the characteristics of frontier towns. The economic opportunities of new industries encouraged larger families and the lure of the city pulled in many from the surrounding areas, as well as from further afield. By 1914, 60% of the population lived in towns, one in three in one of the four main cities.

Such rapid growth brought in its wake immense social problems comparable to those of burgeoning cities in the developing world of today. Rivers, once filled with fish, became open sewers. Formerly elegant mansions were 'made down' to accommodate a dozen or more families and gardens and squares were filled with jerry-built hovels. Wells that had provided a water supply for centuries dried up or became polluted and could no longer meet the needs of both expanding industry and a burgeoning population. Industry contaminated the rivers, polluted the atmosphere and frequently poisoned the inhabitants.

Disease followed remorselessly in the wake of the deteriorating environment. Typhus, carried by the body louse and thriving in dirty housing conditions first reached epidemic proportions in 1818 and returned again and again as an 'unerring index of destitution' striking particularly at some of the young migrants living in cramped lodging houses. Deaths from typhoid, transmitted through food and water and later milk, continued to be a major threat through until the last quarter of the century. Most frightening of all were the recurring waves of cholera which swept across Europe and into Scotland first in 1832, then again in 1848-49, 1853-54 and 1866. Carried through polluted water supplies, cholera was little respecter of social class and took its toll from among those of the better off who had not managed to escape to the country.

While epidemics grabbed the headlines, chronic illnesses like TB, bronchitis and pneumonia were the persistent killers and disablers in towns. Poor and unvaried diet weakened the population. Shared bedding made the spread of infection rapid. Children were vulnerable to measles, whooping cough, diarrhoea and, in the sunless warrens of inner-city closes, to the deforming disease of rickets.

The crises of rapid urban growth gradually forced administrative changes. When epidemics like cholera scythed through the Godly and the ungodly and the rich and the poor alike, it became less acceptable to ascribe them to an act of God or to the fecklessness of the poor. There were calls for action. Medical men, statisticians, and other observers began to expose the extent of the destitution which was developing, and pressed the authorities to step in where voluntary effort had failed. Churchmen and others warned that salvation in the next world and security in this required some sympathy with the most needy in society. Employers recognised that their workforce needed to be healthy. Civic pride overcame civic parsimony.

———— ☙ ————

State of the nation:
the residents of a close at
118 High Street, Glasgow pose in 1868

By the 1840s, with the problems getting worse in cities like Glasgow and Dundee, thanks to a renewed influx of migrants from famine-struck Ireland and from the Highlands, the pressure for action was coming from all directions. A first priority was to get adequate water supplies. Private water companies had long proved themselves incapable or unwilling to respond to the needs of both industry and health. Only massive public investment could solve the problem of taking water from cleaner supplies in the hills. Glasgow got its 'pure' but ultimately harmful soft water from Loch Katrine in the 1850s. Edinburgh's came from St Mary's Loch in the Borders and Aberdeen's from Cairnton in the upper reaches of the Dee. Although dominated by businessmen who would have proclaimed an unswerving belief in private enterprise and in the efficacy of the market, sanitary committees of the town councils began to regulate and control. Streets were lit, sewers were laid, middens and ashpits were cleared away, 'privies' and water had to be available in all new properties; owners were required to whitewash tenement lobbies and stairs. By the 1860s, Medical Officers of Health were being appointed in all the main cities and they learned to use their power and influence to identify and deal with problems. Most of all, the best, like James Burn Russell in Glasgow and Matthew Hay in Aberdeen, were effective publicists and propagandists constantly exposing the horrors of the worst areas of their cities and trying to shame the councillors and the rate-payers into action.

The most intractable problem was housing. By 1850, there was a widespread recognition that overcrowding, ill-health and high mortality went together. Anything from half to more than 70% of families in Scottish towns lived in one or two

SIR HENRY CAMPBELL-BANNERMAN

1836-1908

CB, as he was known, was born in Glasgow, the son of the Lord Provost. He worked in the family drapery business before being elected as the Liberal MP for Stirling Burghs in 1868. A convert to the cause of Irish Home Rule he was a stalwart supporter of William Gladstone. In 1898, he became leader of the Liberal Party and, following the collapse of the Conservative government in 1905, Prime Minister who led his party to a landslide victory at the general election the following year. A pro-Boer he granted the former republics self-government and was closely identified with the campaign to abolish the House of Lords. He resigned from office seven days before he died.

rooms. Attempts to prevent overcrowding by simple regulation and the 'ticketing' of tenements with a metal plaque indicating how many residents were allowed, proved inadequate even with night-time swoops and the arrest of the victims.

Then came improvement movements with local authorities keen to develop their city centres to create squares, public buildings and railway stations which would proclaim the status of their thriving community. The initial tactic was to buy up the poorest property and to demolish it with the expectation that private developers would seize the opportunity to fill the sites with new housing. But, private housebuilders were increasingly concentrating their efforts on providing houses for the affluent who were being attracted to the more salubrious surroundings of the suburbs, accessible thanks to the expanding tramway systems. Paradoxically, the increased regulation of housing discouraged house building aimed at the poorer sections of the population. Slum clearance merely resulted in the problems of overcrowding being transferred beyond the clearance area.

Local authorities, finding themselves to be major slum landlords, slowly and reluctantly, and against the opposition of powerful vested interests, were forced to take upon themselves the task of building houses.

By the 1880s, there were signs that all the efforts were beginning to have some effect. Life expectancy in Glasgow had crept back to the levels it had been at in the 1820s – 42 for men, 45 for women – and continued to improve. The trick was to survive infancy. More than one in every four children died before the age of five. Around 40% cent did not make it beyond the age of 25. Not until the early 20th century did better pre- and post-natal services and better-fed mothers and children bring some fall in the death rates of infants. Nonetheless, the achievements of the Victorians were great and, in judging them, it is perhaps worth remembering that all the efforts of municipal authorities and the state throughout the 20th century have failed to eradicate massive housing problems while the health differential that divides rich and poor remains as distinct and as wide as it ever was.

Glasgow Flourishes

G LASGOW, in 1850, was one of the fastest-growing communities in the United Kingdom, with a population of nearly 330,000. This was a four-fold increase from 1800, largely attributable to the unprecedented number of incomers to the city, especially from other parts of Scotland and Ireland. Manufacturing success in textiles helped to attract the migrants, many of whom sought employment in cotton-spinning and weaving, plus a range of ancillary enterprises. The territory of the city had more than doubled, in 1846, to 5,063 acres, taking in predominantly industrial districts such as Anderston, Calton and the Gorbals and fundamentally redefining the administrative entity of the medieval burgh. Steam was the force powering Glasgow industry and was a potent symbol of the entrepreneurial energy that characterised the city by the mid-19th century. It also represented modernity, in an era of rapid technological change and expanding global markets.

Yet, although the textile and clothing trades together employed over 41% of Glasgow's industrial workforce by 1851, the economic fortunes of the city were increasingly identified with the River Clyde. Over time, the notoriously shallow river was transformed to accommodate substantial harbour developments, allowing Glasgow to become a major port. The abundance of coal and iron in the west of Scotland was a crucial factor in the success of shipbuilding. These resources were readily exploited from the 1830s by the innovative marine engineer, Robert Napier. He went on to inspire a generation of like-minded shipbuilders, many of whom had served an apprenticeship in his yards. For example, John

Elder, who established Govan's Fairfield Shipbuilding & Engineering Company in 1864, was one of Napier's most talented protégés.

The scale of developments was such that during the 1850s and 1860s Clyde shipbuilders produced 70% of the iron tonnage launched in Britain, their output ranging from coal barges to steam yachts and warships. In particular, naval contracts consolidated the

'Clyde-built' reputation around the world for sturdy excellence. The manufacture of steel in and around Glasgow from the 1870s reorientated the base of heavy industry by allowing for even larger vessels to be constructed. Although the progress of the industry was prone to sharp cyclical fluctuations, 1913 was a golden year, when almost a fifth of the world's shipping output was built and launched on the Clyde.

WILLIAM THOMSON
Baron Kelvin of Largs
1824-1907

His was the first house in Glasgow to be lit by electricity, Baron Kelvin having discovered an aptitude for blending pure and practical science.

Born in Belfast and brought up in Scotland from an early age, he was a student at Glasgow University by the time he was 10 and moved on to Cambridge when he was 16. He was appointed professor of mathematics and natural philosophy in Paris at the age of 22. He applied his mind to problems in electrostatics and proposed the absolute, or Kelvin, temperature scale in 1848. He established the second law of thermodynamics.

He became wealthy from the patents of numerous electrical instruments, which were developed and manufactured by his own company in Glasgow. He is buried in Westminster Abbey beside Sir Isaac Newton.

It was ironic that Glasgow became recognised as the shipbuilding capital of the world at a time when the main centres of production, in Govan and Partick, were located outside the boundaries of the city . From the 1850s, the declared objective of civic leaders was to incorporate the outlying districts, which also included prestigious middle-class communities such as Hillhead in the west and

Queen Victoria presides over the Empire Exhibition of 1888 in the 'second city of the Empire'

Pollokshields in the south. As the century progressed, the quest to create the 'Greater Glasgow' briskly built up momentum. After years of intense campaigning by Glasgow Corporation (the municipal authority), the first phase of expansionism was achieved in 1891. Extending over 11,861 acres and with a population of over 560,000, Glasgow was rapidly becoming the 'Second City of the Empire' both in size and status. When Govan and Partick were eventually persuaded to join with the city in 1912, Glasgow's territory covered 29,183 acres and accommodated over a million people.

Up to the 1880s, Corporation leaders were almost invariably Liberals, reflecting the prevailing political orthodoxy of the city. They came overwhelmingly from a business background and shrewdly understood the economic benefits of positive public relations. 'Greater Glasgow' was a slogan that conveyed the city's cosmopolitan credentials and demonstrated that it could compete with the major urban centres of Europe. As part of this purposeful civic image, measures were taken to improve the environment and embellish the landscape. The first custom-designed public park was laid out at Kelvingrove in the 1850s, adding to the traditional open space of Glasgow Green. A powerful symbol of Corporation determination to cleanse and regenerate the city was the Loch Katrine water supply, a major engineering feat sanctioned by parliament as a 'municipal enterprise' in 1855. Although there were vocal complaints from taxpayers about the cost of the project (at over £1m) the official response was that the health benefits of pure water would be incalculable for Glasgow.

Clearing the congested inner city was also a civic commitment. Industrialisation may have broadened economic horizons, but it also brought about extraordinary overcrowding in the old tenement heartland, which inevitably affected the well-being of the community. During the 1860s, suburban Hillhead had a population density of 28 persons to the acre, but the worst city-centre areas, such as the infamous Drygate district, had an incredible density of 1,000 persons to the acre. Contagious diseases flourished in such confined conditions and Glasgow's recurring epidemics were an important reason for the introduction of Loch Katrine water.

The high incidence of respiratory diseases, notably tuberculosis, also impressed the city fathers with the need to create 'breathing space'. The City Improvement Trust was inaugurated in 1866 to clear slum areas, open out thoroughfares for the freer flow of traffic and encourage new building. The role-model was Paris, and although there was scathing criticism of civic pretensions in emulating the French capital, the combined efforts of Corporation councillors and officials did eventually transform the central districts. That architecturally important developments, like the seventeenth-century university, were demolished in the restructuring, forcefully displayed the Corporation's determination to impose modernity on Glasgow.

The City Chambers was a statement in stone to confirm Glasgow's place in the Empire and the world

Bustle of the big city: horse drawn trams amongst the busy traffic on Jamaica Street

The penchant for civic monumentalism continued apace, reflecting 'Greater Glasgow' aspirations and the image of administrative efficiency. The City Chambers in George Square was opened by Queen Victoria in 1888. The sumptuous interior contained marble corridors and rooms richly inlaid with wood from all over the world. The new municipal headquarters consciously paraded Glasgow's global achievements in an era of imperial rivalry. The focus on Empire was used to emphasise the Clyde's importance as a vital trade route. The Empire was also identified with economic success because of the promise of potential export markets as new territories were brought into the imperial orbit. Significantly, from the 1880s, Glasgow Liberalism was confronted by the electoral challenge of Unionism, a populist political ethos that embraced both imperialism and social welfare.

By the 1900s, Glasgow was depicted as a 'city-state' because of its ever-expanding population and much-vaunted civic bureaucracy. 'The Venice of the North' was a title that appealed to city publicists, as it strongly suggested aesthetic and mercantile opulence. Glasgow's world-renowned public tramways were even known as 'the gondolas of the people'. Art patronage was certainly keen in Glasgow at the turn of the century, and Francis Newbery's School of Art made an enduring impact in encouraging the celebrated 'Glasgow Style' of Charles Rennie Mackintosh and his circle. That Glasgow was being assertively promoted as a city of culture was illustrated by the grand opening of the new municipal Art Gallery and Museum in 1901, as the centrepiece of a prestigious and hugely popular International Exhibition at Kelvingrove Park.

Civic pride was by no means an artificially-contrived commodity in Victorian and Edwardian Glasgow. Yet the image often ran counter to the reality of fluctuating economic fortunes and low living standards. There were times of serious industrial recession, as in the winter of 1908. The export market was volatile, and it was primarily the Liberal Government's naval shipbuilding programme prior to the First World War that restored economic equilibrium. For all the high hopes of the City Improvement Trust, housing (and overcrowding) remained one of Glasgow's most intractable social problems. The fear of upsetting private property interests meant that there was timidity in the Corporation's approach to municipal house-building. That the fledgling Labour Party began to take the initiative on this question indicated the changing political direction of the city, which became more apparent after the extension of voting rights to men and women in 1918.

Scots on the Move

1850-1914

✍

Oᴎᴇ of Scotland's greatest exports in this period was people; nearly two million of them. However, just as Scots were leaving, immigrants poured into Scotland from Ireland. This was especially the case after the potato famine started in 1845. Not all Scotland's Irish immigrants were Catholic, about a quarter of them were Protestant and with them they brought distinctive aspects of their culture, namely Orangeism, which had gained a foothold on the Ayrshire coast through returning soldiers and early immigrants at the end of the previous century but remained insignificant for decades. The Protestant Irish found it easier to assimilate into Scottish society than their Catholic co-nationals. Less than 1% of the Scottish population was Catholic, rising to 12% by the end of the century.

Of the Irish immigrants, between a quarter and a third were Protestant, mostly Presbyterians from Ulster who travelled along the shipbuilding nexus between Glasgow and Belfast. They had a vision of themselves as British and Scottish, claiming that they were direct descendants of the plantation colonies of the 17th century. Their loud declarations of loyalty, especially on the 12th of July, the anniversary of the Battle of the Boyne, however, did not endear them to the native Scottish population. Orangeism quickly became associated with drunkenness and disorder and the Scottish middle class believed they could have nothing

in common with this working class Irish rabble. Even the Scottish Conservative Party shied away from courting the Orange vote because an active appeal to Orangeism was likely to alienate many of its middle-class Scottish supporters. Also, the Orange Order was notoriously fickle in its support and even went so far as to denounce leading Scottish Tories who had been part of the government which had permitted the Restoration of the Catholic hierarchy in Scotland in 1878.

Irish Catholics, on the other hand, found themselves strangers in a strange land. Forced to take whatever jobs they could get, they remained firmly on the bottom rung of the Scottish social ladder. Herded into ghettos, and facing hostility from the local community, their identity focused on their church. Catholicism and Irishness mutually reinforced one another.

In addition to Orange antagonism, the Catholic community faced prejudice from the Scottish middle class. Organisations such as the John Knox Society and the Protestant Society actively promoted anti-Catholicism. One leading Scottish clergyman, the Rev James Begg, wrote the best-selling

✍

The diaspora disembark from an emigrant ship at Sydney Cove, Australia, during the 1880s in a scene repeated in many other parts of the world

Hand Book of Popery in the early 1850s and made a speciality of finding former priests who would shock genteel middle-class audiences with tales of chicanery and evil-doing within the Catholic church. Stories that nunneries were filled with the dead bodies of illegitimate children who were the result of unholy unions between priests and nuns provoked genuine calls for the inspection of nunneries. These stories and the former priests who recounted them, however, were all bogus. One of the Rev Begg's favourite former priests, a Canadian charlatan, rewarded his trust by stealing the church collection and was later arrested for brawling outside a brothel in Liverpool.

Whereas Orange anti-Catholicism was raucous and working class, the Scottish middle class added an extra weapon to their armoury of prejudice: racism. Newspapers and journals increasingly depicted the Irish Catholic as ape-like in cartoons and stories. Drunkenness, crime, squalor and lax morality were characteristics impugned to the average Catholic, although by the turn of the century these features were explained not so much by their adherence to Catholicism, but rather on account of their Celtic racial features – limited intelligence, lazy and violent. Indeed, Catholicism was now explained by the fact that they were 'inferior' Celts. The Catholic Irish, too, were a lost cause, too far gone to be worth bothering about. The various Presbyterian churches in Scotland made more effort to convert Africans, Native Americans and Asians than the people resident in their own country.

In addition to Irish immigration, the central belt's growing urban conurbation were fed a constant supply of new people from rural parts of Scotland, especially the Highlands. Migration from the Highlands had largely been of a temporary, seasonal

Emigrants follow the Canadian railroad to their new lives abroad: Scots on the left, Irish on the right

———— ❧ ————

nature in the late 18th and early 19th century, but as conditions got worse, this migration became increasingly permanent. Life in rural Scotland was extremely hard and lonely. Isolation, long hours and little chance of social advancement, all combined to produce an exodus from the countryside.

Whereas the great majority of Scots lived out their lives in a rural environment at the beginning of the 19th century, by 1914 this was down to only 11%. The main problem with rural life was the lack of opportunity for improvement. If you were born a ploughman, you would die a ploughman. You would have the same daily routine for the rest of your life with only a couple of days off in the year. Although cities were renowned as hotbeds of sin, corruption and every conceivable form of human degradation, they at least offered the chance for social improvement. It was this dream that things could indeed change for the better that attracted most people in from the countryside initially. However, in the end most people would be disappointed and would be persuaded ultimately to try their luck abroad.

Emigration from Europe was not unusual, but there is a paradox concerning Scotland. On a per capita basis, Scotland was in the top three of people-exporting nations; Ireland and Norway being the other two with Italy and Portugal making up the top five.

Yet, Scotland was the only industrial nation in this group with a modern economy. The others were primitive agriculture-dominated societies where peasants could only find paid work and potential prosperity in the advanced economy of America's new world. Scotland was very different, so the paradox is this: why should Scots born into a modern

A Scots family observes the Sabbath in their new home in North America

---- ❧ ----

Clearing the Highlands

industrial society emigrate to another modern industrial society?

The answer can be divided into two sections. There were push factors: forces which tended to expel people against their will, such as forced emigration from the Highlands. And there were pull factors: forces which attracted people overseas, such as the prospect of higher wages and steady work. Statistics show that Scottish emigration peaks coincided with downturns in the Scottish economy. It was not a pioneering spirit but unemployment, poor living standards and a lack of opportunity that pushed many Scots out.

Also, a great many itinerant Scots were drawn from the middle class. Doctors, engineers, lawyers, teachers and administrators were produced in great abundance by the Scottish universities. In the 18th century, a third of all doctors in the UK trained in Scotland, leaving the country because there were not enough places in society to sustain them all. Overseas was an important outlet for all the Scottish professional classes.

The transport revolution made emigration easier. In the 18th century,

crossing the Atlantic was a trip undertaken only once in a lifetime. It was an expensive, dangerous journey that took months. By the mid-19th century, the development of relatively safe ocean-going steamers had made fares affordable, and potential emigrants knew that should things not work out, return was always possible. It was no longer a great leap in the dark.

As most European emigrants to America were unskilled peasants from backward societies, the skilled Scottish worker found that his abilities were at a premium in his new country. Foreign companies actively recruited in Scotland, telling workers they could earn twice as much pay for doing the same job. Many Scots already had family connections who could act as the first point of contact with the new world, smoothing the path for finding jobs and accommodation. The average Scottish emigrant in the 19th century was a young, skilled, working-class male from the city for whom the main attraction of emigration was the prospect of an improved standard of living. Yet, not all the Scots were willing emigrants who had been seduced by the promise of a better life.

IN 1846 the Highlands stood on the edge of a social catastrophe. In that year the potato, the main subsistence crop of the people of the region, was hit by a lethal fungal disease which decimated the crops in the crofting townships and continued to have a devastating effect for almost a decade thereafter. Press reports in the autumn of 1846 described how the stench of rotting potatoes pervaded countless settlements along the west coast and throughout the islands. Typhus and dysentery, the classic diseases of famine, spread unchecked among the poor people of the area while death rates among the old and very young started to build inexorably.

The Free Church of Scotland predicted a human disaster on an epic scale – 'the hand of the Lord has indeed touched us' – and proclaimed the emerging calamity 'unprecedented in the memory of this generation and of many generations gone by, even in any modern periods of our country's history'. Contemporaries feared that an Irish-type tragedy was about to be played out in Scotland. In Ireland around one million people died in the terrible years when the potatoes failed, and a further two million people were forced to emigrate because of hunger and destitution.

In the event, however, the Highlands were spared the horrific fate of the Irish. Gradually, mortality rates stabilised and disease failed to reach epidemic proportions. Though the progress of the deadly fungus was just as swift and deadly as in Ireland, the Highlands possessed some key advantages which checked the worst effects of the potato disease. One was the scale of the disaster. In Ireland, the blight brought over three million people to the edge of starvation. In the Highlands around 200,000 were seriously at risk. The real crisis in Gaeldom centred on the north-west and the Hebrides. The central, southern and eastern Highlands were more resilient, with populations less dependent on the potato and possessing economic structures which were more robust and diversified. The concentrated and regional nature of the Scottish famine meant it could be better managed by the relief agencies of the day than the enormous and unprecedented cataclysm across the Irish Sea.

The government stationed two vessels as meal depots at Portree in Skye and Tobermory in Mull to provide alternative food supplies to areas lacking their main subsistence crop. As the principal official in charge of relief put it: 'The people cannot, under any circumstances, be allowed to starve'.

The main impact, however, was made by organised charities. Indeed, the collective response to the Highland famine was probably the greatest single act of philanthropy in Victorian Scotland. The Central Board of Management for Highland Relief raised almost a quarter of a million pounds to aid the stricken population of the north. Contributions flowed in from an amazing array of sources: Scottish expatriates in Canada and India, Edinburgh advocates, colliers, domestic servants, railway workers and even inmates of the country's most famous lunatic asylum, the Crichton Institution in Dumfries. This level of response showed the wealth of

The misery of the clearances is captured in the haunted faces of a Highland family arriving at the quayside as they reluctantly leave their native land for an uncertain future overseas in The Last of the Clan *by Thomas Faed*

Victorian Scotland. It was a society with much higher levels of income than Ireland and already one of the most advanced economies in the world. Scotland, therefore, had the resources to overcome and contain the social crisis in the Highlands.

But the Highlands did not escape unscathed. The officials who organised the distribution of meal in the stricken region were determined that it should not be given away without payment. Virtually all of them shared views about the origins of poverty and the character of the Gael which dictated a much more rigorous approach to relief.

Poverty, in their view, reflected personal failure. Misplaced charity would induce the cancer of pauperism, the habit of the poor depending on the support of others rather than relying on their own efforts. Instead, it was argued that the crisis and the great programme of relief could be used positively as an opportunity to teach the Gael more industrious habits and so prevent another famine.

One of the most influential figures in the entire project, Sir Charles Trevelyan, principal official at the Treasury, viewed both the Irish and 'Scotch Celts' as racially inferior who

had brought disaster upon themselves by their moral inadequacies. To Trevelyan the potato famines represented the judgement of God on indolent people. Therefore, so that the lazy should learn their lesson, relief must be provided only very sparingly in exchange for hard labour. This was the ideological background to the hated 'destitution test' by which a pound of meal was given in exchange for a whole day's work on the building of roads, piers and enclosures. The theory was that only the truly indigent would accept relief on such terms. Today these 'destitution roads' stand

The cliff-top site of Badbea in Sutherland was one of the coastal sites people were 'cleared' to in 1839 to make land available for the more economically viable sheep inland. The community did not flourish and soon it, too, was deserted

*The 1st Duke of Sutherland cleared his
tenants out of their homes in the early
19th century on the grounds that
it would 'improve' their lives, and
allow him to make money from sheep.
His example was to be followed all
over the Highlands*

————— ✦ —————

as enduring monuments to the gravest crisis in the history of the region.

But the relief measures could not prevent the flight of many of the poor. During the famine years, there was an unprecedented exodus from the Highlands. Between the early 1840s and the 1860s, almost a third of the entire population of the western mainland and the Hebrides left for the cities of the Lowlands or sailed across the Atlantic in search of a new life. This was the single greatest and most concentrated diaspora in Highland history and it left entire districts devoid of people and others markedly reduced in numbers. The physical remains of the many communities which disappeared during the famine years can still be seen in the ruined crofting townships and abandoned feannagan (lazybeds) which litter the Highland landscape.

Not all of the movement was prompted by distress, hunger and destitution. Much of it was also induced by coercion from landowners fearful of being burdened with responsibility for an impoverished tenantry and eager to convert crofting land to more profitable sheep walks. In the first few years of the potato famine, many proprietors had come to the aid of their people. However, as the crisis deepened and persisted, a new consensus emerged that the great destitution had unequivocally demonstrated the failure of crofting as a viable economic system. Clearance was therefore given a new intellectual legitimacy. If Highland estates were to reform and modernise, it was argued that they could not support large numbers of indebted tenants and impecunious cottars.

Thus, two years after the potato disease struck, mass removals intensified throughout the western Highlands. Some landowners offered a stark choice between outright eviction on the one hand or removal together with the promise of assisted emigration overseas on the other. More than 18,000 Gaels left in these supported schemes in the 1840s and 1850s. But eviction was only one form of compulsion. The cattle stock of those in rent arrears was confiscated, peat-cutting prohibited and famine relief refused. The strategy was discriminating and pursued with clinical care. The poorest, those most likely to be a burden on the estates, were often the favoured target. As the Duke of Argyll noted, 'I wish to send out those whom we would be obliged to feed if they stayed at home; to get rid of that class is the object'. It was an unyielding philosophy which drove clearance to levels not experienced since the notorious removals in Sutherland. The sheer scope of eviction encouraged one alarmed and experienced government observer to conclude that some landlords risked 'unsettling the very foundations of the social system' and 'depopulating the Highlands by force'. The Scottish famine had unleashed irresistible pressures which would transform Highland society forever.

PATRICK SELLAR

1780-1851

Tᴴᴱ eternal villain of the Clearances, Sellar was born in Morayshire and qualified as a lawyer in Edinburgh before becoming the factor for the 1st Duke of Sutherland just as it was decided that his tenants were surplus to requirements and sheep were the future. Sellar did his master's bidding with uncompromising efficiency and set the standard for what was to follow elsewhere. But the fact was that, at the time, the law was on the side of the landowner and Sellar. His offences were purely moral as he burned and intimidated families out of their homes in Strathnaver in 1814.

Brought to trial later on a surge of public outrage at what was happening to the people of the Highlands, he was acquitted. The clearances continued until the end of the century. He moved to Morvern where he became, ironically enough, a sheep farmer.

The Scots Abroad

There are none so Scotch as the Scots abroad, There's a place in the heart for the old sod.

So sing 'Spirit of the West' a talented group from Vancouver. Between 1825 and 1938 over 2,250,000 Scots departed for destinations overseas. Until recently, few Scottish historians knew or cared what happened to them while those investigating the host countries deemed the emigrants unworthy of attention until they reached their new locations. The extent to which these people

Home from home: the Carnegie mansion beside Central Park in New York

retained a sense of Scottish identity is a more complex question than it might appear. Many who headed for North America, for example, were intent upon assimilating as quickly as possible yet, today, due to the Roots phenomenon and the reinvention of identity, many of their descendants regularly fly the Atlantic in search of their cultural and genealogical antecedents. If the original Diasporeans sought a future, their descendants return in search of a past.

As early as the 17th century, the idea was quite widespread that Scots were somehow programmed for emigration, tough and intrepid as they were supposed to be and well-suited to life in a harsh and alien environment. By the 19th century many not only believed their own mythology but were, furthermore, conditioned by a 'literature of loss' as represented for example by Ossianic

poetry and the verse and novels of Walter Scott. Such people were convinced that an old familiar way of life was over and that a brave new world of opportunity and wealth beckoned. Consequently, some revived and preserved cultures perceived to be on the verge of extinction; others set their faces against the Auld Country which nurtured poverty, tyranny and exploitation. By 1850, Scots were to be found in greater or lesser numbers in virtually every part of the globe from the Arctic to Australasia, from South America to South Africa, India and China. Not all were settlers by any means. Their number included viceroys, governors, merchants, soldiers, civil servants, administrators, explorers, missionaries and teachers as well as shafters, chisellers and conmen of every variety. To most the name of David Livingstone is

familiar; less so are those of John Rae of Orkney who survived incredible treks in the Arctic by following native practice, or Robert Dickson of Dumfries who advocated the creation of an Indian republic extending from west of the Great Lakes all the way to the Pacific.

Almost everywhere they went, the Scots preserved a fairly aggressive sense of their identity, often to the annoyance of their neighbours. In the early 19th century numerous writers more or less created Canada in their own Scottish image. William 'Tiger' Dunlop created a literary circle modelled on the Blackwoods Group in the wilds of Canada West. John Galt, the novelist, and several other Scots founded towns in Ontario. The first settlers were often military men who introduced their sports to Canada – curling, golf, dancing and 'shinny', which became ice hockey. Caledonian Games featured annually throughout the Dominion. St Andrews societies were founded in America as early as 1729 and rapidly spread. Fur traders celebrated St Andrews Day and Hogmanay as did their compatriots when they arrived. Bagpipes were played at many social gatherings in the wilderness. For Gaelic speakers and Lowland Scots alike, the Church provided cultural and linguistic reinforcement as boatloads of Scottish-trained ministers were imported. One year after Thomas

Chalmers founded the Free Church, Canada experienced her own version of the Disruption.

Scots in Canada also controlled publishing and a disproportionate amount of execrable verse, often in Lallans and written by people who had never set foot in Scotland, unfortunately found its way into print. At church socials, curling matches and harvest homes, local bards would compose poems and songs about the Auld Hame. Alexander McLachlan (1818-96), a native of Johnstone, emigrated to become known as the 'Robert Burns of Canada', remaining throughout his life, like his mentor, an impoverished poet. His verse, however, is remarkable

in that he celebrated both of his cultures. He often wrote sentimental effusions in Scots about his boyhood on Gleniffer Braes and the banks of the Cart but he also produced a long poetic sequence on the emigrant experience chronicling the heartbreak of departure, the voyage and pioneer life on the frontier evoking flora and fauna and reporting sympathetically on encounters with the native people. On the eve of the Great War (in which many were to lose their lives) the Scots were failing to maintain their precedence. One of them wrote – 'they seem ever afraid to act as a community and uphold their most sacred ideals, for fear of offending some other national influence; a lamentable

weakness in an otherwise great people'. Harry Lauder was on hand to foster the pap of an ersatz culture on both sides of the Atlantic. But, in 1907, a bank clerk from Glasgow launched his career with his *Songs of a Sourdough* and so Robert Service projected on to the minds of the world the image of Canada which most people now recognise – the Yukon and the Rockies whose awesome landscape was sparsely populated by a host of unforgettable characters who rejoiced in such names as Dangerous Dan McGrew, Sam McGee and 'the lady that's known as Lou', descendants no doubt of the folk who had, so long ago, been programmed for emigration.

ANDREW CARNEGIE

1835-1919

THE weaver's son born in Dunfermline is the prime example of the Scotsman on the make. He emigrated to America with his family at the age of 12 and became the richest man in the world. An astute and ruthless businessman, his fortune was built on steel, but the latter part of his life was devoted to giving away as much of his money as possible. The man who dies rich, he believed, dies in disgrace.

He endowed more than 2,500 libraries in the English speaking world and financed many halls and buildings. In all, Carnegie managed to give away more than £70m, plotting the great giveaway mostly from Skibo Castle in Sutherland where he had returned in 1901 after selling up in the States.

He also dabbled in international politics arguing with the German Kaiser that the commoner, William Wallace, was more significant in terms of Scottish history than the aristocrat, Robert the Bruce. The Kaiser, being imperially minded, preferred the King.

Back home: Carnegie at home in Skibo Castle

GENERAL CHARLES GORDON

1833-1885

The scion of a Scottish family born in England, he saw military service first in the Crimea and then in China in 1860 where he took part in the capture of Peking and the destruction of the Summer Palace before commanding a Chinese force in further operations, forever after becoming known as Chinese Gordon.

An engineer and practising Christian posted to Gravesend in Kent, he spent his spare time helping the poor. In the early 1870s, he set up a network of posts along the River Nile and, in 1877, was made governor of Sudan. Other postings took him around the world until, in 1884, he was asked by the British government to return to Sudan to relieve the Egyptian garrisons that were trapped in rebel territory.

At Khartoum, he found himself beseiged by troops of the Mahdi and held them at bay for 10 months. A relief expedition was on its way to save him but Gordon was killed on the steps of the palace two days before it arrived on the scene, ensuring that he would be forever after idealised as a martyr for the British Empire.

CHAPTER 10

Imperial Scotland
1850-1914

I T IS rather ironic that, though the average Scottish emigrant was male, working class and from the city, the first thing that many people did on arrival in their new country was to set up Caledonian and Burns societies, erect statues to William Wallace, form pipe bands and gather at Highland games. These rather stereotypical images of the Scots were transmitted home and served to further reinforce the kitsch notion of Scottishness. To be Scottish, it would appear, was best done outside Scotland.

The British Empire was an important factor in defining Scottish national identity in the 19th century. The empire allowed the Scots access to the world stage and they grabbed the prospect with relish. It was during the 19th century that the Union became, to many Scots, an imperial partnership. The Scots believed themselves to be natural empire builders and, as they put it, an imperial race.

Increasingly, the Scots perceived their role in the empire as the best way to demonstrate what were thought to be Scottish characteristics. Militarism and martial prowess were sources of great pride. The Scottish press recounted the tales of heroism of the Highland regiments in the campaigns in Crimea, Afghanistan, India and Africa. Furthermore, as these Scottish regiments were commanded by Scottish generals, most Scots believed that the nation made its own distinctive national contribution to British arms. Military parades were an opportunity for the Scots to demonstrate their martial abilities. Soldiering was considered an honourable profession in Scotland, unlike England where more pride was focused on the Royal Navy, and frustrated imperialists who were left at home could act out their military fantasies in the Volunteer Regiments. Organised like the Territorial Army, shopkeepers, bankers, clerks and artisans could drill and parade at the weekend. A moving testament to the popularity of the volunteers, those who pledged to take up arms when the need arose, is to be found in the memorials to the Great War which can be found at the centre of every small village in Scotland.

Trade was another important aspect of the Scottish imperial identity. Locomotives for India, ships to take goods to and from the empire, ventures such as the African Lakes Trading Company and the British East Africa Company were extremely important in reinforcing the link between economic well-being and empire. Scotland as the 'workshop of empire' was one that was enthusiastically endorsed by most Scottish businessmen.

The empire was important in providing jobs for the boys, especially the aristocracy. Almost a third of colonial governor-generals in the period from 1885 to 1939 were Scots. Scots were employed as administrators, civil servants and soldiers in the empire where, according to Lord Rosebery (Prime Minister from 1894 to 1895), Scottish characteristics of hard work, loyalty and trust could be used to best effect. Scottish doctors tackled tropical diseases, engineers built bridges over impenetrable jungle ravines, explorers such as Mungo Park, and James Thomson opened up Africa, missionaries such as James Duff converted heathens to Christianity, and Scottish soldiers and generals such as Sir Colin Campbell, Lord Clyde, who defended and extended the empire, seeing action in the Crimea and leading the relief of Lucknow in India at the time of the Mutiny in 1857.

David Livingstone was the shooting star of missionaries, enhancing Scotland's reputation alongside his own. When Henry Morton Stanley was commissioned by the New York Herald to find Livingstone, presumed lost on the Dark Continent, he uttered the immortal words 'Dr Livingstone I presume' and by doing so paid homage to the service Scotland had performed for the British Empire. He further described Scotland as the nation 'whose energy and enterprise has sent Scotsmen to all countries of the world as pioneeers of discovery, as founders of thriving colonies, as successful merchants and traders, and as useful missionaries and philanthropists'. The eulogy confirmed the impression of Scotland as a natural imperial nation and helped to create the persistent stereotype of the Scot as explorer, adventurer, soldier, administrator and entrepreneur. This was the image that entered the popular imagination, but was it accurate?

It is true the Scots did play a disproportionate role in Britain's imperial expansion, and not only in Africa where Nyasaland, now Malawi, was virtually an exclusive Scottish colony. Nelson Mandela was educated in a Church of Scotland school that had been established in South Africa in the previous century. Elsewhere in the Empire, Scots were equally active, being in the forefront of the East India company, advancement smoothed through clannish behaviour and an 'old boys' patronage network as powerful as any linked to the English public schools. Most of the company's doctors and scientists were recruited from Aberdeen University. It was no surprise that, with Calcutta in the east, the port of Dundee was singled out to be the centre for the international jute trade.

Scots were involved in the Hudson Bay and North West Company with pioneers like Alexander Henry, Thomas Curry, and James Finlay taking the lead. Alexander Mackenzie, a native of Stornoway, was the first European to cross what is now Canada and reach the western seaboard. James Bruce, the eighth Earl of Elgin, was appointed colonial governor of Canada in 1847. Sir John MacDonald was the country's first Prime Minister and the man largely responsible for the construction of the Canadian Pacific Railway. In New Zealand, Prime Minister John Ward talked lyrically of 'friends from the old land' and in Australia echoes of Scotland were apparent in the name of the western city of Perth while in 1889 a capital sum of £1,000 was raised by public subscription to erect at statue at Ballarat, Victoria, to the great patriotic hero William Wallace. Overall, perhaps the most visible demonstration of the all-pervasive influence of the Scots in the Empire is the fact that, to this day, practically every army in the Commonwealth has its own pipe band.

At home, when the Empire was at its zenith, there were plenty of organisations devoted to inculcating the idea that the Scots were an imperial race. Hugely popular magic lantern shows demonstrated that Scottish missionaries were pushing back the boundaries of heathenism. Scots could

Livingstone's original compass and his medical surgery kit are now kept at the museum in his birthplace of Blantyre

DAVID LIVINGSTONE
1813-1873

Born at Blantyre in Lanarkshire, he worked in a cotton mill before educating himself to win a place, at the age of 26, to study medicine at the Anderson's Institute in Glasgow. A devout Christian, the London Missionary Society sent him to Africa. His personal accounts of his journeys through the continent on which he uniquely combined evangelism, medicine and exploration, made him a household name in both Britain and America. He named the Victoria Falls on the Zambezi River and blazed a trail on many routes later used for commercial trade. It was his fame and popularity that prompted the *New York Herald* to send journalist Henry Morton Stanley to search him out, when he was thought to be lost on a quest for the source of the River Nile on behalf of the Royal Geographical Society. His wife Mary, also a missionary, died in 1862 and was buried in Africa. Livingstone died in what is now Zambia. He is buried in Westminster Abbey.

The first European to discover the Victoria Falls on the Zambezi, Livingstone's statue stands beside the river in what is now Zimbabwe

Who's Like Us? Not Them

IT IS A popular notion that the Scots were, if not exactly entirely free from racism, certainly better at getting along with other peoples than their English co-imperialists. After all, wasn't David Livingstone revered in Africa? Didn't 'Chinese' Gordon have a special affinity with other races on account of his Scottish blood? Many Scots at the time thought so, and a large number still do. The truth is, as ever, more complex.

Scots were fascinated by race and racialist ideas. In fact, the Edinburgh anatomist Dr Robert Knox, who collected the bodies supplied by the grave robbers and murderers Burke and Hare in the early 19th century, was one of the original pioneers of racist ideology. Knox, without necessarily trying to promote the superiority of one group of human beings over another, nevertheless, did catalogue the varieties of different peoples into physical characteristics which laid the foundations for subsequent racist ideology The Scots sage, Thomas Carlyle, was a vociferous racist whose notorious publication *The Nigger Question* revealed not only a disdain for Blacks but also the Irish who he described as 'white niggers'. Scottish soldiers during the Indian Mutiny were responsible for the execution of Muslims who were sometimes buried alive wrapped in pig skins. Hindus were wrapped in cowskins and tied to exploding cannons which ripped their bodies apart. Scots settlers in New Zealand cleared the Maori from their lands. In 1919, Glasgow was the scene of race riots. All of which is hardly evidence of a tolerant society.

Scots had always been extensive travellers and this brought them into contact with different peoples.

marvel at the pictures of strange and exotic people and places, secure in the knowledge that the Christianity foisted upon them was of a Presbyterian variety. Scottish museums and galleries displayed treasures of the empire, mostly looted, where the public could see for themselves the fruits of British and Scottish imperialism.

Adverts on Scottish soaps, sweets and tobaccos usually contained an imperial theme. Schoolchildren could collect coupons which showed the flags of the Empire, ships of the Empire,

races of the empire, or even heroes of the Empire. The Boys Brigade, which was founded in Glasgow in 1883, promoted its own muscular brand of Christianity which could be put to its best use in imperial service. The advent of cheap publishing flooded Scottish society with a variety of books, magazines and comics glorifying exploits in the Empire. No matter where you went in 19th-century Scotland, it was impossible to avoid some form of reminder that you were a part of the world's greatest imperial undertaking.

The 17th-century voyager, William Lithgow, spent some time in North Africa. He found it a generally unpleasant experience and his descriptions of the 'heathenish Moor' were not flattering.

The Sahara had been crossed by the Scottish laird, James Bruce, in the early 18th century, and in 1795 Mungo Park set out on his famous exploration of West Africa. The accounts of these travels convinced the Scottish people that civilisation was confined merely to places of white settlement. Africa in the 18th century was best known as a source of slaves, who were used for

Through the imperial window: a popular 'Jolly Nigger Bank' circa 1900. A penny slotted into his hand is then levered into his mouth

labour in the plantation colonies in the West Indies and North America.

The Scots were not extensively involved in the slave trade, but Highland slave owners in America taught their slaves Gaelic so as to easily identify them if they ran away. Many Scottish institutions such as universities and hospitals were left slave plantations by benefactors.

Most of the Scottish literati of the 18th century, however, denounced slavery. David Hume, Adam Smith and Adam Ferguson came out against it, although even their notions regarding the evolution of human society placed Africans at the lower end of the spectrum. Some, such as Lord Monboddo, claimed that Africans were primitives, not far removed from apes.

Scots, in particular women, did play an important part in the campaign for the abolition of slavery, which was outlawed in Britain in 1807 and across the Empire in 1834. Indeed, even before that there was a legal case on whether or not slavery was permitted in Scotland. In the 1770s, a plantation owner had brought back to Scotland a black slave, prompting considerable debate on whether slavery was allowed under Scots law. Finally, in 1779, it was decided that no person in Scotland could be held by the bonds of slavery. Unfortunately for the poor fellow in question, he died before the verdict could be reached.

There was a significant black community in Scotland at the turn of the 18th and throughout the 19th century. Many had returned with merchants and plantation owners as servants. There was considerable social cachet attached to having black servants in the house. The rise of evangelicalism and the anti-slavery movement in the 1820s dispelled these ideas, and in old portraits of merchant families it is possible to see that the

THOMAS CARLYLE
1795-1881

THE most celebrated heir of the Scottish Enlightenment was a stone-mason's son from Ecclefechan in Dumfriesshire. Brought up as a strict Calvinist, he was educated at Annan Academy and Edinburgh University becoming the most prominent of Victorian men of letters, an author and quick-witted social philosopher.

In the context of his times, he was an out and out racist who wrote a book called *The Nigger Question* and was heard to describe the Irish as 'white niggers'. As he grew older he became increasingly right wing, writing pamphlets on the need for duty, obedience and punishment.

The manuscript of his romantic history of the French Revolution was almost burned accidentally by John Stuart Mill's maid but survived. He is buried in the churchyard of his native village.

black servants have been literally painted out of the picture. This was due to a change in attitudes which made black servants socially unacceptable because it was now morally repugnant to have made your money on the backs of slaves.

The issue of slavery again featured in Scottish society at the time of the American Civil War in the second half of the 19th century. The slave-owning southern states had donated a lot of money to the Free Church of Scotland and this was seized upon by its established rival. A campaign was mounted to send the money back and the Free Church, to its great embarrassment, was condemned for promoting and endorsing the evil of slavery.

The growth of missionary activity confirmed Scottish notions of white racial superiority. Lurid tales of cannibalism, infanticide and human sacrifice were used to prop up the notion that Scottish missionaries were spreading civilisation throughout the globe and liberating 'savages' from barbarism. The attitude of the missionaries themselves reveal that their notions, although grounded on racist perceptions, were not entirely racist. Time and time again, missionaries stressed the fact that Africans were ordinary human beings who were not blessed with the benefits of civilisation. Mary Slessor, for example, although a spinster, brought up an adopted African family.

MARY SLESSOR

1848-1915

Mary Slessor in 1898 with four children of her household

BORN in Aberdeen and employed in a Dundee jute mill, she educated herself to become a missionary for the United Presbyterian Church. Inspired by her great hero, David Livingstone, and overcoming contemporary prejudice against lone women, she was sent out to what is now Nigeria to begin her mission in 1876.

Slessor did much to try and improve the living conditions of African women by bringing what moral pressure she could to bear on the African chiefs of the area who were mostly polygamous and ran harems, trying to convince them to change their ways to be more in line with Scots Presbyterian thinking.

She was given British legal authority in territories where she was generally known among Africans as 'Great Mother'. She also liked to practise what she preached and adopted several black children to bring up as if they were her own family.

On the eve of the First World War, she was appointed a British consul in Nigeria.

The Scots were particularly active in attempting to end slavery in Africa. One of Scotland's most famous sons, David Livingstone, acted as an inspiration for many. Scots protested in Edinburgh, in 1867, against the Jamaican Massacres when a plantation revolt had been brutally suppressed. Mary Slessor went out to Nigeria to make amends for the massacre because that was the part of Africa where the Jamaican victims had originally come from. The churches pressed the government to maintain and increase the number of warships on anti-slavery patrols. In the late 1880s and early 1890s, funds and volunteers were sent to support an armed campaign against Arab slavers in Nyasaland, which is now Malawi.

Yet, like most European societies, Scotland was inherently racist. Well-meaning missionaries who endeavoured to improve the lot of the African and Asian did so under the cloak of white racial superiority. Popular literature at the time was replete with racist stereotypes which became worse as time wore on.

Imperial Necessity

IN MAY 1913, Sir Henry Cowan's Bill for Scottish home rule received its second reading in the House of Commons and passed with a comfortable majority. Had the First World War not broken out in August 1914, Scotland would have had its own devolved parliament at the beginning, rather than at the end of the 20th century.

Home rule has a long historical pedigree in Scotland and its birth dates from the same time as the Labour Party in the mid-1880s. To understand why Scotland should so nearly have had its own parliament all those years ago, it is necessary to bear a number of things in mind. Firstly, the latter part of the 19th and early part of the 20th

centuries was a time when ideas about the responsibilities of government were changing. The role of the state was expanding and new mechanisms and agencies were needed. As these agencies had still to be created, there was considerable debate as to what shape or form they should take. Scottish home rule was originally proposed because it was regarded as a practical response to the new challenge facing the British state. Everyone admitted that the Westminster parliament was congested with domestic and foreign matters. Scottish home rulers claimed that the existing system served neither. Imperial and foreign affairs were being squeezed by domestic necessity, while

various important local issues were not receiving the attention they deserved. Home rule was presented as a pragmatic response to the growth of government responsibility.

Secondly, most politicians were searching for a rational way of reforming government into a more coherent system. Scottish home rule was viewed by its supporters as part of an evolutionary development of the empire which in time would lead to the creation of a global United States of Great Britain. Before the First World War, the white dominions of the Empire – Canada, Australia, New Zealand and the whites in South Africa – were effectively managing their own

The condition of poor children in Glasgow in 1910 contrasts with the regal style of King George V and Queen Mary. The cause of Scottish home rule was to be hindered by its link to social reform

domestic affairs. It was argued that this model of development should be applied to the United Kingdom itself. This system of Imperial Federation, it was argued, would help to keep the empire together by giving each of the constituent nations of the empire – the white nations anyway – their own parliaments which would deal with domestic issues and these parliaments would send representatives to the imperial parliament in Westminster which would conduct imperial and foreign affairs. Supporters of Scottish home rule claimed a parliament in Edinburgh was an imperial necessity.

Thirdly, Scottish home rule was seen as a way of keeping things equal with Ireland. 'Home Rule All Round' was designed to apply devolution to the whole of Britain. This would ensure even play between the nations and it was hoped, would remove some of the resentment against Irish home rule.

In Dundee, in 1911, Winston Churchill announced this plan to the world and presented it as a model for the future governmental development

of Britain. Although Churchill was not renowned for having any sympathy for devolution there may have been method in his madness. Many who were opposed to Irish home rule supported the concept of 'home rule all round' for the simple reason that while in principle ceding the right of Ireland to have its own government, it meant that all parts of the UK would have to be treated the same. Knowing this would be contentious – few in England had shown any sympathy for the idea of an English parliament – it would be possible to block Irish home rule until all other parts of the UK were ready for their own parliaments. In effect, it was a perfect stalling device.

Finally, and perhaps most importantly, elements within the Liberal Party had linked Scottish home rule with the cause of social reform and, to a lesser extent, nationalism. While home rule bills had been presented to the parliament in the 1890s, most of these were simply a case of keeping up with the Irish. They lacked specific detail and were rather muddled

inventions. The success of the Liberal Party in the general elections of 1906 and 1910 (two in that year) was down to a commitment to free trade to keep the price of food as cheap as possible, and wider social reform. Due to the influence of a radical ginger group, the Young Scots, the party had moved significantly to the left. Demands for land reform, housing improvements, better health provision and temperance reform – it is worth pointing out that drink was still believed to be a great, if not the greatest, social evil – formed the bulk of their programme.

Yet, in spite of their best intentions, these commitments were continually frustrated at Westminster by a cautious leadership and the interference of the House of Lords. For many Scottish Liberals, 58 of the nation's 74 MPs, it appeared the will of the nation was being thwarted. According to one: 'There is not one piece of radical legislation which would not have been enacted 20 years ago if we had a Scottish parliament.' For many the Westminster system was putting a brake on Scotland's radical aspirations.

By 1911, after the reform of the Lords, a massive campaign was undertaken in favour of Scottish home rule by the Liberal Party. Rallies and speaking tours were organised, more than one million pamphlets published and distributed, MPs were monitored to ensure they gave maximum backing to the cause of home rule. Scottish parliamentarians were urged to forget vain hopes of social legislation from Westminster. For effective social reform a Scottish parliament was a necessity. The extent of home rule demand in Scotland on the eve of the First World War is recorded in a secret Conservative Party memo acknowledging the strength of feeling. Even the arch anti-devolutionist Tories expected that Scotland would soon have its own parliament. It took a war to stop it.

The ubiquitous Union flag appeared on the back of cans of Colman's mustard distributed to all corners of the empire

Age of Mass Democracy

1850-1914

Scottish politics in the mid-19th century was dominated by ideas of civic responsibility. As the vote was confined to the upper and middle classes until 1868, when skilled workers got the franchise, it should come as no surprise to find that politics reflected their aims and aspirations. Notions that government was best left to local councils and that self-regulation was better than state interference were pervasive. Central government did little other than conduct imperial policy, foreign affairs and defence, and its presence was little felt by the majority of people. Taxation was denounced vehemently, and the values of self-improvement and self-help were held up as the best solution for all social ills. Local, rather than central, government was the main focus of political attention, as it was in this area that the most important decisions affecting the lives of ordinary Scots would be taken.

By 1868, the comfortable view of discriminatory politics began to change. For the first time, the majority of the electorate belonged to the working class, albeit only the skilled section that was able to afford to rent a property with a rateable value of £10.

It was in this period that the dominance of the Whig grandees (progressive members of the aristocracy) passed, to be replaced by the radicalism of men who owed their positions in society to talent and ability, not accident of birth. These men, best epitomised by the Provost of Edinburgh, Duncan MacLaren, put a stamp on Scottish politics which would last almost to the end of the century. They described themselves as radicals, although their radicalism was largely confined to economics and their wholesale belief in *laissez-faire* and the power of the market both as an economic and moral regulator. They were opposed to the rights of trade unions, as they believed they

WILLIAM EWART GLADSTONE

1809-98

Scottish parentage allowed Gladstone to establish a personal bond in his political tours north of the Border where he built up a tremendous personal following. Letter writers would inundate the press with complaints if the Grand Old Man was described as English because of his birth in Liverpool and education at Eton and Oxford.

A master of debate, he was Prime Minister in 1868 until he resigned over Irish issues and left Westminster. In the famous Midlothian campaign of 1879, he set the standard for a new breed of modern politician by going out to explain his message to the people. He was returned to Westminster as Prime Minister. Later his Irish home rule bill split the Liberal party until, in 1893, it was passed by the Commons but rejected by the Lords. He resigned in March 1894.

Gladstone is greeted by crowds as he arrives at West Calder during the Midlothian campaign in 1879

were an unnatural interference in the operation of the market. They also believed that free trade was the best solution to international problems, as nations would become economically interdependent and war would be in nobody's interest. Edinburgh hosted the international peace conference in 1856 to promote the concept. Unfortunately, it coincided with the start of the Crimean War.

The success of mid-Victorian Liberal radicalism can be explained by two factors. The first was that many of the values the Liberals espoused were shared by skilled members of the working class, and the second is the dominant figure of their leader, William Gladstone. While the core of Victorian values – self-help, independence, hard work, sobriety and respectability – had their origins in middle-class ideology, they permeated Scottish society. On the surface, it may have appeared that the working class were simply aping their social betters, but the reality is much more complex. Given that there was minimal state interference in social policy, ordinary Scots had no other option than self-improvement as a way to better their lot. By saving money, hard times could be seen off; temperance saved money and avoided the calamitous effect of alcohol on family life which was all too common in Victorian Scotland; self-improvement and education enhanced job prospects and respectability, and independence afforded dignity and self-esteem. Other than a life of crime or sinking into a drink-sodden gutter, there was no alternative. There were plenty of illustrations of the dire consequences of an improvident life at hand in the not-so-respectable working-class communities to enforce the message of self-reliance. That does not mean, however, that the working class bought the middle-class message uncritically. Rather, it was adopted as a means of survival.

The 'dry biscuit of political economy', as Benjamin Disraeli, the leader of the Conservative Party, put it, was hardly inspirational. Indeed, there is evidence that, following the election of 1868, the newly enfranchised electorate was disappointed with the Liberal administration. In 1874, Liberal votes decreased and despondency among the party was complete when they lost the election to the Tories, although Scotland, as ever, was more inclined to the Liberals than England.

Liberal hopes were revived in 1879, when a young Scottish peer, Lord Rosebery, organised a comeback campaign for William Gladstone at the by-election in Midlothian. The campaign was different for a number of reasons. Firstly, it was a Conservative held seat and here 'the People's William' was entering the lion's den against the long-serving MP and landowner, Lord Elcho. It was an act of political courage and daring. Secondly, the event can be seen as a milestone in British political history. Gladstone toured the constituency and spoke at mass rallies to assembled workers. While this may not strike us as unusual today, it was at the time. Gladstone flattered his audience. In speeches which would have most of us bored to tears, he went over the finer points of the Tory budget. Yet people felt that for the first time they mattered. Here was a former Prime Minister who went out directly to meet the people, talked to them in an unpatronising way and made them feel important. As he reminded his audiences, he would go to Parliament because of them. Thirdly, Gladstone focused his campaign around issues of morality and principle. He denounced the foreign policy of the Tory government and condemned its corruption and self-serving ways. The moralising tone of his campaign struck a chord with Scottish voters. Another factor in his popularity north of the Border was the fact that his parents were Scottish and as he regularly, though somewhat misleadingly, reminded audiences 'there is not a drop of blood in my veins which is not pure Scotch'.

The Midlothian campaign was a success and Gladstone went on to win the seat, resume leadership of the Liberal party and emerge as Prime Minister in 1880. For the Conservative Party it was an ignominious defeat illustrating its failure to attract the support of the new middle classes. The Tories, already blamed for the Disruption, were beginning to recover under the leadership of Disraeli in the late 1860s and early 1870s, before shooting themselves in the foot again over the issue of religion. The Conservative government decided it would rescind the rights of patronage in the Church. As this had caused the Disruption in the first place, one might be forgiven for thinking that it would heal the wound in Scottish religious society. It did not.

Disraeli could not understand Scottish ecclesiastical politics. The Free Church believed it was too little too late, and many were now also convinced, after personal experience of being without state support, that no Church should receive aid from the government. The Established Church was outraged because it feared that many Evangelicals and fundamentalists would come back and disrupt their cosy way of life.

WILLIAM COX AND BENJAMIN BOX.
Cox. *"Can you Fight?"*   Box. *"No I can't."*   Cox. *"Then come on!!!"*

Disraeli was never particularly popular in Scotland, whilst Gladstone was hailed as 'the people's William'. From Punch, *1880*

It pleased nobody. Once again, the Conservative Party, electorally speaking, got it in the neck from the Scottish voters.

The Liberal Party was also able to utilise Scottish sentiment to good effect against the Tory party, presenting their main ideological tenets as Scottish characteristics. Hard work and meritocracy were identified as quintessential Scottish characteristics. William Wallace and Robert Burns were used to reinforce the message that it was what you did rather than who you were that mattered. The Tory Party was denounced as representing corruption, privilege and, the greatest bogeyman of all, landlordism.

The Tories were unable to shake off their image as a party that defended the interests of the land-owning class. Their wealth was inherited, not earned. They had caused the Highland Clearances and the famine in Ireland which had overrun the central belt with Irish immigrants. The Tories could not be trusted to govern, it was argued, because they had no conception of the public interest. Their philosophy, Liberals claimed, was pure self-interest. The bogeyman landlord and his association with the Tory Party remained an effective Scottish political propaganda ploy that continued to be used well into the 20th century.

The mid-1880s marked a landmark in Scottish politics. In 1884 the Third Reform Act greatly extended the franchise in the rural constituencies. In 1885, Keir Hardie contested the Mid-Lanark constituency as an independent workers' candidate and went on to form the Scottish Labour Party the following year. The first popular political party in the United Kingdom, the Crofters' Party, won five out of the six crofting seats in the Highlands after a long campaign which was known as the Crofters' War. Many people thought that the turmoil of Ireland would appear in the Highlands of Scotland. In 1885 the Scottish Office and the post of Scottish Secretary were created to help with the administration of governing Scotland. The explosive issue of Irish home rule erupted in 1886 and split the Liberal Party. The

Scottish Home Rule Association was formed to press for the establishment of a Scottish parliament. It was a very tempestuous time.

In many ways, these events were inter-connected. The extension of the franchise and the emergence of a new political doctrine, socialism, which would challenge the Liberal Party for the allegiance of the working class, who by this time made up a clear majority of the electorate, meant that old certainties could not be taken for granted. The traditional ideas of *laissez-faire* – that individuals could improve themselves and that it was that responsibility of the citizen to look after his or her own welfare – had clearly not worked. Increasingly, it was acknowledged that

A grainy and flickering movie camera image shows the Gordon Highlanders parading through the centre of Aberdeen, on their way to the Boer War in 1899

———— ❧ ————

the state had a duty to look after its citizens and that many problems were too difficult to be solved by individual endeavour. Also, given that socialism might emerge as a more attractive political faith because it offered more to the working class in terms of social security, it was necessary to make Liberalism more attractive to traditional supporters to keep them loyal. In spite of their best wishes, governments through the 1870s and 1880s

were increasingly forced to interfere within society, and this entailed the creation of a state apparatus.

The demands for new and, at times, complex legislation meant that there was a need to ensure Scotland was properly catered for. It had long been a standard complaint that Scots law was neglected, usually something to be tagged on to English legislation. Parliament was busy and it was felt that inadequate time was spent on Scottish affairs. The creation of the Scottish Office and the post of Secretary of State would help ease this congestion and ensure that Scotland received greater attention.

The demand for the Scottish Office was also fuelled by nationalist

109

sentiment. Many were disgruntled that the Scots, model citizens of the Empire, received no attention, while the Irish, engaged in parliamentary disruption and terrorism, took up an inordinate amount of time. As one of the leading campaigners for the Scottish Office, Lord Rosebery said: 'Justice for Ireland means everything, even the payment of the natives' debts. Justice for Scotland means insulting neglect. I head north tomorrow with the intention of blowing up a prison or shooting a policeman.'

No sooner had the Scots achieved the much vaunted Scottish Office than they found that the Irish had upstaged them yet again. In 1886, Gladstone declared himself to be in favour of Irish home rule. The effect was to split the Liberal Party. A majority stayed with the Grand Old Man, but a significant minority in Scotland, 16 MPs, could not stomach the prospect of Irish home rule. It was argued that Gladstone had capitulated to terrorism, that it would lead to the disintegration of the Empire and would threaten law

and order and property rights. This new political formation, the Liberal Unionists, would increasingly become closer to the Conservative Party. In 1912, the two merged to become the Unionist Party so the birth of Unionism in Scotland was concerned with the Union with Ireland rather than Scotland and England.

The fact that Gladstone had agreed to Irish home rule annoyed many of his supporters who believed that whatever Ireland was entitled to, so was Scotland. Indeed, the Scottish Home Rule Association claimed in its manifesto that to give home rule to Ireland but not to Scotland would encourage disorder and violence. In any case, the Conservative Party and its Liberal Unionist allies formed the governments from 1886 to 1905, with one brief Liberal interlude, and home rule was effectively shelved.

Although the Conservative party dominated British politics in the 1890s, they remained firmly in third place in Scotland behind the Liberals and the Liberal Unionists. That was the case

until 1900 and the Khaki Election, when Britain was at war in South Africa against the Boers, and jingoism was in the air.

Scottish Liberals had convinced themselves that their nation was immune from such base sentiments. However, they were to be cruelly disappointed. War fever gripped Scotland. The relief of Mafeking was widely celebrated, soldiers on their way to Africa were cheered and anti-war protests were broken up. At the election, the Conservatives and their Liberal Unionist allies won a clear majority of seats for the first time since 1832. It illustrated two things: the power of British imperial sentiment and Liberal complacency.

The war, however, did not go well. It dragged on and was dogged by incompetence and ineptitude as Boer farmers took on the might of the world's greatest imperial power. The Conservatives alienated workers by coming down hard on trade union rights and a scandal about a ploy to import Chinese labour to South African mines raised alarm bells about them doing the same thing in Britain. Just when things were deteriorating, the Conservatives made the situation worse for themselves by proposing tariffs on imports to pay for social reforms like the provision of old age pensions. It divided the Tories, alarmed the working class, but brought some much needed unity to the Liberal Party.

The Boer War had another important impact on Scottish politics. It revealed the precarious state of the British social fabric. The world's mightiest empire had been put to the test by South Africa and found wanting. Recruits from the cities were in poor physical shape and badly educated. In a world of increasing military and economic competition, how could the empire survive unless its citizens were well nourished and

ARCHIBALD PHILIP PRIMROSE
Earl of Rosebery
1847-1929

H E INHERITED an earldom at the age of 19 and went on, after education at Eton and Oxford, to become Lord Rector of Aberdeen, Edinburgh, and Glasgow universities. After organising the Midlothian campaign of 1879 for Gladstone's political comeback, he was appointed Secretary for Foreign Affairs in subsequent Liberal administrations. He replaced Gladstone as Liberal premier in 1894 but lost the following year's general election, briefly remained as party leader and then resigned.

A supporter of the idea of an imperial federation, and an imperialist during the Boer War, he headed the Liberal League from 1902, espousing policies which parted company with official Liberalism. A keen horse-racing man, he owned three Derby winners, the last in 1905.

The slum landlord to his henchman Disease:"Ah, it`s a hard and material age with no sense of the sanctity of custom. Here we have envious Labour fellows panting to destroy that dear partnership which has so long and so profitably united us!"

A pre-First World War cartoon from the Daily Herald

———— ❧ ————

Women Entering the Man's World

IT IS SAID that history is written by the winners. It can also be said that history records the voices of the past. Most of the voices we hear come from the written word and most Scots left no records, words, or voices for us to hear. This is especially the case for over half the population, the women.

While many middle- and upper-class women have left us their thoughts, the vast majority of their working-class sisters left no testimony. Paradoxically, we know more about men's perceptions of women than what women thought themselves. Victorian men divided the world into two parts. One was work and the public sphere, which were the domain of the man; the other was the home and the private sphere, which was the domain, or more accurately the prison, of women. The idea of 'separate' spheres was itself a middle-class idea, but one which was extremely powerful in 19th-century Scotland. It was believed that women were emotional creatures who had an inability to reason. The evidence for such dubious claims was often explained by the fact that men's brains were heavier than women's. It was argued that this so-called inability to rationalise meant women were inherently more prone to corruption. Again, the biblical story of Adam and Eve was used to justify this. Men pointed out that it was only women who became prostitutes, ending up in the oldest profession having worked as factory girls, flower sellers, and in other trades which came into contact with the public. The real reason so many women resorted to prostitution may have been that they were economic

educated? A new buzz term was invented – 'national efficiency'.

Fearful that socialism would take over, the Liberal Party set to work reformulating its policies to produce what was known then as the 'new' liberalism, a similar evolutionary process to that was to produce Tony Blair's 'new' Labour Party from its traditional roots almost a century later.

Social policy, improvements in health, education and housing, became the Liberals' main concern and, at the 1906 election, the party won a spectacular 58 out of the 74 Scottish seats in a landslide victory.

The commitment to progressive policies was also instrumental in keeping the Labour Party at bay. When the Liberals were trounced in 1900, the party, which had separate Scottish and English organisations, decided to enter a secret electoral pact with Labour which would operate in certain constituencies where both parties pledged not to run candidates against one another so that they would have a straight fight with the Tory candidate and not split the anti-Conservative vote. But agreement was reached only in England, not Scotland, where the Conservatives were in such a mess the Scottish Liberals felt they could win handsomely on their own. They did.

Labour was able to win only three Scottish seats before the First World War. The party also had something of an identity crisis. The candidates who won seats professed to be 'good liberals' and none of their manifestos mentioned the word socialism. Before 1914, Labour was contained by the new Liberalism. It would take the upheaval of war to create the conditions for a Labour breakthrough.

Ringing in the new:
Winston Churchill, is heckled by
Miss Molony, a suffragette, as he
canvasses votes from the male electorate
while standing as Liberal candidate in
Dundee in 1908

marginals, but the Victorian male establishment argued, perfectly seriously, that it was because they had been morally contaminated by venturing out in public on their own.

These values were used to keep women out of public life as much as possible. It also explains why women in Scotland received less than half the

pay of men. It was claimed, again quite seriously, that women would be their own worst enemies and only bring suffering upon themselves if they had financial independence.

Ensuring that women did not have sufficient economic means kept them dependent on brothers, husbands and fathers. It was common for women to work alongside men in factories, and even when they did the same job, pressure was applied in both the workplace and the home to ensure they did not campaign for equal pay.

The massive expansion of the teaching profession after the 1872 Education Act was done through the employment of cheap female labour. It was thought that women were 'naturally' suited to looking after children and the sexual division of labour in teaching is best exemplified by the fact that all headteacher posts were occupied by men.

While these notions strike us as ridiculous today, they had common currency and were considered essential to middle-class ideas of respectability. The 'Angel of the House' was expected to look after the children and adorn the husband's home. Yet, even if they had wanted to, most women in Scotland could not aspire to such an existence. For the majority, work was essential to supplement wages. Perhaps as many as one in five women with children had been widowed or deserted, leaving them with no source of income other than the pittance made in sweatshops. Some attitudes were such that Victorian employers found it perfectly moral to employ children in their factories, but not married women – their place was in the home.

However, this state of affairs could not be permanent. Middle-class women, having the time and money, made the first breakthrough. Charity work was considered an appropriate pastime because it chimed in with traditional notions of women as carers and mothers. Yet charity work was important in the development of organisational skills, public speaking and social awareness – all things of which men thought women incapable.

Women were also recruited into politics. Both the Conservative and Liberal parties relied on female labour in their organisations. Prompted by the assumption that no gentleman would shut the door on a lady, women were used as canvassers and in so doing became highly literate in politics and socially aware. Inevitably, female thoughts turned to the vote. Property owning women had been given the vote in local government since 1868, but were denied the parliamentary franchise on the grounds that their husbands and fathers would use the women's vote to represent their own interests. It was argued in the Commons that women should not have the vote because their sentimentalism would not be able to take the country to war when necessary.

The Votes for Women campaign united women because it represented the issue of equality. It has to be remembered that, by 1900, a majority of MPs had been persuaded that women should have the vote; the main disagreement was over a wider reform of the franchise. The Liberals feared that giving votes to women would only create more Tory voters and wanted to extend the franchise to all working-class men and women. (About 40% of men remained disenfranchised.) The Conservatives blocked this because it was believed that this would only create more Liberal votes. The Irish nationalists, who held the balance of power after the elections of 1910, feared that an extension of the franchise would reduce the number of Irish MPs and distract attention from home rule. They would have no truck with it. The quagmire of electoral calculations created an impasse, which led women to take direct action.

The high profile activities of the Suffragettes centred mainly on London as this was the seat of government. Scotland was relatively calm, although there were a number of peaceful marches and deputations sent south to London. The chairman of the Conservative Party, Sir George Younger, did have his house burned down and the golfing activities of the Prime Minister, Henry Asquith, and other members of the cabinet were prone to disruption. As with much else in Scottish society, it would take the impact of war to bring about the change.

ELSIE MAUD INGLIS
1864–1917

BORN in India, she was one of the first female students to study medicine and to overcome gender prejudice by qualifying as a surgeon. In 1901, angered by the continuing prejudice against her from male colleagues and the failure of the medical profession to see the need for better facilities for pregnant women, she founded her own maternity hospital in Edinburgh which was staffed solely by women. In 1906, she helped to establish the Suffragette Movement in Scotland and sent two ambulance units to France and Serbia in the early years of the First World War. She personally supervised the setting up of three military hospitals in Serbia, was taken prisoner by the Austrians and sent home. In 1917, she led another medical team to Russia, but had to pull out after the revolution.

Learning the Lessons of a Good Scots Upbringing

An intake of the country's first female teachers at Crail, Fife, in 1876. Women were needed for the classrooms after the 1872 Education Act made school compulsory for all children between 5 and 13

Scots in the 19th century were pretty smug about their education system, boasting that it was possible for a bright child from the humblest origins to use the education system to rise through the ranks of Scottish society. For example, Robert Burns was the heaven-taught ploughman. David Livingstone was from a relatively poor family but became a respected missionary and explorer. The great Victorian sage, Thomas Carlyle, came from a tiny village. There was, it seemed, no great shortage of Scots who were able to rise to prominence on account of their own efforts and the excellence of the Scottish school and university system.

The belief that Scotland's attitude to education reflected the meritocratic nature of society – in that those who were able would not be held back by lack of opportunity – was a powerful one. The so-called 'lad o' pairts' who, with a sack of oatmeal and his own intelligence, could go to university and prosper was ingrained into the Scottish psyche and lingers to this day.

Yet, the democratic tradition has been much exaggerated. For a start, it excluded more than half the population from the outset. There were no 'lassies o' pairts'; the education system was for boys only and hardly meritocratic or democratic on the basis of gender. What schooling girls did receive concentrated on producing obedient wives and daughters. Women were not allowed to attend university until 1878, and even then the subjects open to them were restricted. The professions feared that women who qualified as doctors or lawyers would depress earnings, as women were paid half the rates commanded by men. These attitudes persisted into the 20th century. No woman doctor was employed at Glasgow Royal Infirmary until 1945, and even then it was a case of needs must because of a shortage.

Scottish education was equally divided on the basis of class. Although working-class heroes were held up as shining examples, they were very much the exception rather than the rule. The Argyll Commission into the state of education (1856), said that as many as half the children in cities did not attend school. The quality of schooling for those who did was shocking. 'Adventure' schools, as they were called, were found to be staffed by drunken headmasters who delegated older children to keep control. The education was rudimentary and involved no more than basic reading and writing.

It was a different story for the upper orders. Charitable schools in the suburbs were increasingly brought under the sway of middle-class parents and fashioned to suit their aspirations. Children were taught Latin, Greek and mathematics. Resources for teaching these labour-intensive subjects were abundant because they were essential for university entrance, the next rung on the social ladder.

The 1872 Education Act created a national system but only by default because it was mainly brought about on the back of the English Act which

THE FIRST 'GLASGOW BOY'

TO THOMAS CARLYLE, writing in 1847, Glasgow had been a sort of 'Dantean Hell… of copperas fumes, cotton-fuzz, gin riot, wrath and toil, created by a Demon'. But for Charles Rennie Mackintosh, the son of a clerk in the Glasgow police force, the spectacular growth of the city at the turn of the century, its rapid industrialization, teeming cosmopolitan population and optimistic internationalism, made it a challenging environment with opportunities for design and production that fuelled his determination to clothe 'in grace and beauty the new forms and conditions that modern developments of life – social, commercial and religious insist upon'. As an architect, interior designer, furniture designer, painter and graphic artist Mackintosh shaped the style of his metropolis, and in return it continues to invoke him today.

The Glasgow industrial and mercantile elite commissioned buildings that expressed their civic pride – in business and commerce as well as in municipal edifices. A member of the loosely-constituted 'Glasgow School' of artists, Mackintosh's contribution was a distinctive form of art nouveau: his designs introduced a new aesthetic of light, rectilinear

'Simply a marvel of the art of the upholsterer and decorator' enthused a Glasgow newspaper about the white and silver and rose interior of the Willow Tea Rooms (1903), Sauchiehall Street, the finest of the dozen or so city tea rooms (or cafés) that Charles Rennie Mackintosh designed for Miss Cranston

decorative detail, sinuousness of line, and innovative use of materials and textures in metalwork, textiles, furniture, stained glass – sometimes working with his wife the painter and decorative artist Margaret MacDonald – and buildings. Those edifices considered his masterpieces, including the Glasgow School of Art (1897–1906) and the Hill House (1902) built for the publisher Walter Blackie overlooking the Clyde, were

similar in their attention to every detail of design to the English Arts and Crafts Movement, but with none of Lethaby's and Voysey's distaste for the machine made. Glasgow was an industrial city and Mackintosh's aesthetic was not a pastoral nostalgia, for Scotland's past was no rural idyll, but a harsh one marked by displacement and poverty.

The verdict of the Modernist architectural historian, Nikolaus

Pevsner wrinting in 1975, was that Mackintosh was 'a juggler with space... the counterpart of Frank Lloyd Wright. The Glaswegian's accolade came much sooner: it was not long before the whole city was 'getting covered with imitations of Mackintosh tea rooms, Mackintosh shops, Mackintosh furniture &c – it is too funny,' his wife wrote in 1904.

sought to create a co-ordinated system of elementary schooling. Working-class children were taught the three Rs with the assistance of the three Bs: Bible, belt, and blackboard. Inspectors checked on schools and payment was on the basis of results, encouraging rote learning. Classes of 50 children would be cajoled and belted into reciting passages from the Bible or times tables to show that they had learned their lessons. The rote method was productive, enabling the maximum number of children to acquire basic educational standards with the minimum effort, but it did not allow bright children to move on to the other, more costly subjects that would have given them a foot in the door at a university.

Official ideology divided children into two types – those who were 'good with their hands' and those who were 'good with their heads'. The expectation was that the latter would come from good homes and the former were to be found among the working class. Good 'hands' were taught to respect authority and be obedient. Good 'heads' were to be inculcated with the

'leadership principle'. Games and a grounding in the classics would turn boys into leaders of men and in the private schools, mirroring the ethos of the English public schools, brutality was often seen as the best way to induce these necessary qualities.

There were economic considerations too. The 1872 Act raised the school leaving age to 14, an unpopular move among the working class. It meant that a valuable earner for the family was kept out of commission. Even supposing that the mythical 'lad o' pairts' did get the necessary schooling to qualify for university, it would have to be a very understanding and enlightened family that would forego present earnings for future potential. By the eve of the First World War, fewer than one-fifth of university students came from a working-class home, and most of these were mature students who had come to education late in life. Most did not graduate. Nevertheless, their very presence was enough to make Scots feel that their education system was somehow special and unique.

SIR HENRY CRAIK

1846-1927

BORN in Glasgow and educated there and at Oxford University, Craik is regarded as one of the most influential figures in the development of Scottish education in the 19th century. He joined the civil service as an administrator and was Permanent Secretary to the Scottish Office for almost 20 years until 1904.

His educational reforms included encouraging the teaching of Gaelic in schools, the introduction of a school leaving certificate, and the dropping of all fees from state primary schools. This last reform meant that elementary education was offered free to any pupil up to the age of 15.

Craik also oversaw the policy of transferring the control of teacher training colleges away from the churches to non-denominational public committees.

CHAPTER 12

Popular Culture

1850-1914

THE way the lower orders amuse themselves has always been a source of fascination and trepidation for those who considered themselves more respectable people. The common folk were accused of having a taste for blood and violence, although their betters were not averse to take a front row seat at bare-knuckle boxing bouts, cock fighting, bear baiting, and dog fighting. This was staple entertainment for the masses, as were lewd and libidinous theatrical performances, which were denounced because, it was argued, they encouraged immorality. For most respectable folk they were a frightening spectacle.

Wild and, at times, brutal behaviour was gradually brought under control. Middle-class wisdom held that idle pleasure for its own sake was a waste of time. Amusement and entertainment had to fulfil the function of either educating or improving. Local authorities progressively tightened up legislation and licensing to bring the more boisterous forms of popular culture under control.

'Rational recreation' was promoted to channel excessive energies into more genteel, sober and worthwhile pursuits. The use of libraries to improve knowledge was heartily approved, garden shows were an opportunity for the green fingered to display their horticultural talents. Visits to museums and galleries helped to inform and improve the mind, and hobbies such as pigeon fancying or playing in a brass band demanded the development of individual skills. These types of activities would teach the

Curling probably originated in Scotland and involves skimming stones across ice or another flat surface (above)

Bare-knuckle fights were popular with a bloodthirsty public, although the government wanted to introduce more worthy pursuits (left)

Golf originated in Scotland in the 15th century. It remains a popular and more accessible sport than in England (right)

working class the virtues of patience, self-discipline and self-reliance.

Recreation became bound up with notions of respectability. Many paternalistic employers actively promoted clubs and bands to keep their employees away from drink, effectively making the workplace the centre of community activity. After work, clubs would meet and bands rehearse in a room provided by the employer, encouraging solidarity and identification. The winning of competitions against other firms induced a sense of company loyalty. It was not unusual for employers to have a presence in the private lives of their staff, organising day trips and giving marriage presents to newly-wed couples.

Pastimes were intended not only to provide people with an interest, but also as a means to build self-esteem. While employers were keen on 'approved' pastimes, it is clear that many people took them up not because they were obliged to but because they enjoyed them. Many of the pursuits were of an individualistic nature. Model building, gardening, playing a musical instrument and reading encouraged many to take a great pride and sense of personal achievement in their expertise and knowledge.

Sport was also subject to the attention and the manipulation of the middle class. Football games between villages, in the early 19th century, often descended into anarchy and violence. The principal objective was to kick a bunch of rags (and, it has to be said, members of the opposition) from a mid-way point between the two communities into the opposing village with few rules other than the requirement to beat the opposition. The potential for mayhem was obvious and frequently fulfilled.

The codification of sport was a process to regulate and formalise behaviour and curb excessive violence.

Queensberry rules for boxing helped to stop bare-knuckle fist fights, although clandestine bouts were still taking place in Glasgow at the end of the 1880s. Rules for cricket and football helped to bring order to games between villages. New games such as bowling and croquet made an appearance in Scotland, helped by the fact that the rules were already written down.

Victorians believed in athleticism. It was considered important to have fit and healthy people. Exercise was an important way of burning up excess energy which otherwise could lead youngsters into trouble. Young men with too much time and too much energy were easy targets for temptations of the flesh. The ideas of the English public school filtered into Scotland. Games were regarded as an important way for young men to both toughen themselves up and control their aggression. 'Muscular Christianity', as it was called, was considered an essential part of the education of the middle class.

Various organisations were created to help channel the excessive energy of youth into more useful pursuits. The Volunteer movement used professional soldiers to instil military discipline among weekend soldiers. The parade-ground drilling and martial training was calculated to give young men that most valued Victorian characteristic, earnestness. The Volunteers, however, were just a bit too pompous for many from the working class and, in any case, the fact that Volunteers had to pay the cost of providing their own uniform acted as a financial disincentive.

Young children were considered better targets for the promotion of healthy minds and healthy bodies. If corruption could be caught in the nick of time, children could be saved from reading trashy novels and instilled with self-discipline which in later life would stop them falling prey to adult vices. Biographies of missionary heroes such as David Livingstone were frequently given out as prizes in schools.

The Young Men's Christian Association, Young Men's Institutes, temperance organisations such as the Band of Hope, and the Boys Brigade, founded in Glasgow in 1883, were designed to make young men sober, moral and tee-total. They offered camaraderie, excitement and adventure, and undoubtedly did help a great many children escape from the drudgery of a working-class life. Just as many children, however, slipped through their fingers.

WEIRD SCIENCE: PHRENOLOGY

PHRENOLOGY was the study of the physical characteristics of the skull which, it was believed, shed light on mental qualities. In short, by examining the shape of someone's head, you could tell if they were intelligent or stupid, emotional or rational, sane or insane. The idea was originally propounded by Johann Caspar Spurzheim and Franz Joseph Gall of Germany in 1800. It received a cool reception in Scotland at first but then began to win over many converts, notably the respectable attention of Dr George Combe at Edinburgh University.

Phrenology opened up the possibility that by measuring the skull and mapping its bumps it was possible to determine a number of important features about that individual and be able to identify

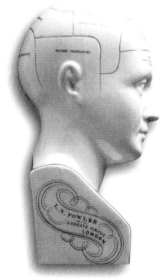

the criminal and the genius. The Phrenology Society had a lot of clout and devoted a considerable amount of time to measuring skulls. It even had the body of Robert Burns exhumed so that his head could be measured to see if there were any bumps on his famous head which could be held out as an indicator of his undoubted literary and artistic genius. The science was popular among amateurs, but encountered increasing hostility from professional anatomists who were unable to accept any cause and effect relationship.

Part of the attraction of phrenology was its simplicity. The notion that skull size and shape provided the key to a person's character had a deceptively scientific ring. But by the mid-19th century its popularity began to wane as repeated attempts to prove the link between physical and mental attributes failed to be established and were exposed to increasing scientific ridicule.

ROBERT LOUIS STEVENSON

1850-94

A CHRONIC invalid from childhood, Stevenson was born into a family of lighthouse builders. He studied engineering in his native Edinburgh but then switched to law to qualify as an advocate in 1875 but never practised. His first book, *Inland Voyage*, was published in 1878 and *Travels with a Donkey* in the Cevennes the next year. After Stevenson married an American, Fanny Osbourne, the romantic fable, *Treasure Island*, was a huge success in 1883 (the location supposedly based on the island of Fidra near North Berwick). *Kidnapped* and then *The Strange Case of Dr Jekyll and Mr Hyde* confirmed his international reputation and remain literary classics. In 1888 Stevenson went to the South Seas to settle in Samoa where he lived out the rest of his relatively short life in a kinder climate.

High Days and Public Holidays

A S THE 19th century ended and the 20th century began, ordinary people had developed a taste for tourism and day tripping. The extension of railways and steamships meant that more and more Scots could travel cheaply around the country. Public holidays, which were increasingly common, proved an ideal opportunity for workers to go on a day out. A whole host of seaside resorts expanded at this time to accommodate the growing numbers who wanted to escape from the gloom and fog of the industrial areas. It was conventional wisdom that fresh air, the sea and the countryside were healthy and that a day trip would do you good. Wemyss Bay, Rothesay, Gourock, Dunoon and Ardrossan catered for the Glaswegians who could travel easily to their destination by steamboat. Fifers could cross the Forth to Granton and Newhaven. The middle class escaped to the remote Highlands, made popular by the journals of Queen Victoria, and new spa towns like Bridge of Allan outside Stirling. By the 1880s, there was a general trend that odd days off were coalesced into a week long, unpaid summer holiday. Friendly societies organised the saving for the holiday when the factory would be shut for a week.

In spite of the best efforts of the guardians of public morality to regulate behaviour, drinking and gambling remained popular. The consumption of alcohol was the greatest social problem, in spite of the best efforts of the prohibitionists, and it was only when higher taxes were introduced during the First World War that inroads began to be made into the extent of consumption.

The 'Kinloch' at Campbeltown after sailing down from Gourock in 1910

121

Gambling was a difficult conundrum for middle-class morality to deal with. It was denounced as a feckless waste of money which encouraged the lazy to believe rewards could be gained without hard work, a clear offence to decent folks' sensibilities. It was also condemned as socially disruptive and the ruin of family life. The Gambling Act of 1853, which outlawed working-class betting shops, was not applied to Scotland and the industry took off north of the border. By the end of the 1860s, Glasgow had 28 bookies shops and Edinburgh 13. In 1874, legislation was extended to Scotland to make it more difficult to bet legally. The middle-class gentleman could belong to a private club, whereas the working class had to resort to subterfuge. A large unofficial industry grew up in which newsagents and street vendors took illegal betting slips. 'Bookies' runners' were children who would carry the slips back and forth and keep a watchful eye out for policemen. Uncontrolled betting, well out of the reach of any authorities, continued at local games of pitch and toss, whippet racing, and card sessions.

JAMES MATTHEW BARRIE
1860-1937

Portobello beach (Edinburgh) came into vogue at the turn of the century as trams and trains brought it within easy reach of the city (left)

Donkeys wait for work on the beach at Prestwick in 1906 (below)

The son of a Kirriemuir weaver, he studied at Edinburgh University and moved to London to begin his career as a writer, including a series of stories set in his home village he called Thrums.

From 1890, he concentrated on the theatre and produced the highly successful social satire *The Admirable Crichton*, but his fame rests on the creation of Peter Pan, the boy who never grew up, in 1904, together with the invention of the name Wendy which has become a relatively common girl's name. Other plays continued Barrie's imaginative journeys into fairyland but, although he considered his later work to be his finest, the public did not agree. He is buried in his native village in Angus, leaving the lucrative rights to the royalties of *Peter Pan* to a London children's hospital.

Far from being an irrational response to the belief that Lady Fortune could provide money without pain, Scottish gamblers embodied many of the qualities of rational recreation. Sports papers were enthusiastically read in the public libraries so that choices at races were based on informed opinion. Just as there were experts at geranium growing, there were experts on horses and dogs. There is little evidence that gambling caused the same social misery as was inflicted by alcoholism. Most gamblers put aside a fixed amount of money for a weekly flutter within the family budget.

The same attitudes prevailed regarding the football pools, which started at the turn of the 20th century, and the tote. Far from being an irrational action, this form of gambling made a lot of economic sense. The amounts involved in playing were small enough that they did not dent the family budget, but the rewards, should they win, large enough to justify the risk. In short, most thought that they could not afford not to play.

WHEN QUOITING WAS THE ONLY SPORT IN TOWN

DICK McBRIDE.   TOM BONE.
49   61

SCOTTISH QUOITING CHAMPIONSHIP. 1908.

QUOITING was a game in which two players or teams of players threw an iron ring, attempting to get it over a pin stuck in the ground some distance away. Players would compete to see who could hit the bull's eye or land closest. It was permissible to try to dislodge your opponent or shunt his quoit out of the way.

It was very much a working-class game which required very little in the way of equipment. Some pins, iron hoops and a small patch of ground were all that was needed for proceedings to get under way. Clubs sprang up all over Scotland and some games could attract several hundred spectators at a time, while the big cash prize games could draw crowds of thousands. Contests held between local communities added an extra layer of

excitement, as villagers turned out to cheer their men on.

It was a physically demanding game – the iron hoops could weigh more than 6lb and games could last several hours. By the end of the 19th century, there were at least 45 clubs in regular competition covering most of the central belt of Scotland.

One reason for the popularity of quoiting was the opportunity it afforded for gambling. Wagers could be made on players and teams, or a combination of both, with the advantage of the bet being settled there and then. Prize money for victorious teams was lucrative as well, and a talented player could handsomely augment his wages. The game was eventually to fall victim to the growing popularity of the more dramatic cut and thrust of football.

Kick-off for a National Obsession

FOOTBALL, Scotland's national sport, has its origins in the pre-industrial era when rival villagers would compete to see which team (there was no limit on the number of players) could kick a bundle of rags into the opposition's territory. It was a conflict with few, if any, rules and, needless to say, it often involved considerable injury to the participants.

Professional football can be accurately dated to 1893 when the Scottish Football Association was founded, and the game was largely confined to working-class communities. The first teams tended to have unifying factors determined by their location. Celtic FC, for example, was formed by Brother Walfrid in 1888 as a healthy outlet for the energies and passions of young Catholic men in Glasgow. By its very nature, Protestants were excluded from membership, laying the foundations for the development of the game in the city along sectarian lines. Rangers FC was founded in 1872 by a group of young men from Gareloch, but when the club moved to Ibrox, in 1899, it drew its support from the skilled, Protestant, working class of the traditional heavy industries. The same type of process created divided loyalties in Edinburgh with Heart of Midlothian and Hibernian, and in Dundee with Dundee Athletic and Dundee Hibs who changed their name to Dundee United in 1909.

It was the ability of football to draw large crowds which led to its commercialisation and professionalisation in the 1890s. A Scottish league was first established in 1890, and paid professionals were legalised three years

Celtic in 1890s

The oldest firm: an early Rangers side (right) that lost the 1877 Cup Final to Vale of Leven; and a later Celtic team (above) in green and white stripes that would soon become hoops

later. Increasing attendances at matches meant that football was a highly profitable business. In 1896, 25,000 fans turned up to watch Celtic play Rangers. In the same year, Celtic's turnover was £10,142, while Rangers raked in £14,076 in 1908, huge sums for their times. Success, then as now, tended to gravitate towards those clubs which could call on a mass following.

Football was a working-class passion and pundits soon acquired highly specialised knowledge of the game which was reinforced by comment in newspapers. It started a Scottish tradition of reading newspapers from the back page. It inspired an emotional intensity, given a sharper edge by sectarian tensions, that could easily turn to violence. Assaults on referees were not uncommon and disputed penalties frequently provoked pitch invasions or a hail of missiles. Rivets from the neighbouring shipyards were regularly converted to flying weapons at Ibrox.

Football was also important in fostering a distinctive national identity. The fact that Scotland ran its own league and that there were international games against the Auld Enemy, England, did much to promote a national dimension in Scottish football. In 1902, for example, 102,000 enthusiastic spectators turned up at Hampden to cheer on the national team against England.

The future was to see the game develop an umbilical link with wider Scottish society. The inter-war years have been described as the golden age of Scottish football when the game provided its followers with a welcome distraction from the torment of the depression and the dreary realities of everyday life. It was also an escape

route, offering fame and fortune to talented working-class youths who would otherwise have little choice but to follow their fathers into the pits or the shipyards. Scottish football's ascendancy was demonstrated by the fact that the nation won 12 out of the 20 internationals against England.

In spite of this success on the national scale, many good players were attracted south by the richer

A capacity crowd fills Hampden Park, the national stadium, in 1910 when Scotland defeated England 2-0

pickings of the English football league. Sectarianism remained an endemic problem, especially in Glasgow where levels of violence scaled new heights.

The Second World War and the resumption of full employment

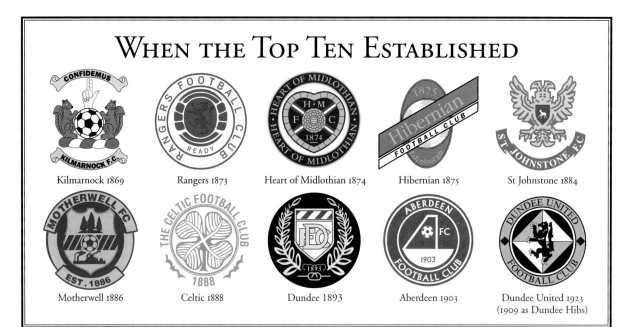

WHEN THE TOP TEN ESTABLISHED

Kilmarnock 1869   Rangers 1873   Heart of Midlothian 1874   Hibernian 1875   St Johnstone 1884

Motherwell 1886   Celtic 1888   Dundee 1893   Aberdeen 1903   Dundee United 1923 (1909 as Dundee Hibs) maintained the popularity of the 'beautiful game' and it arguably reached its zenith in the early 1950s. Thereafter, the impact of television began to affect attendances. The 1960s witnessed a high point with Scotland, despite a generally undistinguished record in the inter-war years, becoming the first team to beat the newly crowned 1966 world champions, England. The same year, 1967, Celtic was the first British team to win the European Cup when it beat Inter Milan in Lisbon. In 1972, Rangers won the European Cup Winners Cup against Moscow Dynamo in Barcelona, although the occasion was marred by crowd trouble. Aberdeen won the same trophy, defeating Real Madrid in 1983.

International football, from the Scottish perspective, reached its nadir in the 1978 World Cup when Scotland travelled to Argentina on a wave of heady optimism whipped up by manager Ally MacLeod, only to have key player Willie Johnston sent home in a drugs scandal, before crashing out of the competition in the first round

having lost to Peru and drawn with Iran, two teams MacLeod had contemptuously dismissed as inferior. Scotland's last game was against eventual finalists, Holland, and perversely they won by the odd goal in five.

On the positive side, although Scotland has never managed to progress past the first round of any World Cup, the behaviour of Scottish football fans, now known as the Tartan Army and considering themselves to be unofficial ambassadors overseas, in the 1980s and 1990s has done much to improve the image of the nation.

The further commercialisation of the sport during the 1980s has had other significant effects. The first has been the influx of foreign players. Rangers' ability to buy new talent was the critical factor in the club's dominance in the 1980s when it matched Celtic's earlier record of nine championships in a row achieved with mostly native-born players. The secure financial foundation of a large fan-base is proving as important in modern terms as when the clubs were first

established last century, ensuring that the Old Firm teams remain the big fishes in Scotland's relatively small footballing pond.

More foreigners entering the game has also meant that Scottish teams are more ethnically mixed and that sectarian divisions, on the field if not in the crowd, have disappeared. As recently as the late 1980s, Rangers first team was exclusively Protestant and when Maurice Johnston, a former Celtic player and practising Catholic signed for the club, it sparked major controversy. Now, the religious faith of new signings is entirely irrelevant.

Rising season ticket prices have meant that the social composition of the most avid followers has shifted towards the middle class and further changes in the culture of the game are being driven by satellite television dictating that more games be played on Sundays and mid-week.

Whatever external forces swirl around football, the essential simplicity of the game allied to the desire for success have been close to the hearts of Scots for more than 100 years now.

Scotland travelled south to Sheffield in 1903 to beat England 2-1. The two countries contest the oldest international fixture in the world, first played in 1872

PART THREE

The Return to Nationhood

1914-2000

THE FIRST WORLD WAR was supposed to be over by Christmas. Thousands flocked to the Colours in anticipation, many of them afraid if they did not join up immediately they would miss the action. The reality, of course, was that the Great War would go on for years beyond the Christmas of 1914 and that it would have a catastrophic effect on Scottish society. It was a war destined to change Scotland fundamentally. The certainties of the pre-war era were swept away in a torrent of upheaval which transformed the political, social, economic and cultural landscape out of all recognition.

The war was largely responsible for creating the social conditions that eventually propelled the Labour Party to political power. The events known collectively as Red Clydeside, although never really of the scale of the significance to inspire a Russian-style revolution in Scotland, were the working class flexing its muscles for the first time. The Rent Strike of 1915 was a clear demonstration of how popular anger could be articulated in direct action which achieved results. When the government was forced to back down, it was a sign that Labour was about to replace the once mighty Liberal Party.

After 1918, the Scottish economy, once the 'workshop of the Empire', lay in ruins. There was no more demand for ships and heavy engineering, export markets for jute and coal had been lost, and the more efficient working practices, brought in during the wartime emergency to deal with manpower shortages, presaged the blight of mass unemployment as rapid military demobilisation put so many men back on the streets without jobs to go to.

The Depression in 1929 made things worse. The political vocabulary in Scotland, throughout the 1930s, was filled with terse phrases such as 'the slum problem', 'provincialisation', 'the southward drift of industry', and 'North Britain, that distressed area'.

But the Depression's effects were uneven. It is undeniable that there were long dole queues and hunger marches, but, at the same time, the average standard of living for most Britons increased faster than at any time in history. Scotland benefited from the positive side as well as the negative side. Its principal problem was that the Depression ripped out its old industrial heart.

It was in response to seemingly intractable social and economic failings that some Scots were motivated to indulge in a serious flirtation with home rule, an issue which had been sidelined since the pre-World War One option of 'home rule all round' had foundered. The economic situation dominated the self-government debate in Scotland. The bottom line was that home rule could not make sense if it meant that the nation was to be bankrupted. If that was the case, the most pragmatic course of action would be to hang on to England, the prosperous partner in the Union, and hope for the best.

In the climate of traumatic social change, Scotland's poets and writers tried to fill a contemporary cultural vacuum. As the nation suffered its worst collapse of self-confidence, the value of Scotland's past history was also called into question and there was a determined attempt to create Scotland anew on the printed page.

The onset of the Second World War in 1939 was almost a relief, given the hardship experienced by most Scots in the inter-war years. Full employment was restored as Britain rearmed to meet the threat of German expansionism, and Scotland's expertise in engineering was once more in demand. The spirit of community forged by the war reinforced the Union and strengthened the State in developing a planned economy. Scotland found common cause, too, in the commitment to social justice in the New Britain that would emerge after 1945.

The war had raised popular expectations for a peaceful future. There had been tacit agreement between people and politicians that the war was not just a fight against the fascist dictatorships, it was also a fight to create a fairer Britain. This sense of idealism was reflected in the general election of 1945 when Churchill was beaten by a Labour landslide.

Building a more socially just Britain was not an easy task. The war had bankrupted Britain and the nation was only able to survive because of American credit. Homes had to be built, schools and hospitals constructed, jobs created and social security paid for. It was a tall order for a bankrupt Exchequer.

The commitment to social justice was popular in Scotland. After all, there was plenty of social injustice for the state to deal with. In the 1950s and 1960s, Scots, as opposed to Scotland, prospered. At a time when productivity and relative economic decline set in, Scotland, paradoxically, enjoyed greater wealth redistribution than at any other time in history. Economic inefficiency paid social dividends!

A powerful apparatus of government control came into being in Scotland. As economic problems mounted, the electorate looked to the state to fix them. The government sought salvation and approbation by pouring public money into high profile and hugely expensive projects. Government bodies in the shape of the Scottish Development Agency and the Highlands and Islands Development Board resolved to fix productivity in out-of-date industries by backing Ravenscraig, the Linwood car plant, and the Invergordon aluminium smelter. The more the state tried to fix the problems, the more the electorate came to rely on the state.

The rise of the SNP after 1967 took place against a backdrop of mounting economic difficulties. The plan for an assembly in the 1970s was a ploy designed first and foremost to stop the SNP. Ill-conceived, badly supported and poorly executed, the scheme seemed destined to fail. The referendum in 1979, although returning a majority in favour, showed that the Scots were deeply divided on the question.

The advent of Thatcherism changed everything. Scots had assumed in the post-war era that the British state was benign. It provided jobs, health care and social security, but Margaret Thatcher was determined to strangle the 'nanny state' and in so doing destroyed what many Scots believed were core British values. As time went on under Tory rule, many Scots began to feel the need to be protected from a hostile, insensitive and alien government. The poll tax, introduced in Scotland a year ahead of England, was greeted with hostility, protest, and refusal to pay, but it was only when there were riots in the streets of London that it was finally withdrawn.

A brash and more self-confident Scottish popular culture was developing alongside the political revival of the home rule question. It was kitsch in many ways, but also challenging and with a sense of its own worth. When Tory Secretary of State Michael Forsyth tried to win over disaffected Scots by returning the Stone of Destiny in advance of the 1997 election, it was widely regarded as a crude political bribe, rather than a well-meaning gesture.

The Labour landslide that swept the Tories from power was followed by a devolution referendum, which confirmed that the 'settled will' of the Scottish nation was to have a parliament in Edinburgh. A political shift in favour of home rule was achieved speedily and with minimal dissent.

CHAPTER 13

The Great War

1914-18

Scotland embraced the onset of war in August 1914 with a patriotic passion. Almost overnight, the divisions which had gnawed away at the fabric of Scottish society were forgotten as mutual necessity demanded they present a united front to the enemy.

Catholic and Protestant clergymen joined the war effort from the pulpit and urged their parishioners to do their Christian duty and fight against the 'heathen Hun' who was evidently a greater danger than either Romanism or Orangeism.

The party political squabbles of the Liberals and the Unionists over reform of the House of Lords, Irish home rule, temperance and the Workman's Insurance Act paled into insignificance against the magnitude of the German threat to liberty and freedom. Normal political activity was suspended as both parties turned over their organisation and offices to recruitment agencies.

Workers and employers who had been increasingly involved in bitter industrial confrontation on the domestic front in the four years before the war found themselves reconciled by the greater menace beyond. The war was temporary salvation for many a middle-class home, returning it to domestic bliss as the women's suffrage movement diverted resources away from winning the vote to the altogether more strategically important

task of knitting socks for the boys in the trenches. The few voices of pacifist dissent were drowned out by the crushing wave of jingoistic euphoria.

It was to be all over by Christmas and young men were caught up in a stampede, all desperate to do their bit for King and Country while they had the chance. Lord Kitchener's appeal for the first 100,000 was greeted with such enthusiasm that the makeshift recruiting agencies were unable to cope with the massive influx. There were shortages of accommodation, food, uniforms and even administrative forms. The *Glasgow Herald* informed its readers that recruitment had to be

suspended as the rush of volunteers to join the Colours overwhelmed the military depots who had to deal with them. By the end of the first week in September 1914, Glasgow was able to boast that it had recruited more than 22,000 men. A raising of the physical standard of entry was introduced the following week to help 'dam the stream' of volunteers. Although recruitment peaked in the first months of war, and by 1915 the physical standard of entry had to be lowered to deal with a manpower shortage, few parts of the UK responded as enthusiastically and consistently to the call to arms as the Scottish nation. Of the 157 battalions making up the British Expeditionary Force, 22 were from Scottish regiments.

The headlong rush to join up cannot simply be explained by blind patriotism. Many joined up believing that the war would be a quick affair which offered a welcome escape from the tedium of boring and unexciting jobs. Some were motivated by more practical and pragmatic reasons. It was widely believed that the war would depress the domestic economy and many sought refuge from unemployment in the forces. The loss of the export market in Eastern Europe for the Fife coalfields confirmed many suspicions and one in four miners joined up. The uptake among the industrial work force was just as great. Employers, carried away with their own patriotism, promised to make up any wage differentials that low army pay might mean and pledged to keep jobs open for volunteers. If patriotism proved an inadequate incentive, many employers promised that cowards and shirkers would face the sack while young women handed out white feathers to shirkers who faced social ostracism. The social imperative for young men to join up was fierce. Peer pressure and the desire to remain with their friends was exploited by the military. 'Pals' battalions comprising friends, neighbours and fellow workers were formed to maintain morale. Even so, demand for cannon fodder could not be satisfied and conscription had to be introduced as the war dragged on into 1917.

The wildly optimistic hope that 'business as usual' would be the norm for the duration of the war was cruelly misplaced. As the casualties began to mount, Scotland had to accommodate itself to endemic national grief and few families were left untouched. It is estimated that 100,000 Scots were among the British total of 745,000. Unlike the Second World War, when recruits were dispersed throughout the armed forces which meant that the

impact of casualties was random, casualties in the First World War were usually specific to local recruiting areas. As pals fought together, more often than not they died together. This meant that local communities experienced collective mass grief rather than individual loss when news of deaths became known. An unlucky shell could wipe out a third of the adult

A mostly female workforce at Clydebank tend to a batch of artillery shells destined for the front. Munitions manufacturers were to be caught out deliberately restricting production to ensure the price paid by the military, and therefore profits, remained high

male population of a small town. To this day, the war memorials in every small village in Scotland are a testament to the sacrifice made by rural society. Similarly, in the cities and larger towns, the death of a loved one who met his end going over the top would probably mean a similar fate for the kin of friends and neighbours. It was with horror and trepidation that local communities followed the reports on the progress of the carnage on the Western Front. Of all the experiences and changes which effected wartime Scotland, none were as traumatic as the loss of life in the killing fields of France and Belgium.

Just as the casualties were piling up in 1915, the much-vaunted social cohesion engendered by patriotism began to break down under the pressure of class tensions. The war greatly strengthened the negotiating muscle of the industrial working class. The desperate need for munitions and men and women to manufacture them

meant that there was a super-abundance of work. Labour shortages meant that wages were driven up and augmented by plenty of overtime. Thousands of workers drifted into the Clyde basin which was the largest centre of armament production in the UK. Trade union membership increased because workers could pay the levy and confidence grew because there was a premium on skilled labour. The benefits of rising wages and almost unlimited overtime, however, was eroded by inflation which meant a 50% leap in the cost of living. The phenomenon that became known as Red Clydeside had its roots in the attempts made by the skilled working class to cling to the gains accrued in wartime.

The government, intent on maximising output, had appointed Lord Weir as munitions controller in July 1915. Weir was an advocate of streamlining and rationalising production. He believed that by 'diluting' the skilled element of the

DOUGLAS HAIG
Earl Haig of Bemersyde
1861–1928

FIELD MARSHALL Sir Douglas Haig was commander-in-chief of the British Army for most of the First World War. He is now considered by many to be responsible for the deaths of hundreds of thousands of his own soldiers.

The former cavalry officer emerged from the war a national hero, and was awarded an estate in the Borders that was paid for by public subscription. On his death, a state funeral was held in Edinburgh.

Forbiddingly remote and awkward in company, the denigration of Haig's reputation began with the war poets Wilfrid Owen and Siegfried Sassoon and has since gained momentum as revisionists argue there were alternatives to the static war of attrition which condemned so many men to near certain death, for little or no tactical advantage. Haig's defenders say that he may have been a flawed character but he won the war.

labour force productivity could be improved and the shortage of labour overcome. Not surprisingly, the engineers regarded this as a threat to their craft skills and resisted all attempts at dilution. Assurances that it was simply wartime expediency were unconvincing and periodic strikes and disputes hit the Clyde throughout 1915. The workers' demands were articulated by the Clyde Workers Committee, an organisation run by shop stewards, many of whom,

alarmingly for the authorities, openly espoused socialism.

Working class discontent was not just confined to the workplace. Over 20,000 workers drifted into the Clyde area within the first year of the war to take jobs in the burgeoning armaments industry. Accommodation was scarce and overcrowding became endemic. Furthermore, landlords, being totally committed to the doctrine of supply and demand, put up rents to cash in. Not only did this eat into the gains which

had come through higher wages, it was seen to be blatant profiteering. Whatever the workers could win with industrial muscle in the workshop, the landlord could easily take away with rent rises. The sense of injustice was reinforced by the fact that the rent rises also hit those vulnerable elements within the community who could not rely on rising wages; the wives and dependants of serving soldiers were badly affected. Landlords were tarred with the brush of unpatriotic behaviour.

Scottish troops follow the pipes and drums as they march towards the killing fields of the First World War

The Rent Strike of 1915 brought it to a head. The fact that it was the community which was seen to be penalised as a whole did more to reinforce a sense of working-class solidarity than the sectional grievances which preoccupied the industrial work force. The profiteering of unscrupulous landlords coincided with the 'shell crisis' in which it was revealed that munitions manufacturers were deliberately limiting production to keep the price of ammunition artificially high.

Government appeals to the patriotism of the rent strikers and munitions workers sounded hollow. Despite the prominence of Labour activists, most demands of the working class of Clydeside were founded on a pre-war sense of fair play, rather than any socialist aspiration. The collective sense of moral indignation culminated in November 1915 when workers downed tools to protest outside the court where rent defaulters were due to appear. Within a matter of weeks, the government was forced to intervene and have rent levels pegged for the duration of the war.

While the claims of the Independent Labour Party agitators that the strike marked a decisive victory in the advance of socialism and the working class may be over the top, there is no doubt that the event was a triumph of people power. The Rent Strike did much to improve the credibility of the labour movement as trade unionists, members of the Co-operative movement and the Independent Labour Party were all instrumental in orchestrating and organising demonstrations. Labour also did well in the workplace as the trade union movement offered socialist activists unprecedented access to the working class. The advances made by workers clearly demonstrated that an independent labour movement did have serious clout. Also, the Liberal Party, which had claimed guardianship of workers' interests in the pre-war era, was increasingly perceived as defending the well-being of the bosses. After all, it was a Liberal government which introduced dilution, passed legislation to regulate work practices, arrested strike leaders and initially supported rack-renting landlords. Any working-class gains came in spite of the Liberal Party, not because of it.

The Liberal government was already being damned as incompetent in its handling of the war when, in April 1916, the Irish community in Scotland was alienated from their former allies by the suppression of the Easter Rising in Dublin. The government collapsed, to be replaced by a coalition, and the squabbling Liberal Party split between Asquith's independent Liberals and Lloyd George's coalition Liberals. It did little to enhance the party's tarnished reputation.

At local level, Labour was able to benefit from growing working-class discontent and, in contrast to the Liberal Party's organisation which had all but collapsed, used its new networks among the trade unions and local communities to further its political message. It was a message the working class wanted to hear as it concentrated on housing, wages, health and social reform.

Just as a new dynamic working-class politics was emerging, the changes wrought by war reshaped political attitudes. Workers on Clydeside may have been simply demanding better pay and conditions without much thought as to how this was to be achieved, but this was not the message picked up by middle-class ears listening to socialist spokesmen relaying their vision of the way ahead. Socialists were taken at their word and the raising of the Red Flag in George Square convinced the authorities revolution was imminent.

The 1919 'riot' in George Square, however, was the result of police insensitivity and poor crowd control. Further demonstrations failed to materialise when the government gave assurances that rent controls would not be lifted in the immediate future. Popular protest by the working class would never again attain the same degree of potency as a political tool. Yet, the real historical significance of the often incoherent agitation surrounding Red Clydeside resided in the psychological effects it would have on the development of both right and left wings of Scottish politics.

Red Dawn Fades

The red flag, potent symbol of socialism and the recent Russian Revolution, is raised in George Square, Glasgow in 1919 just before the troops were sent in

THE decade from 1910 witnessed quite fundamental change in the politics of Glasgow. This was the era of 'Red Clydeside' when the Clyde, like Russia in 1917, was supposedly ripe for a workers' revolution, particularly just after the end of the First World War.

The Marxist, William Gallacher, noted in his autobiography, Revolt on the Clyde, that 'the workers were in a mood to tear up Glasgow by the roots', while fellow revolutionary, John Maclean, appointed Soviet Consul on the Clyde by Lenin, commented in 1920: 'We can make Glasgow a Petrograd, a revolutionary storm centre second to none.'

Subsequently, Red Clydeside has become an issue of furious debate between leftist writers, who believed in its potential, and other historians, who debunked it and declared the whole thing to be untrue or grossly exaggerated and distorted. So what is myth and what is the reality?

The evidence indicates that circumstances and events combined during the period to radically change the way Clydeside people thought and acted, resulting in the creation of Britain's foremost socialist city, with a concomitant marked change in power relationships within society.

In the early years of the 20th century, Glasgow was a major industrial city and port, but one dominated by Liberal politics. There were few strikes and trade unions were weaker than in other British cities. However, even before the First World War broke out, there were signs that the attitudes of Glasgow workers were changing and that they were no longer willing to tolerate grim living and working conditions. The pre-war wave of strikes was sustained longer on Clydeside than in other industrial areas of the UK. Among the many contributory causes were falling real wages, the spread of syndicalist ideas, the growing insecurity of the craftsmen facing de-skilling, technological and managerial changes, and particularly authoritarian work regimes imposed by profit-maximising Clydeside capitalists, who tended to be more anti-union than employers elsewhere.

The all-out strike of 12,000 workers at the previously peaceful Singer factory in Clydebank, in 1911, epitomises this escalating breakdown in capital-labour relations. Overcrowded housing conditions in Glasgow – among the worst in Europe – and high rates of poverty-related disease, such as tuberculosis, made matters worse.

The First World War played a critical role in incubating Clydeside workers' grievances, raising class awareness and drawing workers away from Liberalism towards the left. Several developments defined the Clyde as distinctively radical compared to other parts of Britain.

First, industrial militancy was more intense. The Clyde was the centre of the first major wartime strike in 1915. Thereafter, industrial discontent festered, with skilled metal workers especially disgruntled at the 'dilution' of their labour through the introduction of female and unskilled workers, and the hated Munitions Act which prevented workers leaving one employer for another, a situation described by dissidents as akin to slavery.

What particularly concerned the authorities was the loss of control by official trade union leaders. The workplace discontent was led by radical shop stewards, many of whom were Marxists, syndicalists and Independent Labour Party (ILP) socialists.

They formed the Clyde Workers' Committee (CWC) to co-ordinate action and campaign for an extension of workers' control over industry. The creation of what was effectively a workers' soviet on Clydeside alarmed the establishment which responded swiftly to this challenge to its authority. In April 1916, nine shop stewards were 'deported' to Edinburgh and the CWC newspaper, *The Worker*, suppressed. The Red Clydeside leaders, Maclean, Gallacher, Jimmy Maxton, John Muir, Tom Bell and Jock Smith, were arrested and convicted of sedition.

The public mood was inflamed when, a few days before their trial, a Zeppelin attack resulted in extensive damage and several casualties. A fake letter, supposedly from the Kaiser, was published thanking them for their 'co-operation'. The prison sentences were harsh. Maclean, who had been interned at Edinburgh Castle, was sentenced to three years; Smith 18 months; and Maxton, Muir, Gallacher and Bell one year each.

The industrial action on Clydeside in 1919, however, was of far more serious proportions. It was here that Britain came closest to revolution.

In January 1919, a workers' campaign for a radical reduction in working hours escalated into a strike involving more than 80,000 workers. On the last day of the month, a huge demonstration occupied George Square and, provoked by a police baton charge, the demonstrators rioted, cut tram lines and raised the red flag. Fighting broke out between strikers, ex-servicemen and the police. The whole affair was

famously described to the Cabinet by the Scottish Secretary Robert Munro as 'not a strike, it was a Bolshevik rising'. In response, the government arrested the strike leaders and drafted in troops, tanks, a howitzer and set up machine-gun nests around the city centre. This stabilised the situation.

However, arguably, the most important manifestation of Red Clydeside was not the drama of the riots or disputes over working conditions but the rent strikes of 1915. Exploiting the extraordinary wartime demand for housing, unscrupulous landlords hiked up rents, especially around the shipyards and munitions plants. The women of Partick and Govan organised resistance. Led by Helen Crawfurd, Agnes Dollan and Mary Barbour, together with a number of male ILP activists, the rent

HELEN CRAWFURD

1889-1954

FEMINIST, SOCIALIST and peace campaigner Helen Crawfurd led the fight of working-class Glasgow women against extortionate rent increases during the First World War. The women's militant protest against landlords out to profit from the housing demands around the shipyards and munitions factories of Glasgow, shamed the government into intervening.

strikers proceeded to physically oppose eviction and campaigned vigorously, protesting about the unfairness of rising costs of living when soldiers were away at the front. One placard read: 'While my father is a prisoner in Germany, the landlord is attacking our home.' Workers threatened to down tools in support of the rent strikers.

Faced with such solidarity and effective community action, the government conceded defeat, passing the Rent Restriction Act freezing rent levels and introducing state intervention in the private housing rental market for the first time. It was a great victory for what Crawfurd described as a 'women's fight'.

Moreover, while the patriotism of the majority of Scottish workers was evident, the anti-war movement was also stronger in Glasgow than any other city. Pacifism cut across class and political boundaries, but the agitation of Marxist revolutionaries (especially John Maclean and Tom Bell), ILP members such as John Wheatley and Tom Johnston, and feminist peace campaigners (notably Helen Crawfurd and Agnes Dollan) had wide appeal.

Even the Scottish Trade Union Congress was converted to the campaign for peace, voting unanimously in 1917 for negotiations to be opened to end the war. By this time, the gross mismanagement of the war, evident capitalist profiteering at home and the indiscriminate slaughter at the front had created widespread disillusionment, even disgust.

At times, the particularly repressive actions of the state and employers only served to embitter workers and heighten class consciousness. The political blacklisting and systematic victimisation of the West Scotland Economic League, the infiltration of the unions by police spies, suppression of the press, deportation and imprisonment of workers' leaders, and

JOHN MACLEAN
1879-1923

BORN in Pollokshaws, he worked as a schoolteacher in Govan until sacked in 1915 because of his political activities. He then became a full-time Marxist educator and organiser, charismatic enough to attract more than 1,000 students to his economics classes. He was appointed Soviet Consul on the Clyde after the Russian Revolution, but when the British Communist Party was formed he refused to join, instead setting up a separate Scottish party.

An anti-militarist, he was arrested six times between 1916 and 1923, serving four prison terms for sedition and incitement to strike. His health was broken by prison and he died young, but his position as a socialist and a nationalist is unique in Scottish political history. The Russians have named a street after him in St Petersburg.

the repressive prison conditions served to inflame workers, pushing them further to the Left. The deployment of the notorious 'Black and Tans' in Ireland contributed to the leftward shift in the Glasgow Irish vote.

The actions of the state, particularly in drafting in armed forces to Glasgow in 1919, clearly demonstrated just how seriously it took the threat of a 'Bolshevik rising' in the city.

The era of Red Clydeside saw a transition in political views, with a radical shift to the Left. Membership of the ILP trebled during the war, while votes for Labour and socialist candidates in Clydeside elections increased almost tenfold between 1910 and 1918. The change is most clearly demonstrated in the landslide Labour victory in the parliamentary election of 1922, when 42% of the Glasgow electorate voted Labour, with the Labour party winning 10 out of the 15 Glasgow seats (previously Labour held just one seat in Glasgow). Important here was the swing towards Labour of the substantial Irish vote in the city,

influenced by Labour support for state subsidies for separate Catholic schools.

The 10 Red Clydesider MPs left Glasgow for Westminster to the cheers of a tumultuous crowd of supporters and the chanting of the Red Flag.

Also significant is that there was a greater proportion of workers' leaders on Clydeside with avowedly revolutionary aims than elsewhere. John Maclean attracted literally thousands of workers to his Marxist education classes and the Clyde was the main centre of Communist politics after the formation of the British Communist Party in 1920. Glasgow (like Vienna) developed a vibrant socialist alternative culture between the wars, expressed in things such as the Clarion Scouts, socialist sports movements the May Day rallies, and the Socialist Sunday School.

However, what happened does need to be kept in perspective. The ILP was much more deeply involved and influential in the various manifestations of popular protest from 1910-1922 than were the revolutionaries. Moreover, the

forces of the state were never significantly threatened or the Left sufficiently united for a revolution to succeed. Nor did the revolts on the Clyde provoke other protests elsewhere in Scotland in any kind of domino effect. Divisions between workers, based on occupation, religion and gender continued to fragment and weaken the Clydeside labour movement (which was particularly chauvinist at this time). Nonetheless, politics and social relations on Clydeside were irrevocably transformed during this short period. There was a marked shift in the balance of power – trade unions were strengthened, increasingly recognised by the employers, and state intervention in the housing market was firmly established. Ultimately, of course, it was the Labour party that was the main beneficiary of this crystallisation of class awareness.

To describe Glasgow, in this period, as being on the brink of revolution, therefore, is an exaggeration, but there is no doubt that Red Clydeside was a very real phenomenon, not a myth.

CHAPTER 14

Between the Wars

1918-1939

The world that emerged at the end of the First World War was a very different place from the one that had preceded it. The Hollywood dream factory entered its most prolific phase and cinemas were rivalled only by dance halls as the new temples of popular entertainment. And, while the masses enjoyed the peace as best they could, Scottish politics was dominated by the rise of Labour. On the left, the point at issue was whether socialism was to be achieved by gradualist means or outright revolution. On the right, political priorities were determined by the need to form an anti-socialist bulwark.

The single biggest factor in accounting for the political advance of Labour was the franchise reform of 1918 which almost trebled the size of the electorate from 779,000 in 1910 to 2,205,000 in 1918. Women over the age of 30 were added to the electoral register, but the most important categorisation of new voters was that they were drawn from the working class. Since the war had heightened class tensions and boosted the credibility of both trade unions and Labour Party, one might have expected to see this translated into political change at the 1918 election. But political change rarely follows such a logical path and old allegiances die hard. It was the Unionist Party which emerged as the post-war winner.

The Liberals, still the largest party in terms of seats won, were hopelessly divided, but Labour, although attracting 23% of the votes, could only notch up seven seats. Undoubtedly, the Unionists and their Coalition Liberal allies benefited from the patriotic glow of winning the war and the almost hysterical 'hang the Kaiser' fervour which dominated the campaign. Organisations such as the Middle-Class Union and the People's League supported the best placed anti-socialist candidates.

The good results achieved by Labour in local elections the following year and their progress at the 1922 election – which established it as the largest party in Scotland – were the results of painstaking organisation, which put more and more working-class people on the electoral roll so they could use their franchise.

The failure of the 40-hour strike in 1919 coupled with electoral advances in 1919 and 1922 greatly strengthened the moderate wing of the Labour Party and wrong-footed the proponents of direct action. Furthermore, the trade unions, arguably the single greatest power bloc within the Labour movement, had little interest other than the bread and butter issues which were the mainstay of the rank and file's concerns.

Most of Labour's parliamentary intake of 1922, 'the Clydesiders', had little understanding of Marxist ideology and were principally motivated by a desire to promote and protect the interests of their working-class constituents. There was also an influx of disaffected radical Liberals who would have no truck with

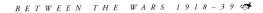

revolutionary ideology. When Labour emerged as the party of opposition in 1922, ultimate power through the parliamentary process was seen as a feasible goal, if not an imminent one. In any case, by that time most revolutionaries had isolated themselves from the mainstream movement. The gradualist strategy was vindicated by the advent of Ramsay MacDonald's minority Labour government of 1924 and its initiation of a limited and pragmatic programme of social reform. Paradoxically, the spectre of Red Clydeside had been most effectively exorcised by the Labour Party itself.

The realignment of the right, which was the other side of the coin in the development of politics based on class confrontation, was more protracted. Both Unionists and Liberals (of all hues) tried to claim the mantle of anti-socialism. In 1918, the Unionists were in the strongest position. The party dominated the coalition government, its organisation was in better shape, it was not divided into factions and its bellicose and hard-line anti-socialist rhetoric was more comforting to a traumatised middle class than that of the Liberal Party. Yet the Liberals had one principal advantage: they had not been significantly dislodged from parliamentary seats. Given that anti-socialism obsessed the politics of the right, the dilemma faced by most Unionists was whether to stand against the Liberal and risk letting in the socialist or to support the sitting MP. The coalition shelved this difficult choice, in 1918, as candidates with the 'coupon' were to be supported by both parties. In Scotland, most Liberals owed their continued parliamentary existence to local Unionist

---

Big Hollywood names in lights attracted the crowds to the Paramount cinema in Glasgow city centre in 1927

campaigners. With a greater perception of the danger of the 'red menace' north of the Border, it was hardly surprising to find Scottish Liberals and Unionists arguing vehemently against the ending of the coalition in 1922. Local agreements made between Liberals and Unionists survived in quite a number of constituencies. The reunited Liberal Party under the leadership of Asquith, still trading heavily on anti-socialism, did well in the 1923 general election by winning 23 seats with just under a third of the vote, helped by the Unionist Party's support for protectionism, which struck a discordant note among an electorate historically conditioned in the faith of free trade.

Asquith's decision to support MacDonald's minority Labour government in 1924, however, destroyed the Liberal Party's anti-socialist credentials. Leaders of the business community who had supported Liberals to keep out Labour howled in unison at this betrayal. The Unionists, meanwhile, made extensive efforts to rid themselves of their crusty image and present a more moderate and conciliatory vision of Conservatism, enabling the party to move closer to the centre ground of politics. Coupled with the moderation of Labour's minority administration which singularly failed to plunge the country into 'socialist anarchy', the Liberals were squeezed out of the centre of British and Scottish politics. At the ensuing general election of 1924, the Unionists were to emerge as the undisputed alternative to socialism and the Liberals ceased to be an effective force in politics. The two-party system based on class interests was now firmly established.

Long-term mass unemployment was a new phenomenon in Scotland. The political values and cultural certainties which had dominated Edwardian society had been swept

away in a tide of class conflict and national self-doubt.

Even before the First World War, although not apparent at the time, the Scottish economy was over-reliant on a narrow base of heavy industries which were inter-connected and interdependent. The drive for munitions, after 1914, killed off what limited diversification had already taken place – in chemicals, car manufacturing and machine tools – and destroyed export markets, particularly in coal and textiles. There was a near total concentration on heavy engineering. This was profitable as long as it lasted, but the war could not last for ever. When it did end, the Scottish economy was badly exposed.

German reparations, Communist revolution, Britain's war debt and financial uncertainty eroded demand for capital investment goods. In the shipyards, restoration of old working practices reduced competitiveness in a market severely affected by the sudden drying up of naval contracts. With shipyards as its largest customer, the steel industry suffered the knock-on effect. While the economy of southern England was revitalised by the new 'sunshine' industries which manufactured consumer durables, Scotland stagnated. All in all, it was a bleak picture.

Scottish industrialists pursued a 'wait and see' policy in the hope that traditional sectors would pick up. To

The Colorado Dance Band play at The Plaza Hall, in Edinburgh, in 1932. Jazz was universally condemned in Scotland as belonging to a degenerate American culture. Churches and politicians bemoaned its influence on the young

male breadwinners. That a woman's place was in the home was ideologically reinforced by reference to vistas of widespread moral collapse and juvenile delinquency. The implosion of the old industrial structure did not entail a similar fate for the patriarchal values which imbued it.

The number of people on poor relief rose from 192,000 in 1929 to 341,000 in 1936. On average, Scottish unemployment levels were almost double those of England, and went over 30% in towns like Motherwell and Airdrie. Whole communities faced economic ruin, including those members of the lower middle class who found the market for their services had evaporated. Unlike the working class, who paid unemployment insurance, the middle class were left to fend for themselves and did not even feature in unemployment statistics. It was estimated that there were 100,000 men 'permanently surplus to requirements' in the west of Scotland at the height of the Depression.

Economic stagnation meant Scotland did little to alleviate endemic social problems of poor housing and health. A Royal Commission of 1917 recommended that 250,000 additional houses would have to be built but cuts in public expenditure dictated that housing targets were lowered. In fact 300,000 houses were built between the wars (two thirds in the public sector) but the number was insufficient to replace old housing stock that was crumbling away. The worst housing tended to be in the unemployment blackspots where there was little enough money for rent, and landlords were prone to save money by endlessly postponing repairs and improvements. The good quality homes that were produced were usually out of the reach of those most in need of them. By the 1930s, constant cost-cutting resulted in councils reducing standards, and

survive the lean times, companies formed defensive amalgamations and investment was pared to a minimum. Often, this meant takeover from London. Scotland lost four of its main banks, and the amalgamation of the railways, which followed the war, transferred management to the south. Thereafter, locomotive repair work favoured Crewe and Derby at the expense of Inverness and Springburn.

The difficulties faced by the Scottish economy in the 1920s, however, paled into insignificance with the onset of the Great Depression in 1929. The statistics make grim reading. In 1932 some 400,000, or 26.2%, of the insured workforce was idle; 20 new factories opened while 36 shut. In 1933, 14

opened and 58 closed. In the following year, 38 opened and 58 closed. In the depressed west central belt the picture was even worse. Rationalisation and the 'southward drift of industry' gathered momentum as companies relocated in the more stable and prosperous markets of England. It seemed that Scotland was in a spiral of terminal decline and that the prosperity of the south was sucking the blood out of it.

The social consequences of economic dislocation were savage and selective. Working class women bore the brunt of the misery. They were deprived of the limited gains made during the war and hounded out of the workplace to make way for traditional

resorting to cheaper materials, therefore producing sub-standard properties. In 1935, overcrowding was six times greater than in England.

The health of the Scottish people was not a great example to the world either. While maternal mortality and infant mortality rates went down in England and Wales, they stayed stubbornly high in Scotland. Experts testified time and again that the average Scot was in poor physical shape. And it seemed the country suffered a spiritual malaise, too, with the Kirk, reunited in 1929 but dogged by the anti-working-class bias of its politics, losing its central position in an increasingly secular Scottish society.

One dismal testament to the failure of Scottish society to provide adequate

Miners kill time playing cards outside an idle pit at Prestonpans, East Lothian, during the general strike in May 1926

economic and social opportunities for its people was the extent of migration to other parts of the UK. For the first time since records began, the 1931 census showed the Scottish population falling, despite a higher birth rate, while south of the Border it rose. The impression was created that the best and most able were seeking a way out and the 'lifeblood' of the nation was being drained.

Yet, it was not all doom and gloom. For those in work, the standard of living in the inter-war era rose sharply and not all areas suffered from

economic dislocation. Edinburgh, for example, was saved by a prosperous financial and services sector.

For the affluent, there were unrivalled opportunities to take advantage of the new range of consumer goods which were flooding the market. Motor cars allowed families freedom to travel the length and breadth of the country. The majority of Scots might have prospered but this in itself could not disperse the sense of crisis which pervaded Scottish society. Most Scots still associated general prosperity with the old industrial structure that was so obviously languishing.

The fundamental problem of structural imbalance in the Scottish economy was never rectified and when activity in heavy engineering was revived in the late 1930s it was because of the urgent need for rearmament as another war loomed.

The Labour Party, abandoning its commitment to home rule, argued that the problems faced by Scottish society were so entrenched that it would take the mobilisation of the resources of the British state to rectify them. What was the point of having a parliament in Edinburgh, it was argued, if it did not have the power to tackle ingrained social and economic problems? By the end of the 1920s, in response to Labour's lukewarm stance on the home rule issue, the National Party of Scotland had been established. Its first foray in the 1929 general election had little impact other than nuisance value. Unionists dismissed the nationalist challenge as the work of left-wing socialists, but nationalism at this stage was only a sideshow.

The major political story of the time was the crisis of capitalism engendered by the Depression. The Labour government, operating within the capitalist system, was impotent to prevent it, exposing the shallowness of the party's attachment to socialism.

The Labour party was decimated at the 1931 general election, and the Scots, along with the rest of the UK, gave a massive electoral endorsement to the new National Government chosen to deal with the emergency. The Unionist Party did best out of this arrangement and was able to secure an electoral hegemony north of the Border which would last until the end of the Second World War.

Throughout the 1930s, Labour directed its energies into rebuilding its organisation while nationalism, encouraged by socio-economic indicators highlighting Scotland's 'neglect' when compared to England, bubbled just under the surface. Unlike in the 1920s, this time it was traditional middle-class Unionist supporters who began to believe Scotland was not getting a fair deal. Usually quiescent allies of the Unionist Party, such as the Glasgow and Edinburgh Chambers of Commerce, complained of Scotland being reduced to a mere province of England. Although the Scottish National Party, formed in 1934 by an amalgamation of the Scottish Party and the National Party of Scotland, was not yet a significant political force, members of the National Government believed that there was the potential for a nationalist upsurge and acted to avert it.

The Scottish Council (Development and Industry) was set up to promote industrial diversification, and numerous semi-official committees and quangos were established to examine and suggest remedies for the beleaguered Scottish economy. The scale of the problems and the limited resources available, however, meant such attempts only scratched at the surface.

Unionists insisted that a nationalist solution would only make the problems worse. Time and time again, it was emphasised that Scotland needed England as an economic prop. Any attempt to abrogate or reform the Union would unleash an economic catastrophe. If things were bad at the moment, it was nothing compared to the economic abyss of nationalism.

In tandem with economic scaremongering, the National Government promoted administrative devolution. What Scotland needed, it was argued, was not self-government, but better government. The Gilmour Report of 1937 recommended the transfer of the Scottish Office from London to Edinburgh as a symbol of national identity and Scottish distinctiveness within the Union. The Glasgow Empire Exhibition of 1938, designed to show off Scotland's imperial achievements, was likewise an attempt to inject a 'feel-good factor' into Scottish politics. Nothing, however, could lift the mood of despondency which permeated the inter-war years. It would take a war to achieve that.

JAMES RAMSAY MACDONALD

1866-1937

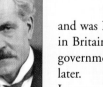

BORN in Lossiemouth, an illegitimate child, he worked as a farm labourer, teacher and clerk before moving south to become an organiser of the British Labour Party. An early advocate of Scottish home rule, he was elected to the Commons in 1906. He was party leader in 1911 until the outbreak of the war when his pacifist attitude held him back. He lost his seat in the 1918 election. He returned to Westminster in 1922 and was Prime Minister in Britain's first Labour government two years later.

In 1929, he was Prime Minister again but lost the support of Labour Ministers and, in 1931, formed a coalition National government with Conservative support, an episode known as the 'Great Betrayal'. He remained at the head of what was effectively a Tory government until 1935, when he handed over to Stanley Baldwin.

Words as Weapons

MEDIEVAL Scottish historians dispute the term Renaissance as used to describe the resurgence of Scottish literature and language in the 1920s, arguing that the real Scottish Renaissance was that of the Golden Age of James IV, when poets such as Dunbar, Henryson and Douglas contributed so much to Western culture.

Modern scholars are also questioning when the great revival of Scottish culture from its Victorian and Kailyard torpor actually began – was it with Robert Louis Stevenson, and is there a host of neglected Scottish writers such as Neil Munro, John Davidson, the Findlater sisters and Violet Jacob, whose achievement has simply been glossed over, since they constantly presented subversive and ironic pictures of Highland and Lowland Scotland, acidly questioning the history and values of a sub-nation?

The re-awakening of modern Scottish writing has been attributed to Hugh MacDiarmid (Christopher Grieve), whose wonderful early lyrics and ferocious journalistic activity certainly created a high-profile movement to revive Scottish culture. If Renaissance implies new affirmation and celebration, however, then perhaps the rebirth of Scottish literature appears with Catherine Carswell's *Open the Door!* of 1920, her portrayal of young Joanna Bannerman's unwillingness to accept dreich convention and sexual repression in her quest for self-realisation. Here, following the carnage of the First World War, was a new fiction which put the predicament of Scottish women on the agenda, and novelists such as Naomi Mitchison, Neil Gunn, Eric Linklater, and Lewis Grassic Gibbon (James Leslie Mitchell) followed with even more challenging new perspectives on Highland and Lowland history, in great novels like *Sunset Song*, the first part of Gibbon's trilogy, *A Scots Quair* (1932-34), and Gunn's *Highland River* (1937) and *The Silver Darlings* (1941). These and many more fine novels re-examined older and false perceptions of Scottish history and society, and – in common with the spirit of the fiction of many small northern nations across Europe after the First World War – created a new mythology of land and sea with folk heroes and heroines who embodied the essential strengths of their ancient races. And MacDiarmid's poetry, culminating in his great long poem which surveyed the state of Scotland's soul, *A Drunk Man Looks at the Thistle* (1926), is a keystone of this Renaissance. MacDiarmid inspired other great poets, such as Sidney Goodsir Smith and the greatest of modern Gaelic poets, Sorley Maclean, and the neglected William Soutar, whose tragic life produced a lyric and epic poetry which celebrated his native Perthshire, the poetic traditions of his country, and his visions of Scotland reborn.

MacDiarmid's notions of Renaissance centred on using Scots and Gaelic as mediums for the rediscovery of older Scottish identities, unlocking buried Scottish culture so that an affirmative declaration could be made of a modern Scotland, linked to its past and the best of European tradition. If an even broader view of Renaissance is taken, whereby other great writers who did not necessarily agree with MacDiarmid's agenda are included, allowing that dissent and ironic treatments can also be part of revival, then the picture becomes even richer. The Orkney poet Edwin Muir, whose argument that Scots was no longer a viable medium so angered MacDiarmid, nevertheless shares many Renaissance

JOHN BUCHAN
Baron Tweedsmuir
1875-1940

BORN in Perth, the son of a Free Church minister, he won the Newdigate prize for poetry at Oxford University in 1898 and went on to write more than 50 books, finding his niche in fast-moving adventure stories like *The Thirty Nine Steps*, published in 1915.

After qualifying in law before the First World War, he was called to the bar in London. He served on the HQ staff during the First World War and afterwards as director of information.

Chairman of the Scottish History Society, he was MP for the Scottish universities for seven years from 1927, before being given a peerage to enter the Lords in 1935 when he was appointed governor-general of Canada – a position he held while also Chancellor of Edinburgh University.

HUGH MACDIARMID
(Christopher Grieve)
1892-1978

THE self-styled leader of the Scottish literary renaissance was born in Langholm, Dumfriesshire, and educated at Broughton High School in Edinburgh. During the First World War, he served with the Royal Army Medical Corps in Greece and France and afterwards married and settled in Montrose to begin work as a writer, publishing his first poems in Scots in the early 1920s. The lyrical verse of *Sangschaw* (1925) and *Penny Wheep* (1926) preceded his *A Drunk Man Looks at the Thistle*, a polemical and philosophical *tour de force* on Scotland's and the Scots' place in the world. In 1931, he married for the second time and went to Shetland. After working in a munitions factory during the Second World War he moved to a cottage at Brownsbank, near Biggar and continued to promote the literary value of Scots as a language.

A founder member of the Scottish National Party, he stood as a Communist candidate in 1963.

beliefs, outstandingly that of a golden age of rural simplicity which underlies the work of Gibbon, Gunn, and so many of the mytho-poetic novelists of the time. 'Our river took a wrong turning, but we haven't forgotten the source', said Gunn speaking for many of the poets, novelists and dramatists of the inter-war years, finding an almost mystical communion with a pre-Reformation and often prehistoric Scotland, a 'dear green place' which perhaps existed only in their creative imaginations but which seemed, to a country that had endured disproportionate losses in the First World War, to be the only way forward and out of parochial, political and economic stagnation, and a kirk-ridden, Kailyard mentality. Rediscovery of the truth behind Scotland's endless internecine warring, the Highland Clearances and ghastly industrialisation went hand-in-hand with exploration of timeless meanings in folklore, legend, and ancient traditions of the supernatural; by going far back in time these writers paradoxically sought to re-create Scottish identity for the future.

The strengths of this modern Renaissance came from several sources, from the great 19th century work in anthropology of writers like Sir James Frazer, whose monumental *The Golden Bough* (1890-1915) inspired Freud and Jung to postulate the importance of the unconscious mind, which in turn inspired Renaissance Scottish writers to look to the surviving folklore and traditions of Scotland for their subject matter, seeing these as the 'collective unconscious' of the nation and as holding its redemptive secrets. Their work sought to explore the stream of consciousness of Scotland through time, as manifested in modern protagonists such as Chris Guthrie in *Sunset Song*, with her intuitive bond with the ancient standing stones which console her in tragedy and loss.

Its weaknesses were that it was still essentially rural in an increasingly technological and urban age, and – perhaps even more significantly – that it worked with national archetypes, so that its protagonists insisted on a notion of racial inheritance which, during the Second World War became utterly discredited through the Third Reich's assertion of purity of race.

Whether out of touch with the new urban realities or politically incorrect, the Renaissance movement stuttered to a halt and lost its momentum after 1945. Indeed, it had almost predicted its own demise; some of the finest work within it is deeply ironic towards its own overblown ideals, as in Eric Linklater's *Magnus Merriman* (1934) which manages both to celebrate and satirise Scotland's uncertain rebirth. Grassic Gibbon's *A Scots Quair* trilogy moved from celebration of the old song of Scotland to dark pessimism over its modernity as Chris Guthrie moved from the countryside to the city. MacDiarmid himself moved from commitment to disillusion, and from the rich humanity of his early lyrics, in a Scots which rivals that of Burns and the great medieval poets, to plainer English and a 'poetry of facts'.

The 1950s would see the new realism of Robin Jenkins and the sceptical depiction of Scotland of James Kennaway and Muriel Spark. This would develop into a revival in the 1960s and 1970s, with the marvellous work of Norman MacCaig, Iain Crichton Smith, and George Mackay Brown, a revival which still continues – but it is a revival which has much bitterness and anger at its heart, in James Kelman, in Irvine Welsh, and their new followers. That said, something of the Renaissance's affirmative belief in enduring Scottish character and country persists, so that their work lives on to inform moderns such as Edwin Morgan, Liz Lochhead and Alasdair Gray.

Contemporary Scottish writing, in all its diversity, still seems to seek a reconciliation between a sense of history and place on the one hand, and an awareness of the randomness of the modern world on the other, and it also increasingly acknowledges its debt to that earlier 20th century Renaissance.

LEWIS GRASSIC GIBBON
(James Leslie Mitchell)
1901-35

BORN a farmer's son, he left Mackie Academy in Stonehaven to begin work as a journalist on the *Aberdeen Journal*, having been inspired to join the Communist Party by the Russian Revolution. In 1919, he moved to Glasgow for a job on the *Scottish Farmer* but was sacked for fiddling his expenses. After a failed suicide attempt, he joined the army and then the RAF as a clerk. He returned to civilian life and published five books under his own name before using his mother's maiden name for *Sunset Song* in 1932. It was written as the first part of a trilogy, *A Scots Quair. Cloud Howe* and *Grey Granite* followed in successive years, but he died before the literary value of his work was properly recognised.

A Home from Home

AFTER 1918, there was an expectation among many that a parliament in Edinburgh would soon become reality. The majority of the country's elected representatives were still, on paper at any rate, committed to home rule. Also, the Labour party, which emerged to supplant the once mighty Liberal party, was if anything even more committed to a Scottish parliament. The war had seen attempts at increased government centralisation, which were denounced as a threat to Scottish self-government and condemned as inefficient.

In the early 1920s, home rule demonstrations attracted thousands of supporters and the Labour party gave the lead to the demand for a Scottish parliament when the Red Clydesiders departed for London in 1922 after Labour emerged as the largest party in Scotland. In 1924, George Buchanan, another Clydesider, introduced a Private Member's Bill for a Scottish parliament. Although the government of the day was a minority Labour administration, it could not stop the bill from being 'talked out' and it was subsequently dropped. This caused outrage among the bill's Scottish supporters and some were barred from the Commons for unruly behaviour.

A second opportunity to present the case for home rule came in 1927 when the Rev James Barr won the ballot for Private Member's Bills. Unlike 1924, there appeared to be little enthusiasm and one of the bill's co-sponsors, Tom Johnston, later admitted the scheme had been badly thought out.

Why should the Labour party have gone so cold on home rule? There were two reasons. First, the economic climate in Scotland had revealed there was massive structural dislocation. With mounting unemployment, trade unionists, who had been stalwart supporters of a Scottish parliament, now believed that small Scottish unions would be easy prey for employers and sought protection by merging

St Andrews House, Edinburgh, opened in 1939 to house the main departments of the Scottish Office. Its architecture has been described as 'unashamedly authoritarian'

JENNIE LEE
Baroness Ashridge
1904-88

A MINER'S daughter from Lochgelly in Fife and a graduate of Edinburgh University, she was the youngest member of the House of Commons when she was elected as MP for North Lanark in 1928. A dedicated socialist, her convictions were dictated by her upbringing. In 1934 she married Aneurin Bevan, the son of a Welsh miner, and, despite her stated feminist principles, consciously stood to one side to allow him to pursue his career within the Labour party. In Harold Wilson's government of 1964, she was appointed Britain's first arts minister. She doubled public expenditure on the arts and was integral in setting up the Open University. Her life is chronicled in two autobiographies, *Tomorrow is a New Day* in 1939 and *My Life with Nye* in 1980.

themselves into larger British organisations. The end of the war had been a time of optimism, but by 1927 there was pessimism in the air and little self-confidence. The general strike had been defeated in 1926 and doubts were raised about the wisdom of home rule.

The second reason relates to the first. As the Scottish economy was damaged and the social costs of this were mounting, it was felt that a Scottish parliament would not be able to make the necessary adjustments on its own. Scotland's problems were such that it would require the full resources of the British state to fix them. John Wheatley argued persuasively that a Scottish parliament which could not tackle these problems was not worth the candle and it was better to work to a British political agenda.

As Labour abandoned home rule, those who believed that a Scottish parliament was necessary coalesced into their own political party, the National Party of Scotland, which was founded in 1928. There were two strands of thought in the NPS. One held that if the party did well enough in elections, it would convince the Labour party to take the issue seriously. The other believed that British parties were intrinsically hostile to the creation of a parliament in Edinburgh and that it could only be achieved by obtaining an electoral mandate from the Scots.

As a single issue party fighting few seats with even fewer resources at the time of the Great Depression, the nationalists failed to make an impact. This led to squabbling and the appearance of a right-wing group known as the Scottish Party in 1932. Both organisations merged in 1934 to form the Scottish National Party, which also had an inauspicious start.

The SNP contained a wide spectrum of people holding opposing views from both right and left wing traditions. Some wanted independence, some devolution, others wanted to win an electoral mandate, others to act as a pressure group. At a time of economic distress and mounting international tension with war looming on the horizon, all the SNP could offer the electorate were platitudes about the 'national' interest.

With the SNP in the doldrums, Labour began to take Scottish home rule seriously again. This was not due to a change in attitude, but a response to the activities of the Conservative-dominated national government.

The state was increasing both its presence and power in Scotland. The Gilmour Report on Scottish administration which was set up in 1935 recommended that government be reorganised in Scotland and that the Scottish Office be relocated to Edinburgh. Many in the Labour party were alarmed by the growing power of the Scottish Secretary of State and the fact that these powers did not seem to be democratically accountable to the Scottish electorate. Believing that Labour and the trade unions were being frozen out of Scottish society, home rule was once again mooted, as a means to put a brake on the growing power of the Scottish Secretary.

The effects of war and the role of Tom Johnston as Labour's wartime secretary reversed this wisdom. Johnston was able to demonstrate what Wheatley had said in the 1920s. An effective operator could use British state apparatus to secure for Scotland social and economic regeneration. The consensus established during the war meant that Labour and the unions would no longer be shut out of the decision-making process and there was now no need for a democratic counterweight. Home rule was dropped again in 1945.

CHAPTER 15

World War Two

1939-45

❧

THE Second World War was not greeted with the same kind of naive enthusiasm that had characterised the outbreak of the century's first all-out conflict. For many, the terrible reality of the Great War of 1914-18 had changed attitudes irreversibly. This was not to be 'the war to end all wars' but the one that would bring an end to civilisation.

Images of the Spanish Civil War had alerted people to the fact that aerial bombardment was now a reality and many were terrified because they knew enemy bombers were now able to drop not only high explosive but poison gas on helpless civilians in the cities. A former Prime Minister, Stanley Baldwin, had said: 'The bomber will always get through.'

It was expected that civilian casualties would be high, and there was a pressing need to evacuate children away from potential targets. The task was enormous. 175,812 Scots were to be evacuated, mainly unaccompanied children and mothers with children under school age. Accommodation had to be identified and prepared and the administrative task of processing, registering, medically examining and allocating places to the evacuees was huge. The psychological effects were traumatic for most families. While some children regarded the whole escapade as an adventure, others were understandably reluctant to leave their families to live with total strangers. Fathers were equally upset at the loss of wives and children. Receiving families in the countryside were anxious about the kind of person they would be asked to take in. In this context, the Second World War was the most disruptive influence on family life in Scottish history.

The initial experience of evacuation was not a happy one. Many of the children had been told that they were going on a day trip and only later did it dawn on them that they were in for a long separation. Some worried that they were being punished for some misdemeanour, and in spite of constant assurances to the contrary, many formed the belief that they would never see their parents again. What was happening to them was simply beyond their comprehension.

Most were from working-class urban communities that had been badly blighted by the effects of the Depression. Medical examiners found a high proportion to be covered in lice and suffering from malnutrition. Photographic and movie images of these refugees which looked as if they had come from the Third World (some wore only a blanket) moved many consciences and gave birth to the idea that never again should so many be condemned to suffer from poverty, a

❧

Children at South Bridge Primary School in Edinburgh are fitted with gas masks in anticipation of bombing raids in April 1939

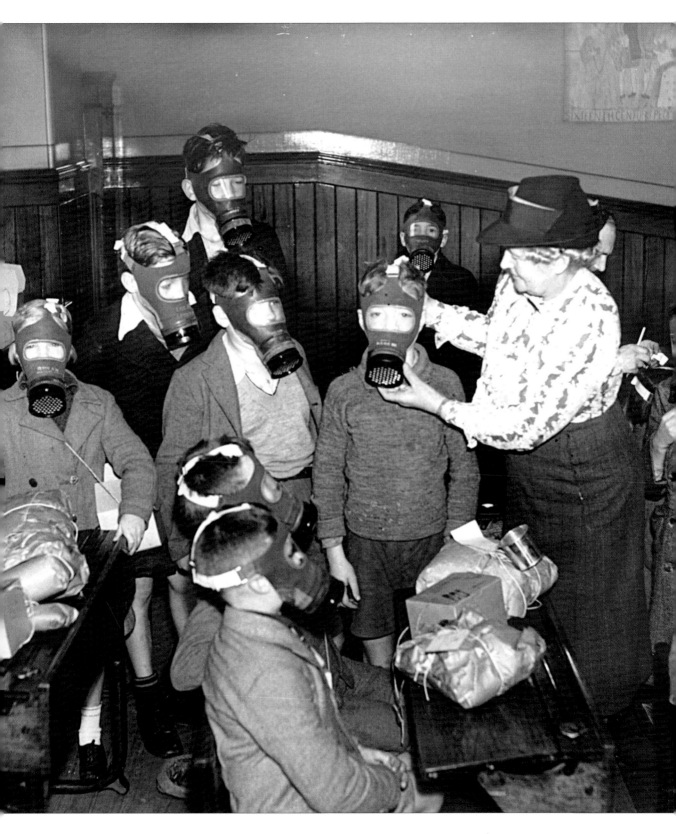

first definite move towards what would become the post-war Welfare State.

Fine ideals of caring for the less better off, however, were difficult to translate into reality as the war began. The welcome for evacuees from their hosts was not always warm. Middle-class families often took in children who had never seen an indoor toilet, some were appalled at their unruly behaviour and their language could be too much for genteel folk to bear. Some reluctant hosts, forced by peer pressures to do their bit in wartime, refused to have 'street urchins' imposed and them and insisted that only children from good homes be placed with them. For their part, the children found life in the countryside strange and unfamiliar and many were unable,

or unwilling, to cope with a diet which did not consist of chips. Social etiquette was confusing for everybody in this clash of cultures. Some farmers took on evacuees as a way of boosting their labour supply. Catholic children sometimes ended up in the hands of Protestant bigots. Many far from well-off families, who took in children, found that their domestic budget was stretched to breaking point and experienced financial difficulties which did not help relationships prosper. Within a few months there were reports of children drifting back to the cities. In any case, there was no immediate bombardment. The 'phoney war' was a period of quiet before the German invasion of France in the spring of 1940. In fact, more people

were killed by road accidents caused by blackouts in the first months of the war than by enemy action.

There is a popular myth that the Second World War engendered a 'Spirit of the Blitz' with all sections of the community coming together to do their bit to help defeat the forces of Fascism. The truth is that the evacuation of poor city children, done for the best of motives, actually helped to magnify the class divide in Scotland.

Rationing was supposed to ensure equal shares for all, but, in reality, there was a vibrant black market where those with the wherewithal could purchase most goods that were in short supply for the majority. With the right connections and contacts, it was still possible to live the high life.

The Dig for Victory campaign was provoked by fears that a naval blockade would attempt to starve Britain into surrender (above)

Classic wartime propaganda produced phrases like 'walls have ears' that have since passed into everyday language (right)

Concrete tank traps on the coast of East Lothian were built to deter a German invasion (left)

❧

Furthermore, although rationing was designed to be fair, it meant that those who were doing heavy manual work received the same food as those who were not.

Conscription into the forces was, as in the First World War, heavily class-biased, with the working class the foot soldiers and those with a better education and social standing routinely channelled into the officer corps. At home, many men were conscripted to work in essential industries, such as farming and mining, and although not reported in the press, strikes became more pronounced as the war went on, indicating increasing class conflict in the workplace. By 1941, there were more than a million days lost due to strikes, and by 1942, the number exceeded the pre-war total.

The whole nation had initially been at risk from a sea-borne invasion. Preparations were made to counteract it by installing tank traps on the east coast, and resistance groups were trained to operate in occupied territory, but once the invasion threat had receded bombing was the main tactic directed against civilians. Statistically speaking, you had more chance of being bombed if you were a member of the working class. The affluent tended to live in residential areas far removed from the dreariness of industry. The working class on the other hand, tended to live beside their places of work and the war industries of the Clyde were a prime target for the Luftwaffe. Ironically, however, the first British civilian killed in a World War Two air raid was James Isbister, a labourer in the remote Orkney hamlet of Bridge of Waith, Stenness, who was in the wrong place at the wrong time in 1940 as a bomber dropped its cargo as it headed for home after an apparently abortive raid on Scapa Flow.

The air attack against Clydebank, when it was finally launched in March 1941, was deliberately targeted and devastating. Over 1,200 people were killed and at least 1,100 seriously wounded. Bombs fell on Edinburgh and Aberdeen but nowhere else in Scotland was subjected to the extremes of the Clydebank Blitz. The raid, two nights of non-stop bombing, saw 500 planes dropping 500 tons of high explosive and incendiary bombs. The fire services were completely exhausted and help had to be drafted in from other areas. The air raid shelters were packed to overflowing and, by the second night, the town had been virtually flattened and burned out. Only seven buildings were left undamaged. Out of a population of 50,000, 35,000 were left homeless. Water, sewerage and electricity supplies were cut, unexploded bombs, collapsing buildings and rubble strewn everywhere made rescue and clean up operations dangerous and difficult. Troops were drafted in to deter looters and it would take more than 800 workers the next year and a half to patch buildings and erect enough pre-fab housing to take the displaced population.

The war brought many newcomers to Scotland. The command of the Polish Free Army was based near Kincardine and Polish soldiers played an important civilian role in the fields, bringing in the harvest of 1940. Commonwealth forces also set up base in Scotland. The Australians, for

example, flew fighter planes out of Drem in East Lothian.

The geographical remoteness of Scotland compared to the European mainland meant that it was an ideal place to house prisoners of war. The first major influx arrived in 1941, after the defeat of the Italian army in North Africa, and by the end of the war there were some 19,000 POWs working on Scottish farms and building the Churchill Barriers in Orkney to prevent submarine attacks on ships anchored in Scapa Flow. The Italian prisoners were added to the considerable number of Italian Scot detainees who were rounded up when Italy entered the war in 1940. Almost all of the Italian detainees were innocent citizens whose crime was an association with their old country which now just happened to be run by the Fascist dictator Mussolini.

Americans also came to Scotland to work at naval bases and on military camps. The arrival of the Americans

A memorial to the Polish paratroopers based at Elie in Fife, 1940-43 (above)

The Clydebank Blitz happened on the nights of March 13 and 14, 1941. Hardly a building was undamaged and 35,000 people out of a population of 50,000 were made homeless (left)

Spitfires of 453 Australian Squadron RAF at Drem, East Lothian in 1942 (below)

engendered much excitement in the local population, largely because of the enormous influence of Hollywood films. Glasgow had the highest per capita cinema attendance in Europe. The Americans were wealthy, brash and had a range of luxury items like chocolates and nylons which were virtually unobtainable by the local population. Although issued with handbooks which tried to highlight 'British sensibilities', the free and easy behaviour of American soldiers shocked many and was the subject of much criticism by the press.

The war was undeniably a time of great romance. The prospect that sweethearts might never see one another again led to an explosion in the number of marriages. The fact was that society was turned upside down and young men and women, previously kept at arm's length by social convention, were allowed to socialise without proscription.

The prospect that one could be killed in action, bombed or invaded led many to think that what time they had together was precious and that life should be experienced to the full. Evidence of increased promiscuity is to be found in a small rise in the number of illegitimate births and in the soaring rates of venereal disease infection, particularly in the ports. Indeed, some military experts claimed the Nazis were using infected prostitutes in Lisbon as a means of passing it on to Allied sailors. The arrival of American soldiers in 1942 caused VD infection to reach almost epidemic proportions – although British soldiers returning form overseas service must take some of the blame.

The massive social dislocation caused by the war and the fact that nobody was left untouched by its

Take your partner: VE Day in Princes Street Gardens in Edinburgh as the nation celebrates the end of the World War Two

FEEDING THE COUNTRY

THE impact of war had an immediate effect on the countryside, as Britain began to worry about its ability to feed its people. By 1939, most of the country's food had to be imported and with supply lines at risk an increase in agricultural production became an urgent priority. Forty district Agricultural Executive Committees were set up to oversee production and maximise input.

Farming was a reserved occupation and vital industry and, especially after the fall of France, measures were taken to ensure that it had an adequate supply of labour. The Women's Land Army and the smaller Women's Timber Corps were created to provide the feminine muscle. Numbering 10,000 by 1943, the women drove tractors, planted crops,

For a healthy, happy job

Join the
WOMEN'S
LAND
ARMY

APPLY TO NEAREST W.L.A. COUNTY OFFICE OR TO W.L.A. HEADQUARTERS 6 CHESHAM PLACE LONDON S.W.1

tended livestock, brought extra land into cultivation, and mended fences.

The work was hard and there were many teething problems as young girls from the city arrived in the countryside with no previous experience of rural life. In spite of the farmers' initial protestations that the women were 'bloody useless', they soon became indispensible. Not only did they restore life to a sector of society sorely affected by social problems in the inter-war years, they achieved the goal of increased production. During the war the production of oats rose by 33%, wheat 32%, barley 72% and potatoes 57%, all of which was due in no small measure to the work of the Women's Land Army.

consequences meant that its end was euphorically celebrated. VE (Victory in Europe) Day and VJ (Victory in Japan) Day in 1945 witnessed scenes of unbridled joy. Huge crowds congregated in every Scottish city, town and village. The streets were packed full of dancing and singing crowds and church bells, silent for the duration as an agreed signal of invasion, rang for the first time in six years. Although the war had witnessed a rise in class tensions and the harmony of everyone 'pulling together' for victory was a largely an invention of government propaganda, there was genuine optimism in the air. There would be a New Scotland as part of a New Britain and the country was to be a more just and caring society. After all, that was why the war had been fought.

The New Britain

1945-67

❦

I N the aftermath of the Second World War, an ideological wind was blowing through British politics that had profound implications for the way post-war Scottish society would develop. The exigencies of wartime had demanded a full and total mobilisation of the resources of the British state. Every aspect of public and private life, from the work people did to the food they ate, was controlled by government. The Scottish economy had pumped out huge quantities of armament production for the war effort with no thought of what would happen once the war was over. Tom Johnston, by far the most gifted Labour politician in Scotland, had been appointed Secretary of State by Churchill's coalition government in May 1941 and he used his position not only to promote the Scottish war effort but also to plan the blueprint for post-war reconstruction. He was able to build on the seeds of corporatism which had been planted in the inter-war years. The committees of reconstruction which he instigated were designed to reflect and combine the different interests of labour, industry and the government. Johnston demanded, and received, substantial powers from Westminster, using the threat of Scottish nationalism and warning that it had shown some signs of stirring into life during wartime by-elections.

The age of corporatism had been ushered in, and Scotland's future, it was decided, could no longer be left to the haphazard fate of the free market. It would have to be planned and managed by experts.

The Clyde Valley Plan was designed to diversify the Scottish economy and reduce its traditional dependence on heavy industry. The mood of social optimism in wartime Britain, which followed the publication of the Beveridge Report, laying the foundations of the welfare state and promising state support from 'cradle to grave', was particularly enthusiastic in Scotland. The revolution in political culture, which expected and demanded that the state be pro-active in guaranteeing the social and economic well-being of all its citizens, was sweet music to the ears of a society which had suffered more than most between the wars. With the welfare state and the managed economy enshrined as a fundamental tenet of British political faith at the end of the war, Scottish politicians had, at last, the answers to the problems which had so persistently defied solution. Furthermore, by setting the example of wringing concessions from the cabinet, Johnston had set the benchmark by which future Scottish Secretaries would be judged in the new Britain.

❦

A street party in Corunna Place, Leith, celebrates the end of the War in 1945

The commitment to the welfare state and the managed economy had a greater resonance north of the Border because there was so much more for government to do in terms of social and economic policy than there was in England. The nationalisation of the key industries of coal, electricity, transport and eventually steel, by Attlee's government – with Labour MPs singing the Red Flag in the chamber of the House of Commons to irritate the Tory opposition – meant the Scottish

Clement Attlee,
Labour Prime Minister in 1945
in an optimistic Britain

THOMAS JOHNSTON
1881-1965

BORN in Kirkintilloch, Johnston started his working life as a journalist after being educated at Lenzie Academy and Glasgow University. In 1906, as a member of the Independent Labour Party he founded the Socialist weekly *Forward* that was to have an influential role in the development of the modern Labour movement. First elected as the MP for West Stirling in 1922, he won twice more with a five-year spell as MP for Dundee.

He was appointed Secretary of State in Churchill's coalition government of 1941 and set up the blueprints for reconstruction of Scotland even as the war was on. He created the Scottish Council (Development and Industry) in 1942. After the war he became chairman of the North of Scotland Hydro Electric Board.

economy was more dependent on central government control than its southern neighbour. Consequently, the Scottish nation came to rely on the British state as the principal determinant and provider of its economic well-being, and look to the Labour Party as its benign protector.

Initial optimism that the Scottish economy would finally be able to diversify away from the traditional heavy industries, was soon confounded and then meekly accepted. The war had cost the British state dear and the welfare reforms of the Labour governments of 1945-51 had put a heavy strain on the British treasury. There were two economic consequences of this. First, government did not have the financial resources to implement a thoroughgoing policy of diversification for Scotland. Secondly, the heavy industries became valuable export earners in the late 1940s and 1950s through European and British imperial reconstruction. It was found that full employment could be achieved within the existing economic framework and,

in the short-run, no structural alterations were needed. It was politically expedient, too, as it avoided antagonising the trade unions, which had no wish to see the power and influence of their industries, and the position of the union leaders within them, diminished.

The Scottish economy was able to boom relatively unchallenged in the early 1950s, largely because there was no international competition from war-ravaged Europe and the Far East, but it was not a situation that could last indefinitely.

By 1958, it was becoming apparent that the Scottish economy was running into difficulties. Dependence on the heavy industries had increased and the failure to diversify was now beginning to tell. Productivity was poor and the economic growth rate of 9% was half the UK average up to 1960. Income per head of population was trailing 13% behind the British average. Foreign companies supplying the new consumer industries began to set up shop while the traditional industries seemed impervious to any notions of modernisation. Management and trade unions colluded to retain old working practices and shunned new investment. In shipbuilding, the family dynasties paid little heed to rationalisation, marketing and design improvement. Deflation and public expenditure cuts in 1957, coupled with the ending of national service, meant the jobless total in Scotland doubled in the space of 12 months to 116,000. The solution to this, best exemplified by the Toothill Report of 1961, was for more planning and better targeted regional assistance. The umbilical connection between Scottish economic well-being and central British state economic policy was now explicit.

Social reconstruction was a key objective of the post-war Labour government, and housing, affected by wartime bombing, neglect, and a shortage of privately rented accommodation, was a priority. It was clear a major house-building programme was required to meet the aspirations of people and politicians. With a consensus that the state was responsible for social welfare, attention focused on council housing but a combination of high standards and lack of building materials produced slow progress. Tower blocks, 'pre-fabs' and 'New Towns' were the pragmatic solutions offered by experts and favoured by the incoming Conservative administrations after 1951. Not only were such schemes more economical, they were the only way the government could be seen to be keeping its side of the bargain. The scale of building was impressive, with 38,000 homes going up in 1954 alone.

The construction plans were, however, soon political claims. The Scottish Office and local authority councillors deployed their influence

More than one million men were de-mobbed and returned to civvy street during 1946

Miners at Loganlea Colliery in West Lothian during the 1950s believed they had jobs for life as employees of the State

to further their own interests, often at the expense of residents. Glasgow District Council kept the Scottish Special Housing Association at arm's length, fearing encroachment into its fiefdom. Zealous councillors and MPs stamped their own brands of teetotalism and anti-capitalism onto new housing estates by denying space for shops and pubs.

Full employment brought relative prosperity to Scotland in the 1950s, and the wages differential with England narrowed for a time. The impact of the National Health Service and increased purchasing power led to a marked improvement in the nation's health. Infant mortality rates decreased, the average height of children increased, people lived longer.

It was a time when the British state was able to deliver on its promises and domestic politics was characterised by a neat balancing act. In the general elections between and including 1950 and 1964, the Unionists averaged 46% of the vote, while Labour averaged 47%. More than anything, the vagaries of the first-past-the-post electoral system accounted for the loss and gain of seats. Political success in Scotland was dependent, as it was in the UK, on the ability of parties to present themselves as the most capable of managing the country. Although there was little difference between Unionists and Labour, either in terms of the share of votes or Westminster seats, the Unionists can be said to have been most successful because Scotland's social structure was more inclined towards traditional Labour voters.

The appeal to the consumer society, in the 1951 election, was set against Labour's record of food rationing and post-war austerity and Unionists were also playing the nationalist card. Nationalisation of key industries was denounced as 'de-nationalisation' for Scotland because control of the

WILLIAM HENRY BEVERIDGE
1879-1963

THE author of the famous report, which laid the foundations for the Welfare State, was born in India of Scottish parentage.

He was educated at Charterhouse public school and Oxford University before setting out on his career as an economist, administrator and social reformer. His first analysis of unemployment was made in 1909. He was director of the London School of Economics from 1919 to 1937 and a member of several economic commissions. His Report on Social Insurance and Allied Services was published in 1942 at the height of the war and proposed 'cradle to grave' provision of benefits for every citizen regardless of social class or income.

Briefly a Liberal MP, he was made a Baron in 1946.

economy moved to London. Socialism was condemned for its centralising tendencies which took no account of the distinctiveness of the Scottish nation. To reinforce the message at the 1955 election the saltire was used as the symbol of the Unionist party. It notched up over 50% of the vote.

An extended family take tea in their Glasgow tenement home in the kind of overcrowded conditions that led to a major expansion in housebuilding in the 1950s. City centre slum dwellers were decanted to outlying estates and new towns like East Kilbride and Glenrothes

The State will Provide

IN the half century since 1945, the role of the British state in Scotland's economy and society has been large and significant – more so than in England.

Government spending per capita in Scotland was well above the rest of mainland Britain. In the mid-1970s, average state expenditure for the UK was £708, but in Scotland it was £866, more than 20% higher. Taxation revenue per head at that time was £730 for the UK, but £695 for Scotland, 5% lower.

The reasons for the enhanced role of the state are numerous. First, the two dominant ideas of the political consensus which dominated British politics between 1945 and 1975 called imperiously for the state to act to eradicate all perceived problems and impose uniform standards. On one hand, the raw Keynesianism embraced by both parties made it almost mandatory that governments should intervene vigorously to stimulate economic activity in underperforming areas. On the other hand, the ethos of the welfare state in social policy required the attainment not just of better health and social security provision, but also of uniform standards across the whole UK. Secondly, of course, there were vital political benefits. Both parties believed unquestioningly that the delivery of better health and social security services, along with the creation of full employment, were the keys to electoral success. Hence, after the 1959 general election, when Labour did markedly better in Scotland than in England, the Conservative government for the next five years sharply stepped up its engagement in Scottish economic development.

The state's prominent economic role in Scotland initially arose because so much of Scottish economic activity in 1945 was geared to basic industry. Labour's sweeping nationalisation programme in the later 1940s had a huge impact in Scotland, where coal mining, transport and steel making were on a larger scale than in England.

As the Scottish heavy industry sector flailed around helplessly from the mid 1950s, government involvement in economic affairs escalated. The steel giant, Colvilles, was effectively compelled by government to build the Ravenscraig mill at Motherwell even though the company harboured serious and, as it turned out, accurate reservations. The abortive effort begun in the 1960s to establish car production on a mass scale at Linwood in Renfrewshire was a government diktat to private manufacturers, with Bathgate and Linwood the result.

The 1960s and 1970s, perhaps, saw state activity in economic matters at its peak, with subsidies, incentives and initiatives dangled in front of businesses in a bid to induce them to settle in Scotland. Between 1961 and 1976, by one calculation, regional assistance to Scotland rose by over 1,500%, and it was receiving a larger share of support than any other British region.

The persistent weakness of the Scottish economy meant that for at least 40 years after 1945, Scottish unemployment levels were about half as high again as English rates, yet wage rates were invariably lower – typically by between 5% and 10%. Additionally, larger family size in Scotland meant that per capita income was well below the British norm. A 1975 study revealed that 24.7% of the worst census districts for multiple deprivation were located in Clydeside whereas, on a strictly proportionate basis, the region should have had a mere 4.3%. These critical social conditions necessitated high levels of state spending.

Nowhere was this trend more apparent than in housing. In England, the state-subsidised public sector took a subordinate share, but in Scotland it was invariably the major partner. By

WILLIAM ROSS
Lord Ross of Marnock
1911-88

THE son of a train driver, born in Ayr, Ross attended Ayr Academy and Glasgow University and then worked as a school teacher until the Second World War.

It was 1946 when he was elected as the Labour MP for Kilmarnock at a by-election. He was to represent the constituency at Westminster for three decades, until he was created a life peer in 1979 and sent to take up his seat in the Lords.

He remains the longest-serving Secretary of State for Scotland, in office for two stints – firstly from 1964 to 1970, and then from 1974 to 1976. He was the politician chiefly responsible for setting up the Scottish Development Agency and the Highlands and Islands Development Board to handle the Labour government's interventionist policies.

1980, 54% of Scottish housing stock was publicly owned, against only 30% in England.

In 1939, the infant mortality rate in Scotland – the most reliable index of wider social deprivation – was a third higher than the UK average. After the foundation of the National Health Service in 1948, the rate fell markedly. Nevertheless, after 1948 health problems associated with poor social conditions continued at higher rates in Scotland: heart disease, alcoholism, tuberculosis, chest and stress-related ailments all underlined this. The upshot was a requirement for more spending in Scotland on health and a better ratio of doctors, nurses, hospital beds and ancillary services than England enjoyed.

By the end of the 1960s, dissatisfaction with the role of the British state mounted as the relative failure of the approaches adopted since 1945 became evident. However, the critiques and

The giant Ravenscraig mill was built to government order by a private steel industry highly sceptical about its viability

———— ☙ ————

solutions differed widely. For some, the problem lay in the constitutional structure: Scottish needs and demands were not being properly articulated in the governmental process, and inappropriate policies were being formulated. What was needed, insisted this camp, was greater oversight of Scottish affairs outwith Westminster – either by devolution of power to a Scottish assembly, or by the achieving of complete independence.

Others took a different reading of the state's shortcomings. They concluded the government could not operate the economy more effectively than the markets, and that welfare spending created a culture of

dependency, sapping initiative and self-reliance. For this group, the remedies were straightforward: the state should retreat wherever practicable.

It was this body of opinion that captured the Tory party in the middle 1970s, and the two decades after Margaret Thatcher's election victory in 1979 saw the implementation of these ideas. Regional aid for industry was cut back throughout the 1980s. State subsidies on housing were almost extinguished, so that by 1995 public sector house-building in Scotland had shrunk from its apogee in the 1950s of 35,000-a-year to a derisory 468 – against 17,000 private sector houses built. The sale of council houses reinforced this trend. Yet, perversely, under the Conservatives spending per capita in Scotland still comfortably outstripped England. The British state continued to play a more significant role north of the Border.

CHAPTER 17

The High Tide of Nationalism

1967-79

THE SLICK presentation of Harold Wilson and the Labour Party seized power from the Tories in 1964. The persistent weakness of the Scottish economy and the raised expectations of its workforce had made Scots receptive to higher bids for their votes. Labour made the bid and cashed in with its thin seven-seat majority at Westminster dependent on 15 constituency successes in Scotland.

Wilson's government, glorying in the application of 'the white heat of technology', immediately embarked on an ambitious project of state-sponsored economic expansion north of the Border. The Highlands and Islands Development Board and regional economic boards were created to oversee a massive public expenditure programme designed to beef up the economic infrastructure by concentrating on health, housing, transport and education. Job creation was a central component of this strategy with the hope that the new employment opportunities created as new industries were encouraged to set up would offset losses in the struggling heavy industries.

Proper economic planning was sacrificed on the altar of political expediency to ensure the government's UK majority by keeping the Scots onside, especially after 1967 when Winnie Ewing won the Hamilton by-election

for the SNP. The Scottish Secretary, William Ross, rammed home the message about the dangers of a nationalist upsurge and screwed more and more money out of the Cabinet. By the late 1960s, public expenditure in Scotland was running 20% above the British average. Poor industrial relations, incompetent and inexperienced planning and planners, wild optimism, oscillating levels of public expenditure and short-term political calculations all combined to produce a litany of economic failure. Full employment and prosperity could only be maintained by unrealistically high levels of public expenditure while a complacent Scottish economy again failed to take heed of warnings and branch out from its heavy industrial base.

The SNP victory at Hamilton terrified the Labour Party because it was a response to the first signs of worsening economic circumstances with rising unemployment and falling standards of living concentrated in Scotland compared with the rest of the UK. The SNP was seen as an effective stick with which to beat Labour. Few endorsed the nationalist manifesto of independence, yet many were impressed with the amount of attention an SNP victory could secure from a nervous British political establishment. However, nationalist progress in the late 1960s was erratic and the party

`WINIFRED EWING

1929-

A QUALIFIED lawyer born in Glasgow, it was her victory in the 1967 Hamilton by-election that established the SNP as a significant political force. She held the seat for only three years, but was then returned to Westminster riding on the crest of the nationalist wave in 1974, as the MP for Moray and Nairn, when she ousted Gordon Campbell, the incumbent Tory Secretary of State. When she lost the Moray seat in 1979, in the election that followed the inconclusive devolution referendum, she was elected, the same year, as Euro MP for the Highlands and Islands. She still holds this position today, and has gained the title Madame Ecosse as a gesture to her elder stateswoman status with the party and in tribute to her flamboyant political style.

She was among the first intake of MSPs to the new Scottish parliament and her seniority made her the obvious choice to call it to order when it held its first public session after being in abeyance for almost 300 years.

won only one seat in the general election of 1970. Labour was still trusted on corporatism and the 1970 Conservative government of Edward Heath proved, in spite of some assertions to the contrary, equally keen to prop up the Scottish economy with state support. The rescue of Rolls-Royce and the Upper Clyde Shipyard, together with increased public expenditure, did nothing to alter the course of Scottish economic development.

The rise of the SNP, in the mid-1970s, was a response to the crisis in British politics inspired domestically by the miners strike and internationally by the sharp hike in oil prices following the Arab-Israeli conflict of 1973. Spiralling inflation, rising unemployment and deteriorating industrial relations demanded immediate and special government attention. The threat of secession from the British state, backed up with the prospect of future wealth from North Sea oil, ensured that Scotland was not ignored. The SNP won almost a third of the vote in the second general election of 1974 and sent 11 MPs to Westminster.

Opinion poll evidence suggests that SNP success was based on a protest vote, as only 12% of the electorate admitted to supporting independence. The protest worked by pushing Scotland up the British political agenda. Again, the Labour government's response to the SNP surge was based on political expediency because its wafer-thin majority in the House of Commons relied on Scottish seats. Devolution as a strategy was promoted, not because it was believed to be worthwhile in itself, but because it was hoped it would take the sting out of the appeal of nationalism.

The second 1974 general election sent 11 Nationalist MPs to Westminster, the largest representation the party has achieved in the British parliament

*(left to right)
Douglas Crawford,
George Reid,
Gordon Wilson,
Douglas Henderson,
Winnie Ewing,
Donald Stewart,
Margaret Bain,
Hamish Watt,
Iain MacCormick,
Andrew Welsh,
George Thompson*

The Scottish Assembly, as proposed by Labour, was more or less doomed from the outset. It would have had few powers and was a poor palliative to the mounting economic problems created by the abandonment of demand management and cuts in public expenditure which were conditions of the loan from the International Monetary Fund which baled Britain out of bankruptcy.

The Assembly also had little support in principle. The SNP were half hearted, viewing it as a stepping stone to independence. Labour commitment was conditioned by an anti-nationalist strategy and the party had a significant hostile element which used every opportunity to sabotage it. The Conservatives, with their business allies, were totally against it despite being in favour of some form of assembly on paper. Neither could the Assembly command sufficient public support.

Although the 1979 referendum had a peculiar clause, which dictated that at least 40% of the electorate would have to vote in favour before it could be enacted, the fact remains that the Scots were deeply divided about devolution. There was a low turn-out and the 'yes' vote was only 2% higher than the 'no' vote. It did not provide a ringing endorsement.

Evidence as to the real political priorities of the Scottish electorate was to be found in the general election later that year, when a substantial proportion of the SNP vote reverted back to Labour in a vain endeavour to block the forces of the Thatcherite free-market economy and hold on to the cosy vision of the British corporate state. However, it was too late. The post-war experiment of a 'new Britain' had failed.

Scotland Says No at First Time of Asking

FOR 18 years, Scottish home rulers insisted devolution was not defeated in 1979. With the Scottish parliament now established, they can now face up to their past.

The anti-devolution forces won the 1979 referendum by all but one standard. The one standard was, however, important. A clear, if small, majority did vote for a Scottish assembly (as it was then styled) but the result was still a defeat. Only 51.6% of those who voted did so in favour of the 1978 Scotland Act.

The expectation that a much larger majority for devolution would be won was evident in the willingness of some pro-devolution forces to participate in what they later described as a 'rigged referendum'. The 40% rule had been passed by Westminster requiring that that proportion of the eligible electorate (not just a majority of those who voted) had to vote in favour of the measure to ensure its implementation. The actual proportion of the electorate which voted 'Yes' was only 32.9%, and if the problems had been realised some pro-devolutionists at least would have boycotted the referendum. By participating they gave the result legitimacy.

Early polls had suggested that the 40% might indeed be overcome. So what went wrong? There were a number of factors which led to the closing of the gap, as indicated by the polls in the late 1970s, between pro- and anti-devolutionists. These were to provide important lessons to those involved in the 1997 referendum. First, there was the 'Winter of Discontent' of 1978-79, months before the referendum held on March 1. The perception of rampant, militant trade unionism, severe economic problems and a tired Labour government coming to the end of a difficult period in office did not augur well for the prospect of a measure passed, however unenthusiastically, by that party.

Labour's campaign material had used the picture of Prime Minister Jim Callaghan when he was at his least popular. By contrast, the Tories, the only party officially opposed to devolution, appeared fresh, united and ready for government.

Second, the parties officially supporting devolution were far from united. Labour sent out confused messages to its supporters with a vociferous and effective minority of key figures openly hostile to devolution. Divisions between Labour and the SNP were unhelpful. Helen Liddell, Labour's general secretary, had infamously remarked that her party would not 'soil its hands' by working with the SNP. This reflected the assumption that victory was already won and both Labour and SNP were determined to claim credit for the setting up of the Scottish assembly and unwilling to share the spoils. The Nationalists, too, were in internal disarray. Then it was an amateurish party with poor leadership, especially when compared with what it has since become.

On the other hand, the Conservative campaign was well-financed and focused. Devolution equals more bureaucracy, more taxation, more politicians, the campaign literature stressed. Abstruse seminars fronted by distinguished professors were organised by the umbrella group 'Yes for Scotland', while its opponents kept the negative message crystal clear, often employing wit in the process. 'Nice Girls Say No' ran one Federation of Conservative Students' sticker of the time, while po-faced pro-devolutionists were explaining the operation of the Judicial Committee of the Privy Council under a devolved system.

The 'No' campaign was successful in projecting an image of unity though

SIR ALEC DOUGLAS-HOME

1903-95

HOME of the Hirsel was born in London and educated at Eton and Oxford University. The heir to a family estate near Coldstream in Berwickshire, he served as Neville Chamberlain's secretary in the years preceding the outbreak of war in 1939. In 1950 he became Minister of State at the Scottish Office and a year later inherited his peerage as the 14th Earl of Home. After the resignation of Harold Macmillan in 1963 he was selected by the 'magic circle' to be Prime Minister but had to renounce his peerage and fight a by-election at Kinross to get into the Commons. He remained prime minister only one more year. On the eve of the 1979 devolution referendum he advised Scots to vote 'no' to the Scotland Bill offered by Labour on the grounds that the Tories would then have the opportunity to bring forward better proposals.

February 1979: Sheriff Peter Thomson, the maverick founder of the Scottish Plebiscite Society, warns that time is running out

⚘

disparate figures, such as Teddy Taylor, still a Glasgow Tory MP, and Robin Cook, still then a Labour left-winger. Through 'Scotland Says No', the Conservatives ran a campaign harnessing business hostility to the idea of devolution. Businesses threatened to leave a devolved Scotland. The Clydesdale Bank sent letters to its customers explaining why devolution was bad for them, while a small band of pro-devolution businessmen attempted valiantly, but unsuccessfully, to counter this message.

The 'Labour Vote No' campaign was designed to encourage doubts among Labour voters. Led by MPs Tam Dalyell and Brian Wilson, it managed to win a court ruling halting party political broadcasts – three to one in favour of devolution – on the grounds that the parties neither reflected public opinion nor were so relevant in a referendum as in an election.

The intervention which was most significant was Lord Home's. Former Prime Minister and Foreign Secretary, this elder statesman and retired Scottish MP had produced a pro-devolution document for the Tories a decade before. But, in a speech at Edinburgh University, Home urged Scots to vote 'No' in order to ensure that a better measure would be enacted – with tax-raising powers, proportional representation and fewer members. Margaret Thatcher, then Tory Leader, concurred and, in her eve of poll statement, promised that a 'No' vote would not mean an end to devolution. Home and Thatcher were unwittingly correct, but only in the long term.

In retrospect, the 1979 referendum was ultimately important in the establishment of the Scottish parliament. Political lessons were learned which ensured victory for the devolutionists 18 years later.

The Saga of the Stone of Destiny

THE STONE OF DESTINY is a legendary, but very real, lump of rock which was an important element in the coronation rituals of the early Scots kings.

Its supposed power to endow kings with legitimacy led Edward I, also known as the Hammer of the Scots, to steal it from its original home at Scone Abbey, near Perth, in 1296. It was his attempt to emasculate the troublesome neighbouring kingdom in the north and show the Scots just who was boss on the British Isles.

Whether or not the English raiding party, which seized the stone, got the right one is a matter for conjecture. The stone has been referred to as a black basalt block covered in intricate carvings, the 'Jacob's pillow', as referred to in the Bible brought to Scotland from the Holy Land.

What the English got was a 335lb of weathered local sandstone. The abbot at Scone, aware the English looters were on their way, may or may not have switched the genuine article for the cover of a cesspit. However, in the final analysis, since it was all about gestures and symbolism, Edward was happy to take any stone from Scone for the purposes of one-upmanship.

The vague myth that Scotland would be independent only if the stone was returned to its home was dented less than 20 years later when, with it safely ensconced in the south, the invading English were routed at the Battle of Bannockburn and Robert Bruce declared the Scottish nation free of outside domination.

A few hundred years were to pass before James VI of Scotland sat on the throne, and on the stone, in England to proclaim himself James I and monarch of both kingdoms. It took another 100 years for the United

Mr Wishart, the Ministry of Works custodian at Arbroath Abbey, keeps an eye on the Stone after it was returned in April 1951

Kingdom to emerge from the 1707 Treaty of Union and another few hundred years before the stone, nestling comfortably in a specially built compartment beneath the coronation throne at Westminster Abbey, leapt back into the public consciousness.

It was in the winter of 1950 that four nationalist-minded students – Ian Hamilton, Gavin Vernon, Alan Stuart and Kay Matheson – strolled into the abbey and nicked the stone. They loaded it into the boot of a car, dropping it on the way so that it broke in two, and headed north for the Border.

The disappearance of the stone became a cause célèbre, once again endowing it with the kind of political significance that had lain dormant for

almost 700 years. The police hunted for it throughout Scotland and eventually, on the promise that the case would not be pursued if the stone was returned, it was left to be found at Arbroath Abbey. The choice of site had obvious political overtones, Arbroath being the title of the famous 1320 declaration 'So long as 100 of us remain alive, we will never give up our freedom but with our lives…' And, as at Scone itself in 1296, an alternative story was soon put about that a fake stone had been substituted to fool the authorities.

Not that it really mattered, unless the Stone of Destiny does have genuinely supernatural powers, since the point of it has always been its symbolism.

And so, the stone was transported back to Westminster Abbey and slipped back under the throne in plenty of time for the coronation of Elizabeth II in 1953, although nationalists and some objective historians pointed out that since there had never been an Elizabeth I in Scotland, the numbering was erroneous. However, the stone beneath the throne was deemed to make her title legitimate.

And there the stone remained, protected by extra security systems, until the second half of the final decade of the 20th century when Scottish Secretary, Michael Forsyth, persuaded the cabinet and the Queen that the Scots might be less hostile if it was sent back north amid much pomp and circumstance. This would show just how seriously the Conservatives took Scotland, where popular support for a devolved parliament ran directly counter to Tory notions of the future integrity of the United Kingdom.

SIR MICHAEL FORSYTH

1954-

SCOTLAND'S most combative post-war Conservative Secretary of State, a conviction politician and supporter of Margaret Thatcher, he was always in a minority both in Labour-dominated Scotland and within his own Scottish party. Educated at Arbroath High School and St Andrews University, he entered the Commons in 1983 as Tory MP for Stirling. After the 1992 general election, when John Major decided a less aggressive style was needed in Scotland, he was moved from the Scottish Office, only to be brought back later in the top job as a bulwark of the Unionist cause and opponent of devolution. In 1997, however, he presided over the annihilation of Conservative representation in Scotland. He dropped out of the public eye and refused to participate in the devolution referendum the same year, starting a new career in investment banking. He remains closely involved behind the scenes in Scottish politics.

Michael Forsyth returns the Stone after 700 years
but it was too late to save the Tory Secretary of State's political skin

Once more, it was all about symbolism but Forsyth's grand gesture, made at the last moment as he saw the final vestiges of electoral support vanishing, did him little good. On St Andrew's Day, 30 November, 1996, the stone was driven up the Royal Mile in Edinburgh under a see-through bubble on the back of a converted army Land Rover while the band of the Royal Marines played and the Royal Company of Archers escorted it up the hill to the castle. But the average Scot in the street seemed more bemused than beholden by the sight of the stone being sent back to be installed as a tourist attraction in Edinburgh Castle.

People either did not care that much, or they resented being expected to be grateful for the return of something which had been stolen in the first place, an attitude reinforced by the official explanation that the stone was being restored to its rightful home.

At the general election of May 1997, Forsyth and the 10 other remaining Tory MPs in Scotland, who alone among the political parties had opposed the least measure of devolution, were all defeated. In the referendum a few months later, 74.3% of the population voted for the re-establishment of a Scottish parliament almost 300 years after it had voted itself out of existence.

The Stone of Destiny, fake or not, is now assured of its place in Scotland and is likely to remain for the foreseeable future although an arrangement exists for it to be borrowed for any coronation ceremony at Westminster. Its own destiny may be to be incorporated as a central feature in the new parliament building under construction at Holyrood.

CHAPTER 18

The Road to Holyrood

1979-99

❦

In 1979, the incoming Conservative government invoked Thatcherism and tried to stamp out all prospect and hope of devolution. John Smith, however, kept the faith and the flame alive inside the Labour Party thoughout the long years in the political wilderness that were to follow the failed referendum.

In the recession of the early 1980s, the old industrial structure was finally swept away by the chill winds of international competition as the state switched off the life support of public finance and Scotland braced itself for one of the most profound periods of change in its history.

The 'Thatcher experiment' forced a radical restructuring of the economy. Paradoxically, the heavy social security costs which then followed were underwritten by the returns from North Sea oil which began to flow into Treasury coffers. Oil perhaps illustrates the greatest indictment of the generic weaknesses of the Scottish economy. Its discovery should have been a great opportunity for Scottish business, but domestic industry was ill equipped and slow to take advantage. Initially, the economy of the American state of Texas derived greater benefit from the discovery of oil in Scottish waters than the Scots themselves.

Once oil was sorted out, it became a major growth point for the Scottish economy during the 1980s along with electronics, tourism, energy and financial services, dragging it more into line with England. Indeed, by the 1990s, the economy was in relatively good shape compared with other parts of the UK and second only to the south east of England in terms of per capita income and low unemployment. On a whole range of socio-economic indicators, Scotland was able to measure up to the European Union average.

But, as Scotland and England became more alike in the social and economic sense, the more they remained apart politically. The greater the social convergence became, it seemed, the greater the political divergence.

Scottish politics has been marked by one striking feature: anti-Conservatism. This has reduced the party of British government in recent years to no more than a rump struggling to maintian its credibility north of the Border, with all representation at Westminster snuffed out in 1997. Much of this phenomenon can be explained in the context of nationalism (with a small 'n').

Margaret Thatcher's attack on the corporate state was interpreted as an attack on a fundamental part of Scottish political culture. Few Scots, even among the middle class, displayed the naked hostility to state intervention which formed such a crucial part of the Thatcherite vision. For all

JOHN SMITH
1938-94

His sudden death, from a heart attack, came just as the Labour Party was completing the process of modernisation that would end the Tories' long period of unchallenged power dating from 1979.

Smith was a QC, educated at Dunoon Grammar School and Glasgow University. He entered the Commons in 1970 and served under Harold Wilson and James Callaghan. He succeeded Neil Kinnock as Labour leader after the disastrous election of 1992, despite surviving a heart attack four years earlier which threatened his career, and used his unimpeachable reputation as a conviction politician to impose discipline and order on a party that seemed to have lost its way in factionalism.

Many Labour supporters regard him as their 'lost leader', the man who made Labour electable again. He retained unswerving support for devolution and is the author of the famous phrase that it was the 'settled will of the Scottish people'. He is buried on the island of Iona.

its manifest faults, the state had played a vital part in improving the lot of a great many Scottish people. Council housing, comprehensive education and the mixed economy were all firmly entrenched elements of Scottish society.

The sense of Scottish, small 'n', nationalism was promoted by the opposition parties, all of whom adopted some form of self-government as part of their manifestos. John Smith and Donald Dewar were long-term champions of devolution within the higher echelons of the Labour party.

Initially, the upsurge in demand for home rule was born out of the frustration that the Conservative electoral hegemony in England guaranteed power irrespective of what happened in Scotland. The poverty of Conservative support in Scotland did not stop unpopular policies such as the poll tax being imposed, in Scotland's case, a year ahead of England. Between 1986 and 1990 Malcolm Rifkind, who had resigned from the Tory front bench on principle because he wanted to campaign for a 'Yes' vote in the 1979 referendum, was the Secretary of State toeing the Thatcherite line.

In Scotland, a parliament in Edinburgh was promoted by opposition parties both as a protective device against hostile Conservative governments and as a measure to stop the escalating demands for political independence. The refusal of the Conservative party to countenance any form of self-government increased the popular perception of the government as alien, English and totally out of sympathy with Scotland.

Conservative unpopularity was not helped by the contradictory nature of its message. The central plank of Thatcherite ideology was the need for people to be self-reliant and stand on their own two feet. It was the message she delivered forcefully in a speech to the General Assembly of the Church of Scotland in 1988 that came to be known as the Sermon on the Mound.

Yet, in Scotland, the Tory party, to answer the claims of nationalists that Scotland only wanted to stand on its own two feet, argued that the Scots had become too reliant on subsidies to be capable of supporting themselves in the modern world. An implicit accusation of being 'subsidy junkies' was never likely to appeal to traditional

Conservative voters in Scotland who were already having a hard time accepting the early imposition of the poll tax, especially when poll tax protests in Scotland were largely ignored, and only riots in London forced the government to backtrack. John Major replaced Thatcher and although the Tories held their ground, both in Scotland and in the south, against the odds at the 1993 general election, by 1997 the party reaped the whirlwind and was not only defeated in the UK but totally wiped out in Scotland.

Finally, and perhaps most importantly, the issue of Britishness itself has determined Scotland's progress in the last quarter of the 20th century. In 1979, the Scottish nation kept true to its sense of British political values which were grounded in the principles of the managed, or at least mixed, economy and the welfare state. In the subsequent and following general elections the English nation rejected what were, to most Scots, core British values. The advent of Thatcherism had, in effect, made it difficult to retain a sense of British identity because it seemed the larger part of Britain did not share what Scotland regarded as British values. In effect, Scots have responded to Thatcher's Sermon on the Mound by taking her at her own word and assuming more responsibility for their own affairs through a devolution, a constitutional arrangement Thatcher abhorred. It is ironic the parliament meets in the chamber where Thatcher made her seminal speech.

⌖

Poll tax protests turned to violence in London in 1990 and helped end Thatcher's grip on power (right)

Three years earlier Margaret Thatcher had arrived in Scotland to deliver her Sermon on the Mound (left)

What's It All About, Jock?

THE opening of the new National Museum of Scotland in Edinburgh on St Andrews Day, 30 November, 1998, stimulated a debate across the nation. Overnight, it seemed, Scots had become experts on museums and their contents. More than 50 years in the making NMS appeared as the morning star to a millennial dawn, as it attempted to illustrate, through its artefacts, several thousand years of prehistory and history.

Like all histories, the museum's version was subjective, though when squawks of dissent and derision greeted the discovery that there was apparently no mention of the great patriot William Wallace, there was a suspicion that the displays represented the establishment view.

Fortunately Wallace was later found lurking in a case devoted to trade but, apart from a few diehards who will forever confuse Mel Gibson with the hero of Stirling Bridge, what characterised the debate was its maturity. Nobody doubted that Scotland actually had a history. The issues were embraced in the same matter-of-fact way that the result of the 1997 referendum had been

———— ❦ ————

Sean Connery's portrayal of James Bond gave Scotsmen a flattering, if unsustainable and undeserved, reflection of themselves

received. Still, some remain to be convinced that politics was not riding on the back of a cultural revival rather than the other way about.

It does not seem so long ago that creative Scots would go off into paroxysms of angst about what it meant to be Scottish as they attempted to explore what was distinctive about Scottish literature, painting, films, theatre and pop music. Such matters now appear to be taken for granted.

Hugh MacDiarmid's reflections on Scottish poets dying to break 'the living tomb' of their people strike few chords with modern practitioners. Novelists of the earlier part of the century such as Gibbon and Gunn, brilliant though they undoubtedly were, now seem to have dwelt upon themes which were archetypically Scottish in a way which modern writers eschew. Alison Kennedy and Janice Galloway, to name only two, deal with universal themes in a Scottish context which is not overly intrusive. Love him or loathe him, Irvine Welsh explores a drug culture which is worldwide and whose victims could as well live and die in Los Angeles or Lisbon as in Leith.

The success of the teaching profession in introducing Scottish literature to the school curriculum has resulted in certain assumptions about that literature among the young so that novelists and poets are unquestioningly accepted in a way that, say, Scottish historians are not. Scottish writers are now part of the literary culture of school students in a way that was unthinkable only a generation ago.

Music has, of course, always been one of the major moulders of cultural identity. Andy Stewart and the White Heather Club traded on one kind of stereotype shored up on an annual basis by Scots ritual indulgence in a

The Stewart clan: Andy (left) and Rod at opposite ends of the musical spectrum but both hugely proud of their Scottish roots and heritage

Shangalang: The Bay City Rollers attracted a worldwide audience of screaming girls with their tartan-draped performances

bathos of maudlin sentimentality every New Year that provided steady work for the Alexander Brothers and Kenneth Mackellar.

Performers such as the tartan-jacketed Rod Stewart and the shrilly chauvinistic Bay City Rollers transferred plaid scarves from the football terraces to the concert halls of the world. Following on more thoughtfully, Runrig and Capercaillie scored massively with their nativist compositions, many of them wholly or partly in Gaelic. A legion of aspiring groups from the central belt, like Nazareth and Simple Minds, achieved hits by playing music which, although distinctive, was ultimately indistinguishable from transatlantic productions. A more overt Scottishness, that could nonetheless claim universal appeal, was shown by groups like The Proclaimers. They presented a harder edge when communicating directly with youth, and not only Scottish youth, whom their elders seemed intent upon trashing.

Certain facets of the Scottish tendency towards dissidence and protest were fostered by jazz bands and folk clubs throughout the land. Experimentation with traditional forms, particularly in Ireland, Canada and some parts of Europe, generated a music which was recognised as 'Celtic' yet internationalist. Bagpipes, for example, were made to perform in ways which gave traditionalists canniptions.

On cinema screens from the 1960s Sean Connery's portrayal of James Bond gave Scotsmen a flattering, if unsustainable and undeserved, reflection of themselves. Television treatments of the works of Lewis Grassic Gibbon depicted powerful and unforgettable women. While movies such as *Local Hero* and *Chariots of Fire* further embellished the 'nice guy' image of humorous Scots, always balanced by a number of nasty Scottish villains.

Big Yins: Billy Connolly's 'banana boots' have acquired glass case status as one of the exhibits at the People's Palace museum in Glasgow

incorrect jokes, are the Scots, relentlessly exploited on comedy shows and in advertisements. The gritty realism of 1960s and 1970s Scottish theatre fed the novels of McIlvanney and Kelman as well as movies which pushed the 'urban kailyard' figure of the hard man to the fore. Urban themes are also central to the work of artists such as Ken Currie, Peter Howson and Joyce Cairns, countered by the more upbeat images of Adrian Wisniewski.

Television has become a major growth area for Scottish culture. In addition to current affairs and news programmes, independent Scottish media companies are successfully promoting Scottish soaps, children's shows and comedy.

Scottish culture, in short, has developed a new confidence and created a sense of its own worth that is not confined to traditional rural or new urban 'kailyards'. The vibrancy of contemporary culture has been absorbed, to some degree, by politics. A neat link over the centuries was evident at the opening ceremony of the parliament when in the chamber Sheena Wellington sang Burns' 'A Man's a Man for A' That' and, outside, there was a concert by Shirley Manson and Garbage.

But Hollywood blockbusters such as *Rob Roy* and *Braveheart*, one dealing with honour and the other freedom, built upon existing Scottish homespun stereotypes which harked back not only to previous movies, but to literary creations of the early 19th century and beyond. Such movies did little for the status of women; Scottish society has remained curiously resistant to the issues raised by the women's movement. Bond, Taggart, Laidlaw and Rebus possibly do not supply good role models. But Billy Connolly apparently does, because the only minority in North America about whom it is still permissible to make politically

Irvine Welsh's iconclastic hymn to drug-sodden youth made the world sit up and take notice of a Scotland shorn of its traditional myths

THE NEW SCOTS

THE 20TH CENTURY has seen a large number of immigrants make Scotland their home. The Irish influx was more or less halted by the Depression of the 1920s but they remained the biggest group of New Scots in the period up to 1945 as other nationalities joined them.

At the outbreak of the Second World War there were 3,000 Italians living in Glasgow, the third largest community in Britain after London and Manchester, with many population pockets in small towns. Italians set up numerous ice cream parlours and fish and chip shops, establishing the fish supper as a traditional Scottish meal, while maintaining close contact with Italy. The appearance of Fascist clubs in the 1920s and 1930s was due more to social reasons than politics but it was a strong motivating factor in the internment of many immigrants on Italy's entry into the war in 1940, sparking anti-Italian riots.

Eastern Europe has also provided Scotland with immigrant communities, matching the Italians in numerical terms. Escaping from Tsarist 'Russification', there were Poles and Lithuanians in Scotland before the First World War, mainly working in the Lanarkshire coalfields. The Russian Revolution of 1917 and the Communist invasion of the Baltic states increased these numbers. During the Second World War, the Polish Free Army was based in Scotland with many exiles staying after the Soviet domination of Poland after 1945.

It was in the 1950s that immigrants began to arrive from the Indian sub-continent in significant

Bronzes by sculptor Sir Eduardo Paolozzi are installed at the new Museum of Scotland. Born in Leith in 1924 of immigrant Italian parents, he was interned during the war but is now part of the establishment

numbers to add to the 500 Sikhs and Hindus who lived in the central belt, although most preferred to take their chances in England where there were better job prospects. The expulsion of Asians from African States in the 1960s led to a greater presence in Scotland.

Scottish notions of themselves as a tolerant people were not always borne out by their reactions to the newcomers. Racist taunts and assaults were matched by endemic institutionalised racism that is still regarded as a problem today. There are now 50,000 Asians, about 1% of the population, who are New Scots. This includes Chinese and

Vietnamese, but the biggest group is Pakistani. As shopkeepers, they have made an indelible mark on Scottish society and, like the Italians before them, have altered the nature of Scotland's cuisine, making curry the favourite dish.

The English have emerged as a significant community in Scotland over the last 30 years, travelling north to take up a wide range of public sector and university jobs in the 1960s and 1970s. In recent times, the English have made a significant contribution to the Highlands by restoring smaller country hotels and revitalising the tourist industry.

A Landslide Followed by a Tidal Wave

THE GENERAL ELECTION on 1 May, 1997, ended 18 years of uninterrupted Conservative government in Britain. Labour's landslide victory put Tony Blair in Downing Street with a majority of 179, even larger than that achieved in the immediate post-war election of 1945, although the actual share of the vote at 45% was four points lower than Harold Wilson secured in 1964.

For the Conservatives, it was an unmitigated disaster. They were left with the lowest number of MPs since 1906 and the party lost every one of its 11 seats in Scotland and a total of seven Cabinet ministers across the country. Its share of the vote at 31% was their worst performance since 1832, although they did not descend to the 28% depths plumbed by Labour in the 1983 election.

The Nationalists made a few gains at the expense of the vanishing Tories but it was the scale of Labour's victory both in Scotland and in England and Wales that eclipsed all else, even the coincidence that the election was held on the 290th anniversary of the Treaty of Union which had abolished the original Scottish parliament.

Attention immediately turned to the devolution referendum promised in Labour's manifesto. There had been internal party wrangling over the referendum. Blair, assuming the leadership after the death of John Smith, had insisted on it although many in the Scottish party believed it unnecessary because a parliament was, in Smith's words, simply 'unfinished business' which needed no further legitimacy. Blair, however, argued that the mandate given by a referendum would pre-empt any blocking tactics which were expected from the still Tory-dominated House of Lords. This was sufficient to convert the Shadow Secretary of State,

Tony Blair, defender of the Union

———— ❧ ————

George Robertson, who had earlier publicly opposed the idea of a referendum, but it created an antipathy between many party members in Scotland and the London headquarters. Another source of tension was the two-question format, asking first if a parliament was wanted, and then separately if it should have tax-varying powers of up to 3p in the pound. This was interpreted, and not only by Nationalists, as further evidence of Blair's relative coolness towards the principles of devolved government. The counter argument from Blair's supporters was that a clear and unequivocal endorsement was required to ensure subsequent legislation was not delayed at Westminster.

Whatever, the motivation, one of the new Labour government's first acts was to introduce a bill to allow the

referendum. The date was set for 11 September and the campaigns got underway. Every political party supported the 'Yes Yes' option, apart from the Conservatives who, despite having many convinced devolutionists in their ranks, realised that it would have been just too hypocritical to reverse party policy so soon after taking a vehemently anti-devolution stance that had been comprehensively rejected.

The 'No No' campaigners were hamstrung politically and ineffectual, practically, while all the other major parties joined forces to jointly state the case for a 'Yes Yes' vote. The leaders of Labour, SNP, and Liberal Democrats shared platforms in what was to be a very one-sided campaign which was briefly suspended less than two weeks before the vote when the Princess of Wales was killed in a Paris car crash.

The result was never in doubt and, when it came, it was like a tidal wave. On the day, a total of 72% voted 'Yes' in favour of a parliament, and 60% added a second 'Yes' that it should have discretionary tax powers. Unlike 1979, support was uniformly spread across the country with every single region voting for the creation of a parliament, and only two, Orkney and Dumfries and Galloway, wishing to deprive it of the tax powers.

Clackmannanshire was the first to declare: 80% and 69%. Fife was the last: 76% and 65%. In between, the figures stacked up to show that a devolved parliament with tax-varying powers was indeed the 'settled will' of the people. East Renfrewshire, which until May had been a Tory stronghold, voted 'Yes Yes', 62% and 52%. Stirling, where former Tory Secretary of State, Michael Forsyth, lost his seat despite raising the spectre of the 'tartan tax', voted 68% and 59%. In West Lothian, where the local MP Tam Dalyell was one of the few Labour rebels to oppose devolution, the result was 80% and 68%.

The four cities made their choice: Glasgow 84% and 75%, Edinburgh 72% and 62%, Dundee 76% and 65%, Aberdeen 72% and 60%. The overall turnout at 57.8% was ten percentage points down on the general election figure but respectable enough to offer no crumb of comfort to opponents of devolution.

Tony Blair welcomed the result unreservedly. 'It was,' he said, 'a good day for Scotland, a good day for Britain, and a good day for the United Kingdom.' His controversial decision to hold a referendum had been entirely vindicated. The outcome brooked no argument. The result surpassed even the requirements of the 40% rule that had been designed to emasculate the vote in 1979. The will of the people could not now be denied.

The political truce was also over, with the parties now making individual preparations for the first exclusively Scottish parliamentary elections in

All pals for the referendum, SNP leader Alex Salmond, Secretary of State Donald Dewar, and Hollywood star Sean Connery, a celebrity advocate of independence

DONALD DEWAR

1937-

THE FIRST First Minister in the reconvened Scottish parliament, he was Secretary of State following Labour's 1997 election victory.

A contemporary of John Smith's at Glasgow University, he was first elected to Westminster when he won the Aberdeen South constituency in 1966. He lost it in 1970 and spent eight years practising as a lawyer before returning to the Commons in the Garscadden by-election of 1978. Chief opposition spokesman on Scottish affairs from 1983 and a lifelong supporter of devolution, he was chosen as the man with the best pedigree to oversee the first devolved Scottish Executive. Elected as an MSP in 1999 he, with several MPs from other parties, will hold a dual mandate until the next British general election, when he will stand down from Westminster.

almost 300 years. Labour abandoned the old Royal High School on Calton Hill which had been long been expected to be the home of the new parliament. It was now ruled out as too small, although it was suggested it had become too much of a 'nationalist shibboleth' for Labour to bear. A brand new building was commissioned on the site of an old brewery at Holyrood to be ready in 2001. It was decided that for the first few years the parliament would meet in the General Assembly Hall of the Church of Scotland on the Mound in Edinburgh.

A Scotland bill was drafted and began working its way through the legislative machinery at Westminster. Its first sentence, 'There shall be a Scottish parliament', was to come true in less than two years.

The Start of the New Song

THE first Scottish parliament since 1707 met in the summer of 1999. It was achieved by the consensus of almost all the Scottish people and most political parties and validated by a decisive vote in a national referendum which gained substantial majority support from all regions of the country and all social classes. It was indeed 'the settled will' of the Scottish nation.

The contrast with 1979 could not have been more dramatic. Then, legislation had been conceived for motives of expediency to see off the SNP rather than for genuine reasons of constitutional reform. Nevertheless, many saw the result as a failure of nerve and a comprehensive refutation of the claim that there was indeed a deep-seated national demand for Scottish devolution. In a celebrated cartoon in the *Glasgow Herald*, James Turnbull drew a lion refusing to leave its cage even though the door had been flung open. The caption read: 'I'm feart!'

Yet, less than two decades after the debacle of 1979, a strong national consensus on home rule had been achieved and a new Scottish parliament with much fuller powers than the discredited assembly had convened in Edinburgh. The Scottish middle and professional classes who were sceptical two decades ago were now supportive. Institutions such as the universities, strongly opposed in the 1970s, now warmly embraced devolution. The business community made little protest and committed itself to working with the parliament. The silence from all those traditional supporters of Unionism in the 1997 referendum campaign was almost audible. Clearly a change had occurred in attitudes during the 1980s and early 1990s. What had happened in these decades to cause such a transformation?

Scotland experienced a traumatic process of de-industrialisation in the early 1980s which brought pain and suffering to many communities. Decline and adjustment were inevitable but the process was hastened by the refusal of the Conservative government under Margaret Thatcher to provide the kind of state support and protection to which Scottish industry had been accustomed since 1945. Between 1976 and 1987 manufacturing capacity in Scotland fell by almost a third and by an even greater proportion in the west central heartlands of heavy industry.

At the same time a cleavage opened up between Scottish and English voting patterns. While the Conservative vote north of the Border fell into terminal decline, the Tories in the Midlands and south of England continued to pile up huge majorities and establish a veritable monopoly of power at Westminster. Mrs Thatcher's governments rejected the Union as a partnership to be worked out through a consensus and as discussion combining Scottish and London interests. No account was taken of the consistent rejection of Conservatism in Scotland. From the Tory perspective, the cancers of state control, corporatism and welfare dependency would have to be removed there as elsewhere in the UK.

Indeed, Mrs Thatcher showed her utter contempt for the subtleties of the Union relationship by imposing the poll tax first in Scotland as an experiment in what soon came to be regarded as a detested form of primitive and regressive taxation. The attack on the corporate state went down almost equally badly, not least because the Scots had gained more than most from the welfare state reforms post 1945 and regarded the new market philosophy as destructive of the community values they saw as central to their national identity.

All this gave a new impetus to the cause of home rule. The Union, which had been so benign from 1945, was now also seen to have the potential

The parliament in session in its temporary home on the Mound

The Queen processes up the Royal Mile to formally open the new parliament

———— ❧ ————

for repression. Nor was there any machinery in the British constitution by which specifically Scottish interests could be safeguarded in the event of permanent English majorities at Westminster. Under earlier governments, this problem had rarely surfaced. Now, the Scottish people were brought face to face with the awesome reality of the absolute authority of the crown in parliament. As Canon Kenyon Wright, chairman of the Scottish Constitutional Convention, put it: 'We realised that our real

enemy was not a particular government, whatever its colour, but a constitutional system. We came to understand that our central needs, if we were to be governed justly and democratically, was not just to change the government but to change the rules.'

But it was only after another Conservative victory, in 1987, that the movement 'to change the rules' began in earnest. The Campaign for a Scottish Assembly had kept the torch of devolution alight after the fiasco of 1979, but for much of the 1980s, it was

virtually a voice crying in the wilderness. In 1988, a group of 'prominent Scots' appointed by the CSA issued 'A Claim of Right for Scotland' which stated the intellectual case for a parliament and recommended the establishment of the Constitutional Convention drawn from all the political parties and Scottish institutions.

In the event, neither the Conservatives nor the SNP took part. However, the absence of the nationalists probably made Labour more willing to make the kind of concessions, as in the important area of proportional representation, which in the 1997 referendum campaign helped to make the overall structure of the proposed parliament more acceptable to opinion outside the central lowlands than the assembly proposal of 1979. This was to be a devolution measure which was thought through rather than one concocted, as before, on the hoof. Crucially, too, it came with the support of representatives of Scottish trade unions, churches, local government and other organisations. The Labour party, which alone could deliver home rule at Westminster, was at the heart of the process and so could not easily renege on its commitments.

Amid some alarm in Scotland, however, Tony Blair proposed two referendums following a white paper that would be brought forward after a Labour general election victory. The decision suggested some anxiety about the prospects for devolution and brought back unhappy memories of 1979. But the huge Labour majority made those concerns irrelevant. The positive popular response to the referendums gave further legitimacy to the bill and possibly eased its passage in the House of Lords. The most far-reaching constitutional change in the Union of Parliaments since 1707 was achieved with remarkable speed and minimal dissent.

The Beginning of a New Song

I N July 1999 after almost three hundred years, Scottish history seemed to change its direction. Queen Elizabeth travelled north to open the new parliament and amid the pomp and circumstance of the royal visit, a republican note was struck with the singing of Robert Burn's 'A man's a man'. All agreed that it was a peculiarly Scottish event. On the occasion of the sitting of the last Scottish parliament, when it agreed to vote itself out of existence, Lord Belhaven bemoaned the passing of independence with the comment 'there's an end to an auld sang'. Belhaven's pessimism should be contrasted with the optimism which greeted the opening of the new parliament. Within a remarkably short period of time, the nation has been utterly transformed. The industries which were so important to our history have all but vanished to be replaced with electronics, petro-chemicals, banking and insurance and tourism. Glasgow, which was once second city of the empire, has been overtaken by Edinburgh as a new centre of economic dynamism. The nation of John Knox has given way to a secular and multi-cultural society. The 'blackness and despondency' which was often characterized as the hallmark of Scottish culture has been replaced with a new sense of identity which is confident and vibrant in its new found sense of Scottishness. And to cap it all, the nation has a new political sense of itself in the shape of its own parliament.

Scotland now has 143 MSPs (Members of the Scottish Parliament) and in the election of April 1999 the Labour Party won most seats, but not enough to form a government and had to rely on its Liberal Democrat allies to form a coalition government. The Scottish National Party (which advocates complete independence from Britain) emerged as the opposition. The Scottish parliament has power of legislation in 'domestic' issues with the London government retaining control over defence, foreign affairs and macro economic policy. While all may agree that the opening of the new parliament was the opening of a new chapter of Scottish history, there is no certainty as to how this chapter will end. The question many are now asking, and will continue to ask for some time, is whether the Scots having tasted political power will thirst for more leading to independence?

For many commentators, there is a belief that independence will be the final outcome of devolution. Indeed, a recent opinion poll by NOP showed that two thirds of Britons believe that Scotland will have an independent government within a generation. The argument that the creation of the Scottish parliament will lead to an inevitable drift towards independence is based on the following simple premise. If devolution works, then many Scots will assume that the parliament will perform better if it is given more powers. Members of the Scottish parliament will demand greater control of 'reserved' areas currently the preserve of London and devolution will lead to independence by stealth. Alternatively, if the Scottish parliament fails to realize the expectations of the Scottish people, then blame will focus on London because it has retained too much control. In order, to make the parliament work, it is argued, the reserved powers of Westminster should be brought under Scottish control which would lead to independence. In either scenario, it is claimed, independence will be the final outcome.

Yet, in spite of the alluring simplicity of this thesis, there are many problems which make it very difficult to predict with any degree of certainty the final destination of the devolutionary journey. Firstly, the whole concept of political independence is one that is increasingly difficult to realize in a world which is dominated by the global economy and trans-national groupings such as the European Union. Whereas the idea of the nation state made perfect sense in the latter part of the nineteenth and first half of the twentieth centuries, its role in the modern world has become increasingly obsolete. As the power of the European Union grows, national sovereignty in its traditional guise will become redundant. Monetary Union, co-ordinated defence and foreign policies, harmonized taxation, the Social Chapter which defines individual rights, the abolition of border controls and uniform environmental laws, all which were once the powers that defined the classic nation state, are increasingly gravitating towards Europe. It is not entirely beyond the bounds of possibility to suppose that the Scottish parliament will be unable to take 'reserved powers' from London in the next generation because these powers will have moved to Europe. If this is the case, and most commentators are inclined to agree that it is not a case of if but when, then the Scottish parliament currently enjoys the powers that would be appropriate in a federal Europe. Even if the SNP were to make an electoral breakthrough which secured a mandate for independence, it would only have these powers for a short time before handing them over to Europe. It is also highly significant that the Scottish parliament has already begun to make itself heard within the European Council of the Regions, demonstrating that Europe is just as an important forum for government as London.

While ethnic nationalism has re-emerged in the world, especially in Eastern Europe and in the Balkans where it has often had disastrous results, it should not be thought that the reawakened sense of Scottish nationhood is part of this phenomenon. Scottish national identity has not been based on notions of race or ethnicity. Instead, it has been founded on 'civic nationalism', that is all who live in Scotland are part of the Scottish community regardless of origins or place of birth. In line with this way of thinking, all resident in Scotland are entitled to vote in the Scottish parliamentary elections. In any case, with European citizenship and an increasingly international mobile workforce, the differences between national citizens and residents have become blurred. Furthermore, the awakening of Scottish national identity has not been founded on a profound sense of grievance. Although the Conservative administrations of the 1980s and 90s were deeply unpopular in Scotland, it has to be borne in mind that the Scots were not held in the Union against their will. Most Scots have voted for political parties committed to retaining links with England. Scotland is currently the second most prosperous part of the United Kingdom, on most socio economic indicators it attains the European average and exports more per head of population than Japan. While there are significant pockets of deprivation, it can not be said that socio-economic grievances have fuelled Scottish nationalism. Indeed, as the pages of this history have shown, the relationship with England has been a close one and it would be hard to envision a scenario where that did not continue.

So in a world where the nation state is becoming increasingly redundant what can the Scots do with their new found sense of national identity? Firstly, because Scottishness is associated with civic nationalism and not based on ethnicity, it can be held up as an antidote to the strident and racialist notions of nationalism which are emerging to plague the world. Also, the Scots have set a premium on cultural, rather than political identity and although many in Europe are worried that integration could lead to the loss of distinctive national characteristics, the Scottish historical experience demonstrates that it is possible to exist within a political union and still retain a strong sense of national identity. Secondly, the Scots have shown that national identity is as much about a state of mind as anything else. Without a political apparatus for over three hundred years, culture, history and community were the essential elements in maintaining the Scots' sense of themselves. There is no reason to think that it will be any different in the future.

A Guide to Further Reading

General Histories

In the last two decades there has been an explosion in the writing of modern Scottish history. So much so that even the specialist historian finds it difficult to keep up with the latest literature. Those who wish a general overview of the period should consult T.M. Devine's magisterial *The Scottish Nation 1700–2000* (London 1999) for the latest synthesis of modern research. Two older volumes are still of considerable value; William Ferguson's *Scotland Since 1689* (Edinburgh 1968) focuses on the political development while the social aspects are covered in T.C. Smout's *A History of the Scottish People 1560–1830* (London 1969) and *A Century of the Scottish People 1830–1950* (London 1986). The last four volumes of the *New History of Scotland* published in various editions by Edinburgh University Press, though somewhat dated, are a useful source of information. They are: Rosalind Mitchison, *Lordship to Patronage: Scotland 1603–1745*; Bruce Lenman, *Integration, Enlightenment and Industrialization: Scotland 1750–1832*; Olive and Sidney Checkland, *Industry and Ethos: Scotland 1832–1914* and Christopher Harvie, *No Gods and Precious Few Heroes: Twentieth Century Scotland*. The economy of modern Scotland is well served by R.H. Campbell, *Scotland Since 1707: the Rise of an Industrial Society* (Edinburgh 1986) and Bruce Lenman, *An Economic History of Modern Scotland* (London 1977). Cultural history is covered in the four-volume series *The History of Scottish Literature*, general editor Cairns Craig (Edinburgh 1988). A number of journals are devoted to the subject: *The Scottish Historical Review* and *Scottish Economic and Social History* cover the broad expanse of time, while *Scottish Affairs* deals with more contemporary material.

Union, Enlightenment and Transformation

The Darien Adventure is covered in: George Pratt Insh, *The Company of Scotland Trading to Africa and the Indies* (London 1932); T.C. Smout, *Scottish Trade on the Eve of the Union, 1660–1707* (London 1963) and John Prebble, *The Darien Disaster* (London 1968). The Union of 1707 has remained a contentious issue in Scottish history gravitating between those who see its creation largely in political terms and those who favour an economic explanation. Politics take pride of place in William Ferguson's *Scotland's Relations with England: A Survey to 1707* (Edinburgh 1977) and P.J. Riley, *The Union of Scotland and England* (Manchester 1979). The economic arguments are ably rehearsed in Chris

Whatley's *Bought and Sold for English Gold: Explaining the Union of 1707* (Dundee 1994). J. R. Young, in a recent article, draws our attention to the important international aspect of the Union in 'The Parliamentary Incorporating Union of 1707: Political management, Anti-Unionism and Foreign Policy' in T.M. Devine and J.R.Young (eds.), *Eighteenth Century Scotland: New Perspectives* (East Linton 1999).

The Jacobites have received more attention from romanticists than serious historians, although there is now a corpus of scholarly work which cuts through the tartan myths surrounding Bonnie Prince Charlie and his valiant followers. Foremost in the Highland charge against myth is Bruce Lenman in two excellent studies: *The Jacobite Risings in Great Britain 1689–1746* (London 1980) and *The Jacobite Clans of the Great Glen* (London 1984). Allan Macinnes provides us with the most comprehensive account of clan politics, economy and society in his *Clanship, Commerce and the House of Stuart, 1603–1788* (East Linton 1996). M.G.H. Pittock's *Jacobitism* (London 1998) examines the phenomenon from a cultural perspective.

The Scottish Enlightenment has been one of the most productive seams in Scottish history, although it must be said that much of the material it produces is narrowly biographical or excessively intellectual. A number of scholars, however, have managed to integrate the various components to produce 'rounded' histories of the Enlightenment. David Allan's *Virtue, Learning and the Scottish Enlightenment* (Edinburgh 1993) charts its origins from the Reformation. Those who think that Scotland was an intellectual desert before the eighteenth century should consult Alexander Broadie's *The Tradition of Scottish Philosophy* (Edinburgh 1990) for a surgical removal of their ignorance. Richard Sher demonstrates the important role of the church in promoting enlightenment thought in his *Church and University in the Scottish Enlightenment* (Edinburgh 1985) and Annand Chitnis provides us with an important social history in *The Scottish Enlightenment* (London 1976). The importance of history is demonstrated in Colin Kidd's excellent *Subverting Scotland's Past* (Cambridge 1993).

The transformation of Scotland during the 'long' eighteenth century has been well served by a number of valuable collections of essays; T.M. Devine and R. Mitchison (eds.), *People and Society in Scotland, Vol. I 1760–1830* (Edinburgh 1988); T.M. Devine and J.R. Young (eds.), *Eighteenth Century Scotland: New Perspectives* (East Linton 1999); R. Mitchison and

N. Phillipson, *Scotland in the Age of Improvement* (Edinburgh 1998) and R. A. Houston and I.D. Whyte (eds.), *Scottish Society 1500–1800* (Cambridge 1989). For Scottish economic development in this period see T.M. Devine, *The Tobacco Lords* (Edinburgh 1975) and Chris Whatley, *The Industrial Revolution in Scotland* (Cambridge 1997). The agrarian revolution is charted in T.M. Devine, *The Transformation of Rural Scotland* (Edinburgh 1994) The shady world of Scottish politics can be illuminated by reading: R. Sunter, *Patronage and Politics in Scotland* (Edinburgh 1987); A. Murdoch, *The People Above* (Edinburgh 1979) and J.S. Shaw, *The Management of Scottish Society 1707–1746* (Edinburgh 1983).

Industry, Empire and Democracy

In the field of urban history, Glasgow has proved itself 'miles better' with two volumes which chart the rise and heyday of the city in T.M. Devine and G. Jackson (eds.), *Glasgow: Beginnings to 1830* (Manchester 1995) and W.H. Fraser and I. Maver (eds.), *Glasgow 1830–1912* (Manchester 1996). A. Slaven's *The Development of the West of Scotland* (London 1975) provides a useful survey of the main lines of Scottish economic development in the nineteenth century, but should be supplemented with Clive Lee, *Scotland and the United Kingdom* (Manchester 1995). Social history is well served by W.H. Fraser and R.J. Morris (eds.), *People and Society in Scotland, Vol. II 1830–1914* (Edinburgh 1990). The Highlands are covered in T.M. Devine's *Clanship to Crofters' War* (Manchester 1994) and *The Great Highland Famine* (Edinburgh 1988). The social history of religious adherence is charted in Callum Brown's *Religion and Society in Scotland Since 1707* (Edinburgh 1997). For those interested in the political and social fallout of religious division and sectarianism see; S.J. Brown and M. Fry (eds.), *Scotland in the Age of Disruption* (Edinburgh 1993); G. Walker and T. Gallagher (eds.), *Battle Hymns and Sermons* (Edinburgh 1990); E. McFarland, *Protestants First* (Edinburgh 1990) and M. Mitchell, *Irish in the West of Scotland 1797–1848* (Edinburgh 1998). The history of Scottish women is explored in two volumes edited by E. Breitenbach and E. Gordon: *The World is Ill Divided* (Edinburgh 1990) and *Out of Bounds* (Edinburgh 1992). The campaign for the vote for women is covered in E. King, *The Scottish Women's Suffrage Movement* (Glasgow 1978).

Politics are covered in: M. Fry, *Patronage and Principle: A Political History of Modern Scotland* (Aberdeen 1987); I.G.C. Hutchison, *A Political History of Scotland 1832–1924* (Edinburgh 1986); C. Harvie, *Scotland and Nationalism* (London 1998) and R.J. Finlay, *A Partnership for Good* (Edinburgh 1997). For an illuminating insight into the relationship between Scotland and Britain in the mid-nineteenth century see G. Morton, *Unionist Nationalism* (East Linton 1998). Education is covered in R. D. Anderson, *Education and the Scottish People* (Oxford 1995) and D.J. Withrington, *Going to School* (Edinburgh 1997). The Scottish role in the British Empire is a new area of research and is best found in the forthcoming three volume series *Scotland and the Empire* edited by T.M. Devine, R.J. Finlay and J.M. MacKenzie. Those wishing a cogent overview of the subject should see J.M. MacKenzie, 'Empire and National Identities: The Case of Scotland', *Royal Historical Society Transactions* (Cambridge 1998). On the Scottish role overseas see: R.A. Cage (ed.), *The Scots Abroad* (London 1985) and T.M. Devine (ed.), *Scottish Emigration and Scottish Society* (Edinburgh 1992)

The Battle for Britain and the Struggle for Scotland

A good overview of the Scottish experience since 1914 is to be found in T.M. Devine and R.J. Finlay (eds.), *Scotland in the Twentieth Century* (Edinburgh 1994); D. McCrone, *Understanding Scotland: The Sociology of a Stateless Nation* (London 1992) and L. Paterson, *The Autonomy of Modern Scotland* (Edinburgh 1996). The experience of war is charted in E. McFarland and C. MacDonald (eds.), *Scotland and the Great War* (East Linton 1999). Political developments can be charted by reference to A. Marr, *The Battle for Scotland* (London 1992); J. Mitchell, *Strategies for Self-Government* (Edinburgh 1996) and A. Kemp, *The Hollow Drum* (Edinburgh 1995). On the political parties there are: I. Donnachie, C. Harvie and I. Woods (eds.), *Forward! Labour Politics in Scotland* (Edinburgh 1988); M. Keating and D. Bleiman, *Labour and Scottish Nationalism* (London 1978); J. Mitchell, *Conservatives and the Union* (Edinburgh 1990); C. MacDonald (ed.), *Unionist Scotland* (Edinburgh 1998); J. Brand, *The National Movement in Scotland* (London 1978) and R.J. Finlay, *Independent and Free: Scottish Politics and the Origins of the SNP* (Edinburgh 1994).

Marjory Harper demonstrates the continuing outflow of people from Scotland in *Emigration from Scotland Between the Wars* (Manchester 1998), while Bashir Maan provides a readable account of the Asian experience after 1945 in his *The New Scots* (Edinburgh 1992). The economic problems of the post war era are explored in R. Saville (ed.), *The Economic Development of Modern Scotland 1950–1980* (Edinburgh 1985), while the increasing role of government is explored by A. Midwinter, M. Keating and J. Mitchell in *Politics and Public Policy in Modern Scotland* (London 1990). The history of rivalry between Scotland's two most famous soccer clubs, Celtic and Rangers, is charted in Bill Murray's *The Old Firm* (Edinburgh 1984).

INDEX

Page references in *italics* indicate illustrations.

NOTES ON AUTHORSHIP

John R. Young 'The Matter of Union'; Colin Kidd, 'A Nation Betrayed'; Lizanne Henderson, 'A Different Story from the Dark Side'; Chris Whatley, 'Engines of Change Start to Roll'; Gerry Caruthers, 'What is Scottish Culture?'; Chris Harvie, 'Trains Take the Strain in a Shrinking Country'; W.H. Fraser, 'Rise of Town and City'; Irene Maver, 'Glasgow Flourishes'; T.M. Devine, 'Clearing the Highlands'; Juliet Gardiner, 'The First "Glasgow Boy"'; Arthur McIvor, 'Red Dawn Fades'; Douglas Gifford, 'Words as Weapons'; Iain Hutchison, 'The State Will Provide'; James Mitchell, 'Scotland Says No at the First Time of Asking'; T.M. Devine, 'The Start of a New Song'. All other material written by E.J. Cowan, R.J. Finlay and William Paul.

PICTURE CREDITS